AFRICAN POLITICAL, ECONOMIC, AND SECURITY ISSUES

AFRICA

THE STATE OF THE CONTINENT FIFTY YEARS AFTER THE LIBERATION

AFRICAN POLITICAL, ECONOMIC, AND SECURITY ISSUES

Additional books in this series can be found on Nova's website under the Series tab.

Additional e-books in this series can be found on Nova's website under the e-book tab.

AFRICAN POLITICAL, ECONOMIC, AND SECURITY ISSUES

AFRICA

THE STATE OF THE CONTINENT FIFTY YEARS AFTER THE LIBERATION

OLAYIWOLA ABEGUNRIN
EDITOR

nova publishers
New York

For permission to use material from this book please contact us:
Telephone 631-231-7269; Fax 631-231-8175
Web Site: http://www.novapublishers.com

Library of Congress Cataloging-in-Publication Data

ISBN: 978-1-62948-561-4

Published by Nova Science Publishers, Inc. † New York

CONTENTS

List of Tables

ACKNOWLEDGMENTS

The editor is very grateful to the various contributors for meeting the deadline for their submissions. I thank all my friends and colleagues who have encouraged and supported me in producing this collection of essays on *Africa: The State of the Continent Fifty Years after the Liberation.*

Special thanks go to Professor Ali A. Mazrui, of The State University of New York at Bingmington, for his contribution and to be the first to submit his chapter, which gave me encouragement to pursue the effort to get this book published. I thank Professor Mae C. King for finding the time to contribute a chapter on "Sudan, Development, Peace and U.S. Constituency for Africa," to this book.

My deepest gratitude to Dr. Balla M. Keita for editing the entire manuscript and his valuable suggestions, and to Araba Evelyn Johnston-Arthur, my Teaching Associate, for her support in copying of the manuscript, and other documents for this book and for filling in for me in teaching my undergraduate classes in the cause of putting this book together. I am grateful to Benjamin Machar who read and edited some of the chapters in this book and his valuable editorial suggestions. Finally, I express my gratitude to my family, especially my wife Funmilola Atoke Emiola Abegunrin and my children for their moral support throughout the period of editing this book. I thank the publisher, for being penitent with me after many delays in finally getting the manuscript for this book together.

Olayiwola Abegunrin, Ph.D.
New Carrollton, Maryland and
Washington, D. C., June 2013

LIST OF ABBREVIATIONS

AAMS - Associated African and Malagasy States
AAP- African Action Plan
AAPC- All African People's Conference
AAPSO- Afro-Asian People Solidarity Organization
ACP- African Caribbean and Pacific Group
ACCORD- African Centre for Constructive Resolution of Disputes
ACDHRS- African Centre for Democracy and Human Rights Studies
ADB- African Development Bank
AEC- African Economic Community
AFL- Armed Forces of Liberia
AFRC- Armed Forces Ruling Council
AFRICOM- African Command Center
AGOA- African Growth and Opportunity Act
AHSG- African Head of State and Governments
AIAI- Al-Itihad Al-Islami of Somalia
AIDS- Acquired Immune Deficiency Syndrome
ALF- Africa Leadership Forum
AMISOM- African Mission for the Security of Somalia
ANC- African National Congress (of South Africa)
ANZUS- Australia, New Zealand, and United States
AOPIG- African Oil Policy Initiative Group
APC- African People's Congress
APEC- Asian Pacific Economic Cooperation
APEF- Asian Pacific Economic Forum
ASAS- Association of Southern African States
AU- African Union (formerly Organization of African Unity)

AWCPD- African Women's Committee on Peace and Development
AZAPO- Azanian People's Organization
BBC- British Broadcasting Corporation
BCEAO- Banque Centrale des Etats de I'Ouest Africaine
BCM- Black Consciousness Movement
BEECOM- Black Economic Empowerment Commission
BP- British Petroleum Company
BSA- British South African Company
CA- Cooperation on Africa
CAN- Christian Association of Nigeria
CAP- Common Agricultural Exports
CARICOM- Caribbean Economic Community
CB- Central Bank of Nigeria
CD- Campaign for Democracy
CEAO- Communaute Economique de I'Afrique de I'Ouest
(Economic Community of West Africa)
CEAPL- Economic Community of the Great Lake
CENND- Conference of Ethnic Nationalities of the Niger Delta
CFA- Communaute' Financiere Africaine
CIA- U.S. Central Intelligence Agency
CIAS- Conference of Independent African States
CLO- Civil Liberty Organization
CMP- Concert of Medium Powers
CODESA- Convention for a Democratic South Africa
COMESA- Common Market for Eastern and Southern Africa
CONSAS- Constellation of Southern African States
CORE- Congress of Racial Equality
COSATU- Congress of South African Trade Union
CPA- Comprehensive Peace Agreement
CPP- Convention People's Party
CSCE- Conference on Security and Cooperation in Europe
CSSDCA-Conference on Security, Stability, Development,
and Cooperation in Africa
DFI- Direct Foreign Investments
DMO- Debt Management Office
EAC- East Africa Community
ECA- United Nations Economic Commission for Africa
ECGD- Export Credits Guarantee Department (British)
ECOMOMOG- ECOWAS Monitoring Observer Group

ECOSOCC- Economic, Social and Cultural Council
ECOWAS- Economic Community of West African States
ECU- European Currency Unit
EDF- European Development Fund
EEC- European Economic Community
EDB- European Development Bank
EFCC- Economic Financial Crimes Commission
EMCAP- Economic Management Capacity Building Program
EPA- Economic Partnership Agreement
ESCOM- Electricity Supply Commission of South Africa
ESKOM- Electricity Supply Commission of South Africa
EU- European Union
FAS- Femmes Africa Solidarite
FAWE- Federation of African Women in Education
FBI- (U.S.) Federal Bureau of Investigation
FCD- Forum for Community Development
FDI- Foreign Direct Investment
FIFA- Federation International Football Association
FMG- Federal Military Government
FNLA- Frente Nacional de Libertacao de Angola
FCS- Foreign Service Commerce
FAO- Food and Agricultural Organization
FRELIMO- Frente de Libertacaio de Mozambique
GDP- Gross Domestic Product
GEAR- Growth, Employment and Redistribution
GOSS- Government of South Sudan
GNP- Gross National Product
GRAE- Revolutionary Government of Angola in Exile
GSM- Global System Mobile Communication
GSP- Generalized System Preferences
GWOT- Global War on Terror
HDI- Human Development Index
HIPC- Heavily Indebted Poor Countries
HIV- Human Immunodeficiency Virus
HOA- Horn of Africa
HRVIC- Human Rights Violations Investigation Commission
IASPS- Institute for Advanced Strategic and Political Studies
ICPC- Independence Corrupt Practices and Other Related Offense Commission

IFI- International Finance Institutions
IFP- Inkatha Freedom Party
IGAD- Inter-Governmental Authority on Development
IGO- Inter-Government Organization
ILO- International Labor Organization
IMF- International Monetary Fund
ING- Interim National Government
ISDSC- Inter-State Defense and Security Committee
IRFG- International Religious Freedom Group
JACC- Joint Agricultural Consultative Committee
JMC- Joint Monitoring Commission
LURD- Liberian United Reconciliation for Democracy
MAGHREB- Permanent Consultative Committee of the Maghreb (North African Consultative Committee/NACC)
MAP- Millennium Action Plan
MCA- Millennium Challenge Account
MEND- Movement for the Emancipation of Niger Delta
MODEL- Movement for Democracy in Liberia
MOSOP- Movement for the Survival of Ogoni People
MPLA- Popular Movement for the Liberation of Angola
MSF- Medecins sans Frontieres (Doctors without Borders)
MTN- Mobile Telecommunications Network
NAACP- National Association for the Advancement of Colored Peoples
NADECO- National Democratic Alliance
NAFTA- North American Free Trade Area
NATO- North Atlantic Treaty Organization
NCNC- National Council of Nigerian Citizens
NCP/NIF- National Congress Party/National Islamic Front
NDC- National Democratic Congress
NEPA- National Electric Power Authority
NEPAD- New Partnership for African Development
NEPU- Northern Element Progressive Union
NGO- Non-Governmental Organization
NIC- Newly Industrializing Countries
NIEO- New International Economic Order
NIIA- Nigerian Institute of International Affairs
NIPSS- National Institute for Policy and Strategic Studies
NIS- Newly Independent States
NDPVF- Niger Delta People's Volunteer Force

NLC- Nigerian Labor Congress
NNDP- Nigerian National Democratic Party
NNOC- Nigerian National Oil Corporation
NNPC- Nigerian National Petroleum Corporation
NP- National Party of South Africa
NPC- Northern People's Congress
NPFL- National Patriotic Front of Liberia
NSF- Namibian Solidarity Fund
NTF- National Trust Fund
OAS- Organization of American States
OAU- Obafemi Awolowo University-(Ile-Ife, Nigeria)
OAU- Organization of African Unity (now African Union)
OECD- Organization of Economic Cooperation and Development
OEF- Operation Enduring Freedom for Somalia
OIC- Organization of Islamic Council
OPEC- Organization of Petroleum Exporting Countries
OSCE- Organization for Security and Cooperation in Europe
PAC- Pan-African Congress of South Africa
PAFMECA- Pan-African Freedom Movement of East and Central Africa
PAFMECSA- Pan-African Freedom Movement of East, Central and Southern Africa
PAIGC- Partido Africano da Independencia da Guine e Cabo Verde
PCP- Popular Congress Party
PDP- People's Democratic Party
PHCN- Power Holding Company of Nigeria
PNDC- Provisional National Defense Council
PRC- Provisional Ruling Council
RDP- Reconstruction and Development Program
RENAMO- Mozambique National Resistance Movement
REPA- Regional Economic Partnership Agreement
RTZ- Rio Tinto Zinc
SACP- South African Communist Party
SACU- Southern African Custom Union
SADC- Southern African Development Community
SADCC- Southern African Development Coordination Conference
SADF- South African Defense Forces
SADR- Saharawi Arab Democratic Republic
SAFCOL- South African Forest Corporation
SAF- Sudan Armed Force

SANDF- South African National Defense Force
SAP- Structural Adjustment Programs
SARF- Southern African Relief Fund
SAYROC- South Africa Youth Revolutionary Council
SDP- Social Democratic Party
SEATO- South East Asian Treaty Organization
SFBC- Swiss Federal Banking Commission
SMC- Supreme Military Council
SANNC- South African Native National Congress (later ANC)
SPA- Strategic Partnership with Africa
SPLM/A- Sudan People's Liberation Movement/Army
SPLM/A-N- Sudan People's Liberation Movement/Army-North Sudan
SSF- Salam Sudan Foundation
SWAPO- South West African People's Organization
TAC- Technical Aid Corps
TEC- Transitional Executive Council
TFG- Transitional Federal Government for Somalia
UANC- United African National Council
UDEAC- Central African Customs and Economic Union
(Union Douaniere et Economique de l'Afrique Centrale)
UDF- United Democratic Front
UDI- Unilateral Declaration of Independence
UDHR- Universal Declaration of Human Rights
UIC- United Islamic Court for Somalia
UMBC- United Middle Belt Congress
UMEOA- West African Economic and Monetary Union
UNAIDS- United Nations AIDS
UNCED- United Nations Conference on Environment and Development
UNCTAD- United Nations Conference on Trade and Development
UNECOSOC- United Nations Economic and Social Council
UNECA- United Nations Economic Commission for Africa
UNHCR- United Nations High Commissioner for Refugees
UNICEF- United Nations Children Fund
UNIDO- United Nations Industrial Development Organization
UNESCO- United Nations, Educational,
Scientific and Cultural Organization
UNITA- National Union for the Total Independence of Angola
UNIA- Universal Negro Improvement Association
UNO- United Nations Organization

UPA- United Party of Angola
USEUCOM- United States European Command
USSR- Union of Soviet and Socialist Republic
WACH- West African Clearing House
WAEMU- West African Economic Monetary Union
WB- World Bank
WFP- World Food Program
WILDAF- Women in Law and Development in Africa
WMD- Weapon of Mass Destruction
WTO- World Trade Organization
ZANLA- Zimbabwean African National Liberation Army
ZANU- Zimbabwean African National Union
ZAPU- Zimbabwean African People's Union
ZIPRA- Zimbabwean Independence People's Revolutionary Army
ZUPO- Zimbabwe United Peoples Organization

NOTES ON THE CONTRIBUTORS

Olayiwola Abegunrin is Professor of International Relations and African Studies, Department of Political Science, Howard University, Washington, D.C. He is former Chair of Department of International Relations, Obafemi Awolowo University, Ile-Ife, Nigeria, where he taught for many years. He was a Visiting Professor in the Departments of Political Science and Africana Studies, University of North Carolina at Charlotte, 1989-1991. He has held teaching positions at Woodrow Wilson Department of Government and Foreign Affair, University of Virginia, Charlottesville, and University of Maryland, College Park. He has authored, co-authored, edited and co-edited eight books; he has contributed chapters to many books and published several articles in referred journals. His latest book is *Africa in Global Politics in the Twenty-First Century: A Pan-African Perspective*, Palgrave Macmillan, 2009. He serves on Advisory Board of many journals and he is a member of Academic Advisory Board of Global Studies, *Africa*.

Sabella Ogbobode Abidde is an Assistant Professor in the Department of Political Science at Alabama State University, Montgomery, Alabama. He obtained Ph.D. from Howard University, and between 2007 and 2009, he was a Fellow of the Ryoichi Sasakawa YoungLeaders Fellowship Fund (SYLF). His teaching and research interest includes, African Politics, History, African American Studies, and International Studies. Dr. Abidde has presented papers at many academic conferences. He is also currently a columnist for Nigeria's newspaper *The Punch.*

Dr Joseph Aihie, currently a Lecturer at the Department of Political Science, University of Benin, Nigeria, was educated at the University of Ibadan and Igbinedion University, Okada. He has held a teaching position at the Igbinedion University where, he was former Acting Head of the Department of International Relations and Strategic Studies.

Dr. Abiodun Alao is a Senior Research Fellow at the African Leadership Centre, King's College London. He has published extensively on African security issues. His latest book in this regard is *Mugabe and the Politics of Security in Zimbabwe*, Montreal: McGill-Queens University Press 2012. He obtained a doctorate in War Studies from King's College London.

D. Elwood Dunn is The Alfred Walter Negley Professor of Political Science at The University of the South, Sewanee, TN. where he has been on the faculty continuously since 1981. Before coming to Sewanee he earned a Ph.D. degree from American University in 1972, taught at Seton Hall University, New Jersey and served in the government of his native Liberia as the Minister of State for Presidential Affairs in 1979. He is author of more than 10 books and book chapters on West African society and politics and numerous articles on international affairs.

Mae C. King is Professor of Political Science, Department of Political Science, Howard University, Washington, D. C. She taught in the Department of Political Science, University of Benin, Nigeria, 1975 to 1989. Her teaching and research interests focus on African Politics, U.S. Foreign Policy towards Africa, and Third World Political Theory. She has written several referred articles, many book chapters and many books on Nigerian and African politics. One of her authored books is *Basic Currents of Nigerian Foreign Policy,* Howard University Press, 1996.

Charity Manyeruke is Acting Chairperson and lecturer in the Department of Politics and Administrative Studies, Faculty of Social Studies, University of Zimbabwe, Harare. She was born in Marondera, Mashonaland East Province of Zimbabwe. She obtained her Ph.D. in Political Science from University of Zimbabwe. Her research and teaching interest focus on International Economic Relations; International Law; Politics and Governance in Africa. She married to Shingirai Manyeruke, with two children, Victor and Nyasha.

Ali A. Mazrui is the Albert Schweitzer Professor in the Humanities and Director, Institute of Global Cultural Studies at Binghamton University, State University of New York, Binghamton, New York. He is author, co-author and editor of more than twenty books, including *Towards A Pax Africana* (1967), *The Power of Babel: Language and Governance in the African Experience (*1998*) Black Reparations in the Era of Globalization* (2002), *A Tale of Two Africas: Nigeria and South Africa as Contrasting Visions* (2006), and the Politics of War and the Culture of Violence (2008), as well as numerous articles in scholarly journals, and public media. In addition to his written work, he is the creator of the BBC Television series *The Africans: A Triple Heritage* (1986). Professor Mazrui is a consultant to many International Organizations and Corporations, and member of Advisory and editorial board member of many academic Journals.

Getachew Metaferia is Professor of Political Science, Morgan State University, Baltimore, Maryland. He is the Director of International Studies in Department of Political Science, Morgan State University. Dr. Metaferia was a recipient of Fulbright-Hayes Awards to Myammar and Thailand in 2002 and to China in 2004. His teaching and research focus on Comparative Politics, African Politics and International Studies. He has authored and edited three books. His latest book is *Ethiopia and the United States: History, Diplomacy and Analysis*, New York: Algora Publishing, 2009.

James Pope received his PhD from Howard University in political science. His research interests are interdisciplinary and include Africana history and politics, human rights and international law, social movements, revolutions, and race. Dr. Pope is an Adjunct Professor in Department of Political Science, Howard University; is a research fellow with *TransAfrica Forum* and was a human rights education Facilitator with Amnesty International.

INTRODUCTION

The genesis of this book started from the Africa forum held at the Ralph J. Bunch International Affairs Center, Howard University, organized by the department of Political Science and the Ralph Bunch International Affairs Center on November 9, 2010. The aspirations and survival of Africa rested on Africans shoulders. Is Africa, with its vast wealth in both human and natural resources, on the path to realizing its enormous potential? Or is it in danger of becoming a failed continent in the twenty-first century? *AFRICA: The State of the Continent Fifty Years after the Liberation* considers the challenges and opportunities that the continent, its peoples and its leaderships now face, while it offers rich and sobering analyses of Africa's current political and economic situations.

Year after year, and in country after country, individuals and organizations have devoted their time, resources and intellect to tackling the *African wahala (*African problems). Some notable scholars in this regard include Bereket Selassie, Ali A. Mazrui, Sulayman S. Nyang, Julius E. Nyang'oro, F. Ugboaja Ohaegbulam, Georges Nzongola–Ntalaja, Mario Azevedo, Robert H. Bates, Layi Abegunrin, E.C. Ejiogu, Robert Edgar, Toyi Falola, Cyril Obi, Lonzen W. Rugira, and many others. The African Studies Association (ASA) is the foremost academic organization/association on and about Africa, in North America. It relentlessly probes the continent.[1] The theme for its 2011 annual conference was *"50 Years of African Liberation,"* from which the title of this

[1] The ASA was founded in 1957, with the primary goal of promoting the study of the continent in all academic disciplines. There are currently 1700 due paying members and institutions subscribed to the ASA. The organization convened its 54th annual conference from November 16th through the 19th at the Marriott Wardman Park Hotel, Washington DC. A multitude of people, including researchers, ivory-tower based scholars, public intellectuals, and students and various organizations, partook in the intellectual pursuit.

book is adopted. According to the association, "The period 1960-1961 marked a watershed in the history of the continent, when the largest number of African countries gained independence. These transformations signaled the beginning of five decades of struggle for democracy and development. Since then, there is much to celebrate: Today, Africa has the highest number of democracies since 1960; institutionalized apartheid has been eliminated in South Africa; and women are emerging as political leaders. At the same time, the fifty year mark provides us with an opportunity to reflect critically on the complex ways that history has unfolded on the continent."[2]

In this twenty-first century, the able peoples of Africa are once again focused on the arduous task of nation-building after decades of despotism, military coups and profligacy all-over the continent, starting with the first military coup d'état led by Sergeant Emmanuel Bodjolle and Colonel Etienne Gnassingbe Eyadema that overthrew and assassinated President Sylvanus Olympio of Togo on January 13, 1963. General Eyadema eventually ended up ruling Togo as a military head of state for thirty-two years, 1963-2005.

African countries are facing myriad of problems, such as political instability, military coups, civil wars, underdevelopment, the rising HIV/AIDS pandemic, human rights abuse, and rampant corruption all over the continent after fifty years of independence. This book has argued that one of the reasons why the African dreams have not been realized is; first, the project for a United States of Africa by Kwame Nkrumah failed because it was modeled on the false and shaky unity without honest commitment. Similarly, because it is modeled on the European Union and therefore, the African Union is bound to face the same fate. The second, is lack of committed and visionary leaders; Third mismanagement of the African resources, Fourth, too much dependence on their former colonial rulers, Fifth, rampant corruptions, and finally lack of good governance, accountability and transparency.

The shallowness of transplanted European institutions is best illustrated in the Belgian Congo (the Democratic Republic of Congo). The so-called Congolese National Army mutinied within a month of independence. The richest province at the time, Katanga (now Elizabethville), declared its

---

[2] The following seventeen countries gained independence in 1960, (1) Republic of Benin, (2) Burkina Faso, (3) Republic Cameroon, (4) Central African Republic, (5) Republic of Chad, (6) Peoples' Republic of Congo, (7) Democratic Republic of Congo, (8) Republic of Gabon, (9) Ivory Coast, (10) Republic of (11) Madagascar, (12) Republic of Mali, (13) Republic of Mauritania, (14) Republic of Niger, (15) Federal Republic of Nigeria, (16) Republic of Senegal, (17) Republic of Somalia, Republic of Togo. Consequently, 1960 was called the year of African Independence because 17 countries became independent in that year. This was largest numbers of African countries to achieve independence in one year.

secession soon after. Then President Joseph Kasavubu, and the Prime Minister Patrice Lumumba, declared each other illegitimate, and before too long the latter was viciously assassinated, on January 17, 1961, just six months after his country's independence. A Belgian Sociologist Ludo De Witte has shown in his book, and a Congolese scholar Georges Nzongo-Ntalaja have also shown in his book that, "the Belgian ruling class and its representatives in collaboration with CIA in the Congo were directly responsible for Lumumba's assassination."[3] Since the 1960 millions of people have died, and hundreds of thousands of women have been raped. Democratic Republic of Congo has remained the ultimate example of Africa's chronic instability. Somalia in the Horn of Africa is a typical example of a failed state; a country that had no functioning government for (since 1991) twenty-one years.

The arbitrary and artificial boundaries the colonial overlords created all over Africa have made it hard to integrate the populations into real nations. Africa South of Sahara continues to be haunted by perennial ethnic rivalries, while Arab Africa has suffered from periodic conflicts between Islam and secularism and now mass revolutions starting in Egypt in November 2010, had spread all over the region. Post-colonial African economies have suffered from shortages of skills and rampant corruption. According to Professor Ali A. Mazrui, "The three codes of conduct of Africa, indigenous, Islamic and Western have created moral incoherence, at least for the time being. Indeed, the Somali militants seem to have traversed a whole span from pastoralism to piracy."[4] On the other hand, the continent has produced two Secretaries Generals of the United Nations, Boutros Boutros-Ghali, and Kofi Annan, and dozen Africans have won Noble Prizes, predominantly for peace, literature and physics, but still no peace and stability continental-wide.

But what are the signs for the next fifty years of post-independence Africa and particularly for the African peoples in the twenty-first century? Most of the continent is still in a pre-democracy era, and many elections are notoriously and fraudulently rigged. However, most African countries stand a good chance of becoming democratized, if the leadership would allow fair, free and credible elections to take place. The real test is when an incumbent president or political party allows itself to be peacefully voted out of office, and not once, but at least twice. Ghana, which has led the African South of Sahara in the attainment of independence in 1957, has satisfied this condition,

[3] See Ludo De Witte, *The Assassination of Lumumba*, Paris: Karthala, 2000, pp. 128-132. Also see Georges Nzongola-Ntalaja, *The Congo from Leopold to Kabila: A People's History*, New York: Zed Books, 2002, pp. 106-112.

[4] Ali A. Mazrui, "An African Half-Century," *The Guardian*, London, December 7, 2010, p. 7.

and Botswana has followed Ghana in this game of peaceful political transition. The new and apartheid free South Africa is likely to continue peaceful democratic good governance.

However, this book is about how to move beyond the problems of the past five decades, promote good governance, peace, stability and address human rights issues in the African World, and achieve the very best possible results for Africa and its peoples. Most importantly, it is also what is still to be done to realize those early dreams of African leaders like Kwame Nkrumah of Ghana, Emperor Haile Selassie of Ethiopia, Gamal Abdul Nasser of Egypt, Julius K. Nyerere of Tanzania, Patrice Lumumba of the Democratic Republic of Congo, and Sekou Toure of Guinea in an entirely reordered, better and tougher context for the twenty-first century Africa.

In: Africa
Editor: Olayiwola Abegunrin

ISBN: 978-1-62948-561-4

Chapter 1

FIFTY YEARS OF AFRICAN LIBERATION: PROMISES, CHALLENGES AND FAILURES

Sabella Ogbobode Abidde
Assistant Professor, Department of History & Political Science
Alabama State University, Montgomery, Alabama

INTRODUCTION

According to anthropologists and archeologists who study the origin of mankind, human beings descended from hominids whose origins, millions of years ago, can be traced to Central Africa [1]. And the continent itself, according to Robert D. Kaplan is the mother of all continents: the continent from which all humans acquired their deepest genetic traits [2]. Essentially, therefore, human beings, no matter their race, color, statement of belief, and current habitat all have African ancestry. This belief, and the understanding of human origin, has always set the African and the African continent apart [3].

For thousands of years, the continent flourished; giving birth to a multitude of kingdoms, empires and collection of ethnic groups that roamed the large expanse of the continent. They lived and flourished in relative peace and prosperity. Although the continent was not isolated or completely unknown to the Europeans and Asians and others in other part of the known world, still, it was an enigma to most. And a few years after the Age of the Renaissance [4], the Portuguese formally ventured into the continent [5]. Other

European nations followed (in order to satisfy their curiosity; proselytize and to civilize the Africans; and to establish trade and diplomatic connections) [6].

Trade

Trade in natural resources was the focal point of the Europeans. Over time, however, legitimate trade in resources metamorphosized into trade in human beings. Slave trade, or more precisely, the Trans Atlantic Slave Trade, which began in the 15th century lasted until the 19th century, devastated the continent and its people. While no one knows, with any degree of certainty how many Africans were taken and sold as slaves, the estimate ranges from ten million, at the lower end, to fifty million [7]. What seems certain is that the vast majority of slaves were taken from the West and West Central African regions with Brazil and the Caribbean as the final destinations for most of them.

Slavery impacted continental and Diaspora Africans in ways that are yet to be completely understood. Nonetheless, we know that the trade in humans impacted the continent in terms of its economy, demography and talent pool, and politics. We also know that the continent's culture and psyche was severely damaged. However, about one hundred and fifty years after the end of slavery [8], Africans, at home and abroad, continues to suffer from what has come to be known as the Residual Effects of Slavery [9].

Several other factors have and continue to impact the continent, and these include colonization, the first and second world wars, the Cold War, globalization, and neocolonialism. In ways that have been documented and in ways that are still being investigated these factors contributed to the stunting of the continent. For instance, the Berlin Conference of November 1884-February 1885 called for by Portugal, but organized by the first Chancellor of Germany, Otto von Bismarck, formalized the colonization process whereby Africa was carved up and divided amongst European countries [10]. The domination of Africa South of Sahara (Black Africa) came to an end when individual African countries began to gain independence, starting with Ghana in 1957.

During the colonial period, the continent was carved into 55 colonies with the lion share going to Britain and France, followed by Portugal, Germany, Spain and Italy. In the end, countries like Angola, Mozambique, Zimbabwe, Algeria, and Guinea Bissau gained independence through armed struggle; while countries like Nigeria, Tanzania, Ghana, Uganda, Gambia and Senegal gained independence through negotiated settlement. Nonetheless, the decolonization and transition process was difficult for virtually all African countries. For instance, many countries were forced or induced to introduce western-styled democracy and this made governing difficult for countries with steep tradition in Africa-styled democracy. What's more, the social, political, economic and cultural systems and processes that were forced on the continent led to a series of internal and cross-border problems.

PRE- AND POST-INDEPENDENCE CHALLENGES

A critical appraisal of modern Africa by both Afrocentric [11] and Eurocentric [12] scholars reveals several factors as to why the continent is the way it is after several years of independence. Both perspectives, in spite of the occasional optimism, agree that the continent is mostly stagnant: undeveloped in some areas, underdeveloped in others and plagued by disorder, poverty, and volatility in all areas. Even for Africans, the continent is a continuous body of complexities and complications and of almost impenetrable landscape.

The Africa continent nags and confounds in spite of the "causes, effects, and roadmaps" that have been propagated and submitted by different schools, scholars and institutions. From Marxism to Modernization and from Dependency to other systems of thought that are cogent or feeble, palpably silly or condescending hypotheses about Africa abound. Some commentators believe that it is impossible to understand Africa without having a deep understanding of the suffering and calamities wrought by slavery and colonialism on the continent. They think that without slavery and colonialism Africa would have been a thriving and prosperous continent.

During the pre-independence period, African nationalists made several promises to their people vis-à-vis political reform and participatory democracy; economic growth and development; constitutional reforms and civil liberties. In one African country after another, nationalists made lofty promises. Sadly, in every one of these countries, the people were betrayed. According to John Isbister, "nowhere has the promise of independence been more cruelly betrayed than in Africa. In most countries, any semblance of democracy disappeared, and one-party states became the norm for decades" [13].

Man's inhumanity to man also became the norm in the continent. Isbister noted that "Apartheid South Africa was the greatest tragedy to Africa" [14.] Other such tragedies include the continent's seemingly unending wars in places like the Democratic Republic of Congo; and the genocide in Rwanda; the civil wars in Liberia, Sudan and Sierra Leone, the fragmentation and total collapse of state in Somalia and the never-ending food crisis in Ethiopia. Today, searing poverty, preliterate conditions, and ecological disasters are fast becoming a permanent feature of the continent's landscape. To provide social programs or development or improve their infrastructures; many countries had to borrow or rely on foreign aid. Taking in totality, Africans are worse off than they were in the first decade of their independence.

Roel Van Der Veen's 2004 instructive tone, "What Went Wrong With Africa" [15] is a modern account of why Africa is the way it is while other continents prospered; and about how globalization, lack of viable institutions and democracy and other factors have impacted the continent. All these problems account for why Africa is vastly under-developed. "Why, despite the rising prosperity elsewhere in the world and widespread changes that took place on the continent itself, Africa failed to break free of poverty after gaining independence" [16]. How did a continent so rich in human and natural resources ended up being the most famished and underdeveloped of all continents?

Africa is not unique in any way. Virtually every negative that has ever happened in Africa has happened elsewhere. [17] But while other continents are putting their houses in order development variables are adrift in Africa. For instance, there is no linkage between the government and the people. What's more, African leaders weaken and corrupt their own institutions; they manipulate the poor and the uneducated; they play sectional and ethnic politics; they do not differentiate between public and private interests thereby illegally enriching themselves; they have no respect for human life and human dignity; and they rely on coercive agencies to do their biddings. All of the aforesaid have compounded Africa's problems.

What are Africa's main problems and challenges? These include internal factors such as corruption both at the personal and institutional level; poor culture of savings and investment; inadequate macro and micro economic policies; high level of illiteracy; lack of viable economic, political and social institutions; a self-loathing mentality which assumes everything Western is better than Africa's; and the unfounded expectation on the part of Africans that the western countries will come to their assistance.

External factors include the lingering effects of slavery and colonization; interference in Africa's domestic affairs by western and non-western nations; the insidious effects of globalization and westernization; exploitation of the continent's human and natural resources by foreign powers and other entities;

and the sometimes insidious effects of the international political and economic system. In addition, African countries, through the Structural Adjustment Programs, policies instituted and dictated by the International Monetary Fund and the World Bank, are forced to remove subsidy on such staples as bread and rice on which African masses are dependent on.

Other conditions, such as free trade, open markets and the liberalization of the economy tend to stunt the continent's industrial space; hence, the majority of African manufacturers are unable to compete with their foreign counterparts. And in some cases, African markets became the dumping ground for foreign goods. Furthermore, the terms of trade and balance of payment were never in favor of Africa. Consequently, the continent became and continues to be the world's dumping ground for inferior goods and services. Today, Africans are mainly consumers, as opposed to being producers of goods and services.

COUNTRIES CASE STUDIES

In the years before or immediately following political independence, rarely was the African leaders without a development philosophy or a governing worldview. Their positions were generally well enunciated; but due to endogenous and exogenous reasons, most of these leaders failed in their pursuit of their economic, social, and political agenda. Their promises came to naught because "promise is not performance; and philosophies are easier to enunciate than to put into practice. Moreover, a proclamation of good principles is not a pledge of good intentions" [18]. According to Damachi, these leaders couched their promises and visions in one form of ideology or another. Kenneth Kaunda of Zambia for instance espoused Humanism; Seretse Khama of Botswana ideology was of Harmony; Mohammar Gaddafi pursued Arab Islamic Socialism; Marien N'Gouabi of the Congo was interested in Scientific Socialism; and Julius Nyerere was all about Ujamaa-Socialism and Rural Development [19].

Fifty years after independence, all the aforementioned countries still lag behind in terms of development. In all these countries, there is a high degree of needs that are not being met by the government or by the private sector. And indeed, they all performed poorly on the United Nations Development Program on Human Development Index [20]. Of the 185 Member states of the United Nations that were profiled, Zambia ranked 164; Cote d'Ivoire rank 170; Botswana, 118; Tanzania 152; Congo 137; and Libya 64. Nigeria ranks 156 and is a microcosm of what is wrong with the African continent. In spite of her human and natural resources, she is still a beggar-nation. She is a beggar-nation because, amongst other factors, she has been ruled by a succession of mostly corrupt and functional illiterate leaders. The greed and the excesses of Nigerian leaders is a major source of Nigeria's development crisis. This gluttony is manifested in the level and pervasiveness of corruption and other economic, political and social ills of the country. Nigerian leaders and their elites generally do not draw a demarcation between what is public and what is private and so they feast on the public treasury.

Some of the obstacles to Nigeria's development are (1) low productivity; (2) misuse and mismanagement of capital for investment and savings and for credit and ability to borrow from abroad; (3) the conditions for foreign trade in terms of unfavorable balance of trade and balance of payment; (4) lack of viable institutions; (5) personal and institutional corruption; (6) marginal health care services and education; and (7) rapid increase in population. For much of its existence as a nation-state, Nigeria has been governed by third-rate leaders who, along with their cronies, have plundered the nation's wealth and ruined the country's institutions. It is a country that is living well below its potential. It is also a country that has managed to curtail its people's hope, aspiration, and possibilities. It is a country that cannot conveniently provide public goods such as security, public infrastructures, and an enabling environment for decent living [21].

Foreign Aids

Moreover, there is the insidious politics involved in foreign aids. Over the long run, foreign aids do not serve any real purpose. The corruption and politics of foreign aid aside, what good would it do any self-respecting people to continually depend on handouts? What does our penchant for handouts tell the world about us? Today, most African countries depend on foreign assistance to stay afloat. These aids are injurious to a continent's psyche: it encourages laziness and indolence; and makes receiving countries dependent on donor countries. Over the long run, receiving countries become indebted to donor countries and in due course become an appendage to the donor countries. The West, as a rule, does not give a cent out of the sheer goodness of their heart. These are capitalist countries and not charity organizations; and capitalism is all about profit and self-interest.

African leaders and their political elites should be allowed to roast in the inhumane conditions they have created. These can be done if the West (1) denies African elites and ruling class funds and any kind of investments in western nations, (2) denies African leaders, along with their proxies and family members, medical treatment in hospitals in the West [22]; (3) denies the children of these leaders access to western education; (4) except for meetings at such places as the United Nations, decline all visa applications by African leaders; and (5) grants members of the civil society the right to sue African leaders in western courts, especially in the case of theft, money laundering, and crimes against humanity. The aforesaid steps need to be taken by Western Governments if the African-malignancy is to be arrested. What the West owes Africa are not foreign aid, not handouts, not grants and definitely not loans.

What Africans Should Do

The revival and strengthening of the legislature and the judiciary; the education and reeducation of the people and the introduction of a new political and governing system would be in order. Most Nigerians, for instance, are weary and wary of the military establishment. Still, they ought to fashion a governing system that allows for military institutions and civil governing structures to coexist. For instance, the American or British style system does not seem to augur well for Nigeria's peculiar condition. Most foreign aids are not aids in the real sense of the word since most of the allotted money/material/service never makes it to the intended enclaves; and even when they do, such aids never achieve the intended impact.

Consolidate Nation States

There are countries in Africa that shouldn't have been nation-states in the first place. These are countries that are just too small, too poor, vastly undereducated, lacking human and natural resources and are not ready to be truly independent states. Some of these countries should have formed confederations or at best, teamed up with other countries to form one independent state. But pride and undue nationalistic feelings "convinced" them they needed independence. Unfortunately, flag independence does not pay workers' salaries, pave roads, build schools and hospital, eradicate diseases, provide for public infrastructures and other life' necessities.

Thus, decades after "political independence," these countries do not have the wherewithal to administer their own affairs as they are constantly in need of foreign aids and other forms of assistance from the West or from other countries that would listen to their pleas for help. For instance, Rwanda, Burundi and Uganda would have been better off as one single country; just as Republic of Benin and Togo should have been a single country, ditto Senegal and Gambia. Same can be said of Burkina Faso, Mali, and a host of other African countries. Aside from historical reasons, what business does Swaziland and Lesotho has to be independent countries? Wouldn't' they have been better off as an integral part of South Africa?

Profits from Foreign Direct Investment

Profits from FDI (or any sort of investment) should be restricted from being taken out of the continent (no less than 35 percent in 5 years). Such windfalls should be reinvested in the continent. True, capitalism and globalization allows for unimpeded investment and roaming of profits, the fact is that the continent is not economically strong and politically buoyant to allow for such unregulated economic practice. Globalization or not, Africa needs this sort of protection from global sharks.

Abolish the Military

In virtually every African country, the military (navy, air force and army and paramilitary) has been used to oppress and punish the populace, and are sometime used to usurp constitutional rule. Only the Police and the national intelligence service should be retained. No sub-Saharan African country truly needs an army. None! A small militarized peace keeping unit may be constituted, and controlled by regional bodies like the Economic Community of West African States or the larger African Union.

BUDGETARY CONTROL

At least for the next two decades, upward of 75 percent of the total budget be spent on education, health care, and water and sewage treatment plant and on the other fundamentals of development (basic human needs). Of this amount, no less than 25 percent should be spent on education and healthcare. This could be reduced by 5 percent each year after the first 11th year but must at no time fall below 10 percent. Other areas of the economy are transportation and housing should be privatized. And indeed, it should be illegal for governments to engage in White Elephant Projects like stadiums, airports, shopping malls, and seaports.

Discourage Ethnicity: questions and references to ethnicity and religious affiliation should be deleted in private sector and government documents, i.e. employment applications, voter's registration card and school admission forms. In contesting elections, only residency and other qualifications should matter. Also, more than 50 percent of secondary schools must be boarding schools with no more than 70 percent of the student body being indigenes. Boarding schools helps with the detribalization process.

REVERSE MIGRATION OF AFRICANS

Overseas/diasporan Africans must, on their own volition, return to their respective countries to help with the economic, social and political process. For too long, the general argument has been that the political, economic and social space is not conducive, secured or big enough for all those who may wish to return home. This sort of reasoning is outdated, and a copout. Some of the continent's best and brightest are in exile, leaving some of the continent's dumbest (and brightest criminals) to rule and to plunder.

THE WEST'S OBLIGATIONS TO AFRICA

The United States and other western nations must stop behaving as though there is nothing wrong with the African continent. Or that they can continue to exploit, or encourage the exploitation of the continent without dire consequences. They cannot turn blind eyes to the excesses of the elites and the continent's leadership. By their actions and inactions they encourage theft and all kinds of illegal and unethical behaviors. The Western Powers encourage antidemocratic behaviors; and also wholeheartedly encourage the illegal trading of dreams, hopes and aspirations. But most of all, they encourage the underdevelopment of a whole group of people and their land. What does the world owe Africa? Simple: encourage and help the African people so they can put a stop to the bastardization of their peoples, land, and develop viable institutions [23].

It is impossible to tell, with any degree of certainty, how Africa would have turned out without slavery and colonialism [24]. All we can do is guess, make conjectures. Nonetheless, considering the fate of other peoples in other continents, and considering also the history of the continent, it is safe to say Africa too would have had its fair share of historical-unavoidable. Overall, one does not share in the excessive romanticism of the continent and its past; moreover, one does not have a hangover over slavery and colonialism. The time to move on has long gone. But unfortunately, too many Africans, encouraged by African leaders and continental elites, and some scholars, have made it fashionable to blame slavery and colonialism for all the ills of the continent.

There are religious leaders who harps fatalism into the consciousness of their followers. However, a sizeable number of Africans have refused to take personal responsibility for the continent's failure and recklessness. Day in and day out, they wait for a God or for a Rawlings with magical wand. In addition, they look to the West for direction and for handouts.

In spite of the aforesaid, Africans themselves must take back their own continent; they must take back their own countries. The West can help, but for the most part, Africans must do the unthinkable and the painful to regain their world. As it is, Africans are afraid: they are afraid to sacrifice their conveniences and their lives, and are very much afraid to venture into an uncertain future. This timidity is more pronounced in the post-independence generation, a generation that is given to immediate gratification, laziness and gullibility. For the most part, they imitate absurdities from other regions, especially from the west.

After fifty years that most of African countries have gained independence, the continent continues to have a striking resemblance to the Africa of the 18th and 19th centuries. Any wonder then that some commentators have insinuated that the continent was better off colonized. Indeed, in one country after another, the conditions are similar, similarities that are manifested in low quality of life. In virtually every country, the average African has been betrayed by the political leaders, intellectual class, the military cadre, and by the civil society (selling out to the oligarchy and to foreign agents).

For Africa to advance, certain unorthodox steps have to be taken. The suggestions here can be improved upon. However, one must take into consideration the fact that for more than fifty years, all types of paradigms and approaches have been rendered and tried to no avail [25]. It is time to think and act unconventionally. Trepidation will not help. Fear will not help. Dithering will not help. And neither will the little-little things. Virtually every African country lacks the fundamentals of development. They lack the infrastructures.

Of all the problems facing the African continent, weak institutions and the crisis of governance, the enmity between the rulers and the governed, the inability to draw lines between public and private goods, preliterate and fatalistic citizenry, the sheer stupidity and low self-esteem of African leaders, and the question of good and visionary leadership is the most pressing. Beginning with Ghana in 1957, to South Africa in 1994, contemporary Africa has not had more than five first-rate leaders. Since leadership is the bane of the continent, why not act on it?

THE FIFTY YEAR VERDICT

Up until the twentieth century, the vast majority of people who lived on planet earth were poor, weak, uneducated, superstitious, and prone to diseases and natural disasters. But the industrial revolution, which begun in nineteenth century Britain and which gradually spread to other parts of the world changed all that. This was practically the beginning of human progress since the revolution positively affected all aspects of mankind, in terms of gender role, the nature and structure of society, the role and place of science, technology and the arts. It is a different world we live in today even if a sizeable number of people still live in agrarian condition. Countries with industrial base or mobility are either absent or weak are mostly in the global south: South America, Asia, and Africa.

Of the three zones, Africa, as data and everyday realities have shown, is perhaps the least developed. It is not as if the African continent does not have the wherewithal to grow, to develop and to prosper. It does! And in some places, it has all the ingredients it will ever need, in abundance. There are times when it is impossible, or even imprudent, to generalize as to why the African continent is still crawling. Nonetheless, several factors, such as endogenous and exogenous have contributed to the continent's sad and painful condition.

The Role of Academic/Intellectual Organizations

Whether the continent and its people will ever move out of its preliterate condition is subject to debate and to academic probing. Year after year, and in country after country, individuals and organizations have devoted their time, resources and intellect to tackling the African wahala (African problems). Some notable individual scholars in the field of African Studies include Bereket Selassie, Julius E. Nyang'oro, F. Ugboaja Ohaegbulam, Mario Azevedo, Sulayman S. Nyang, Ali Mazrui, Georges Ntalaja-Nzongola, E.C Ejiogu, Cyril Obi, Robert Edgar, and Robert H. Bates. The African Studies Association (ASA) is the foremost academic organization/association on and about Africa, in North America. It relentlessly probes the continent [26].

The theme for the 2011 was "50 Years of African Liberation, in which this book has taken its title. According to the association,

> The period 1960-1961 marked a watershed in Africa, as the largest number of countries gained independence.
>
> These transformations signaled the beginning of five decades of struggle for democracy and development.
>
> There is much to celebrate today, Africa has the highest number of democracies since 1960; institutionalized apartheid has been eliminated in southern Africa; and women are emerging as political actors. At the same time the fifty year mark provides us with an opportunity to reflect critically on the complex ways that history has unfolded on the continent" [27].

Hence, the organization invited scholars, students, commentators and others to "reflect on the many achievements, challenges and disappointments the past five decades have heralded" [28]. Indeed, many achievements are associated with the continent; but for the most part, the last fifty years have been a history of catastrophes, mysteries, wars, famine and hungers, of coups and counter coups, and of man's inhumanity to man. Across the continent, and in specific places like Nigeria, what we see and what we have experienced, are failed leadership; weak and fragmenting institutions; a debased political and economic space; the manipulation of the poor and the weak; the theft of public funds, and many other socio-cultural and socio-political calamities.

In more recent times, we see the sickening emergence of dynastic rule at all levels of governance. The African peoples themselves seem helpless and unsure of what to do. It is as if several decades of poverty, abuse, rape and deprivation have caused them to lose their voice and their courage. We especially see this at the academe where, unlike the 1960s to the mid-1980s, when the Nigerian university system was a bastion of activism. The Nigerian intellectual class from which many courageous ideas and ideals emanated has yet to recover after being emasculated and asphyxiated by successive authoritarian and military governments. We seem to forget that a nation without its intellectual class has no hope of significant successes. This is where Nigeria, the so-called giant of Africa is today. Fifty years plus after liberation, she wobbles and gropes aimlessly.

During the colonial era, several African leaders traversed the continent selling dreams and making promises. Frankly, the list is very impressive: Kwame Nkrumah, Sekou Toure, Félix Houphouët-Boigny, Tafawa Balewa, Julius Nyerere, Haile Selassie, Leopold Senghor, Ahmadou Ahidjo, Patrice Lumumba, Leopold Senghor, Nnamdi Azikiwe, Jomo Kenyatta, Agostinho Neto, and many more. These men and several dozen more men and women made promises. They failed. Ironically, all the men and women who followed in their footstep or by way of military coups also failed. Successes, or whatever that counted for success, were, frankly, marginal.

But beyond the independence ceremonies, what other gains and advancements can one say have accrued to the African after five decades of liberation? What lasting economic and/or political gains are there to note or to celebrate? In what ways did the liberation of the continent helped women, children and minority groups and their interests? For many countries, industrialization is not even at the horizon. Why is there not a single African country where basic needs and human security has been advanced? From Mauritania to Somalia, and from Egypt to South Africa, is there an ideal African country?

The cost of political struggle and liberation was heavy. It was exorbitant. But what have the everyday African gained after all these years? And therefore, when 50 Years of African Liberation is studied by groups, individuals and institutions, the results are about to be the same; several decades of unmet promises; mounting and increasingly complicated challenges, and unwarranted failures. Fifty long and painful years later, the struggle continues. But for how long must the Africans continue to struggle in order to escape the odious, the insidious, and the lecherous system they live in?

Across the continent, the only groups of people who can claim any measure of success are the elite, the oligarchies or the nouveau riche (the new rich). The oligarchies, especially, have stolen and continuing stealing more. In addition, they have hijacked the judiciary and the legislative system. In concert with their foreign partners, they continue to enslave the people. This is where we are today. If one were to be generous in his assessment, one could say that a few African countries are on the rise, and that they are about to turn the corner. Just a few! But fifty years after independence, is *just a few*.

In the case of Nigeria, it is difficult, if not outright impossible for one to imagine the country "being on the rise" or "turning the corner." Why not? The answers are simple: The political will is not there. The leadership quality is not there. The institutions are not strong enough. The people are not ready and are not in the right frame of mind yet. What's more the ethnic and religious dynamics of the country makes liberation and genuine progress difficult. We may have to wait another fifty years. Sad, isn't it?

THE MILITARY IN AFRICA

One cannot discuss Africa pre and post-independent Africa without mentioning the role and place of the Armed Forces. Indeed, the military has played a very prominent role in the development and underdevelopment of the continent. During the colonial era, for instance, they helped to maintain law and order. And in the post-colonial era, especially in West and Central Africa, they inserted themselves into politics [29]. The Nigerian Armed Forces, for instance, have a mixed record: adept at coups; and like their counterparts in many parts of the continent, it has largely been seen until very recent times as a destabilizing force in the domestic affairs of the nation. Overall, there have been five successful coups in Nigeria: in 1966, 1975, 1983, 1985, and 1993. But in spite of its penchant for coups, the Nigerian Armed Forces has had a long history of peacekeeping missions abroad. For instance, it was an integral part of peacekeeping engagements under the United Nations, and as the core elements in ECOWAS/ECOMOG and African Union-led peacekeeping efforts in places such as Liberia, Sierra Leone [30], and Sudan [31]. Since the last coup in 1993, Nigeria has enjoyed a prolonged period of stable government.

CONCLUSION: HOPE FOR THE FUTURE?

According to *The Economist*, "after decades of slow growth, Africa has a real chance to follow in the footsteps of Asia" [32], The magazine went on to say that "over the past decade six of the world's ten fastest-growing countries were African. In eight of the past ten years (2000-2010), Africa has grown faster than East Asia, including Japan. Even allowing for the knock-on effect of the northern hemisphere's slowdown, the IMF expects Africa to grow by 6 percent in 2011 and nearly 6 percent in 2012, about the same as Asia (see the GDP map of Africa)."

The Economist went on to say that significant and measurable changes are taking place in the continent: "labor productivity has been rising. It is now growing by an average of 2.7 percent a year. Trade between Africa and the rest of the world has increased by 200 percent since 2000. Inflation dropped from 22 percent in the 1990s to 8 percent in the past decade. Foreign debts declined by a quarter, budget deficits by two-thirds" [33], But in spite of the bright lights, we are cautioned:

Optimism about Africa needs to be taken in fairly small doses, for things are still exceedingly bleak in much of the continent. Most Africans live on less than two dollars a day. Food production per person has slumped since independence in the 1960s. The average lifespan in some countries is under 50.

Drought and famine persist. The climate is worsening, with deforestation and desertification still on the march [34].

We are also reminded that some countries praised for their breakneck economic growth, such as Angola and Equatorial Guinea, which are oil-sodden kleptocracies. Some that have begun to get economic development right, such as Rwanda and Ethiopia, have become politically noxious. Congo, now undergoing a shoddy election, still looks barely governable and hideously corrupt. Zimbabwe is a scar on the conscience of the rest of southern Africa. South Africa, which used to be a model for the continent, is tainted with corruption; and within the ruling African National Congress there is talk of nationalizing land and mines [35].

The African continent is full of contradictions. On the one hand, all evidence points to its continuing growth and development. After all, all the resources and factors necessary for advancement can be found on the continent. What's more, the vast majority of the people are hardworking and resilient. But on the other hand, this is a continent that has gone through several peaks and valleys, and its people constantly being oppressed by their leaders. Beginning in the 1960s, in one country after another, African leaders, be they military or civilian in dispensation have been physically chaining and mentally abusing their peoples. What's more, they collaborate with foreign and domestic agents and saboteurs to loot their own resources.

Many of today's African leaders and elites are no different from Europeans who showed up in the continent in the 15th century to partake in the enslavement of African peoples and the destruction of the continent. Essentially, slavery and the economic exploitation of the continent have not ended, only that it has taken a new shape and a new form, what Kwame Nkrumah called *Neo-colonialism*. Considering the state of the continent, therefore, liberation total freedom from oppression and poor human needs is at least another fifty years away. Promises were made, but the continent and its people are, today, deluged with challenges and problems. In the estimation of Chinua Achebe, the African continent is "a place of strange, bizarre and illogical things, where people don't do what common sense demands" [36]. And that's precisely the problem. Indeed, development statistics may point to those things that are economically possible. It is not as if the continent is completely hopeless. No. It is a continent and a people capable of greatness. But beyond the statistics and the hope are the practical things the continent needs to do.

Nigeria is a microcosm of the African continent. During the 2012 Seoul Nuclear Security Summit in South Korea [37], the Nigerian president, Mr. Goodluck Ebele Jonathan, promised to transform the Nigerian economy to rival those of the four Asian Tigers [38] within the next few years (even though he had only two years left in office). His promise was unrealistic [39]. It is the type of promise African leaders have been making to their people since independence, but to no avail. Moving various economies in the continent, from agrarianism to manufacturing and service based, has been an uphill battle. For Nigerian or any African country to replicate to any degree of success, such country or groups of countries must be able to produce a succession of good leaders who encourages and pursues strong and enabling institutions; a national culture that emphasizes savings and investments; good leadership, accountability, and transparency, the provision of quality education and other basic needs.

They also must promote national integration, and drastically cut down on waste and corruption. But beyond the obvious are the fact that African countries must be serious about development and about what it means to be a part of the global community in the twenty-first century. But the first things first: provide basic needs, infrastructure, and also repair the inherent deficits that greatly hinder the continent's growth and development. Eradicate the complex system of patronage, endemic corruption, inefficiencies in the private and public sectors, nepotism, state violence and public crimes, and the personalization of the rule of law; and a decomposing political system and structure that makes governance very difficult. If these problems, that are endogenous and exogenous in nature, are properly addressed, Africa will rise. The next fifty years, therefore, may look vastly different from the preceding fifty years. A hopeful, bright and thriving future it might be.

What are the alternatives to a hopeful, bright and thriving Africa? Africans cannot afford the alternatives – alternatives that might include secessionist movements; religious, resource, ethnic conflicts and associated social dislocations; new and the spread of diseases; youth restiveness; and a general breakdown of law and order and social mores. Those who think these are not possible should take a second look of the Africa of the last quarter-century. What they see will only worsen.

REFERENCES

[1] Edward H. Judge and John W. Langdon, *Connections: A World History to 1650*, New York: Pearson Press, 2012.

[2] Ibid.

[3] In spite of the widespread belief that Africa is the origin of the humans, several scientists, have argued that human origin may not lie exclusively in the continent. For instance, see the work of Vinayak Eswaran, Henry Harpending, and Alan R. Rogers, "Genomics refutes an exclusively African Origin of Humans," *Journal of Human Evolution*, vol. 49, issue 1, July 2005, p.1-18.

[4] The Renaissance was a cultural movement that began in Northern Italy and spread through Europe. It began in the 14th century and lasted through the 17th century. It positively affected virtually all areas of life and avocation in terms of music, arts and culture, philosophy, and politics. For a detailed understanding of this movement, please see: J.H Plumb (June 19, 2002), The Italian Renaissance published by Mariner Books; revised edition. See also Paul Johnson, *The Renaissance: A Short History*, published by Modern Library, August 6, 2002.

[5] Malyn Newitt, editor, *The Portuguese in West Africa, 1415 – 1670: A Documentary History*, New York: Cambridge University Press, 2010

[6] See M. Alpha Bah "Legitimate Trade, Diplomacy, and the Slave Trade" in Mario Azevedo, editor, *Africana Studies: A Survey of Africa and the African Diaspora*, Durham, NC: Carolina Academic Press, 2005.

[7] Ten million was the initial estimate given by Philip Curtin. 12-15 million is a more realistic figure. According to M. Alpha Bah (2005), "J. Oliver Martins gave an estimate of 20 million, while W. E. B Dubois, J. D. Fage, and Basil Davidson estimated it to be in the range of 50 million."

[8] Britain, for instance, abolished slavery in 1833. In the French colonies, slavery ended in 1848. In the United States, slavery ended after the 13th amendment to the US Constitution in 1865.

[9] See Nathan Nunn, "The Long-term Effects of Africa's Slave Trades" in *The Quarterly Journal of Economics*, February 2008. See also Rodney, Walter. *How Europe Underdeveloped Africa*, London: Bogle-L'Ouverture Publications, 1972.

[10] Eleven European powers took part: the Netherlands, Austria-Hungary, Belgium, France, Italy, Denmark, the United Kingdom, Russia, Spain, Sweden-Norway, and the Ottoman Empire. The US took part in the deliberations as an observer.

[11] For a cogent understanding of Afrocentricism, please see Molefi Kete Asante (August 2, 2000), "Afrocentricity: Toward a New Understanding of African Thought in this Millennium", University of Liverpool accessed 11, February 2009. See also Adeleke, Tunde. "Will The Real Father of Afrocentricity Please Stand?" Western Journal of Black Studies No. 25, 21-29, Spring 2001. Also see Armstrong, Ketra L., "Black Students' Responses to Afrocentric Communication Stimuli." *Journal of Black Psychology,* 31, 67-86, February 2005.

[12] For Eurocentricism, please see Blaut, James M, Eight Eurocentric Historians, Guilford Press, New York; Brahman, John (1995), "Universalism, Eurocentrism, and Ideological Bias in Development Studies: From Modernization to Neoliberalism." Third World Quarterly 16, 1, 121-140; and Brahman, John, "Universalism, Eurocentrism, and Ideological Bias in Development Studies: From Modernization to Neoliberalism." *Third World Quarterly,* 16, 1, 121-140, 1995.

[13] John Isbister, *Promises Not Kept: The Betrayal of Social Change in The Third World,* West Hartford, CT: Kumarian Press, 1998.

[14] Ibid.

[15] Roel Van Der Veen, *What Went Wrong with Africa*, Amsterdam, New York: KIT Publishers, 2004.

[16] Ibid.

[17] Until 1723 when Peter the Great converted house slavery into house serfs, slavery was a major institution in Russia. For a fuller account, please see Historical survey Ways of ending slavery in Encyclopedia Britannica (http://www.britannica.com/blackhistory/article-24160). And according to Suzanne Miers, in 1841, there were about 8 or 9 million slaves in India. For this account please see http://www.yale.edu/glc /events/cbss/Miers.pdf. And in the Americas, slavery dates back to the Aztec. Essentially, therefore, virtually all the inhabitable continents have had slavery in one form or another. Today, many of the countries in these countries are either developing or have supercharged economies. It is only in Africa that slavery and colonization seems to have stunted growth and development.

[18] Ukandi G. Damachi, Leadership Ideology in Africa: Attitudes toward Socioeconomic Development, New York: Praeger Publishers, 1976.

[19] The detailed exposition of these ideologies can be found in Ukandi G. Damachi's book, "Leadership ideology in Africa." Kaunda's Humanism is said to be derived from the African culture; Houphouet-Boigny's ideology is culled from capitalism; Seretse Khama's Kagisano, or Harmony, is based on unity, peace, harmony and a sense of community; Julius Nyerere's Ujamaa is an ideology that centered on socialism and rural development; Marien N'Gouabi development worldview is based on what he termed scientific socialism; and Muammar Al-Ghaddafi's ideology drives from Arab-Islamic socialism. See Ukandi G. Damachi Ibid.

[20] The Human Development (HDI) is a summary measure of human development. It measures the average achievements in a country in three basic dimensions of human development: a long and healthy life (health), access to knowledge (education) and a decent standard of living (income). Data availability determines HDI country coverage. To enable cross-country comparisons, the HDI is to the extent possible, calculated based on data from leading international data agencies and other credible data sources available at the time of writing. For a full explanation of the HDI and its role, see: http://hdr.undp.org/en/countries/ accessed 02/20 /2012.

[21] Daniel Jordan Smith, *A Culture of Corruption: Everyday Deception and Popular Discontent in Nigeria*, Princeton, NJ: Princeton University Press, 2007.

[22] According to Channels Television, a private television station in Nigeria, The Minister of Health Professor Onyebuchi Chukwu, would soon

recommend that paid overseas medical service for public officials be discontinued unless of course such services and treatments cannot be carried out in Nigeria. Such treatments and services have been a burden on the Nigerian treasury. In addition, the availability of such option accounts for why the ruling class, along with high-ranking members of the civil service, has been reluctant to upgrade the Nigerian health care system. For complete media coverage, see “FG to bar officials from foreign medical trips:” http://www.channelstv.com/home/2012/04/14/fg-to-bar-officials-from-foreign-medical-trips/ accessed April 5, 2012.

[23] There is the belief amongst Africans that the western nations of Europe and North America really do not care about the continent so long as they have unhindered access to Africa’s raw and cheap materials, and so long as the people of the continent continues to buy foreign goods and services. Africa, essentially, is basically an afterthought vis-à-vis the international political economic system.

[24] The British Broadcasting Corporation (BBC) QUOTED Mohamed Shaibu Abdulai, as saying that Africa's loss of millions of the strongest men and women during the slave trade is one reason for Africa’s slow growth and underdevelopment. He went on to say that “"The slave trade actually prevented the coming into being of an agrarian revolution in Ghana, and likewise an industrial revolution. Because before you can industrialize you need to have stable agricultural production. So slavery has a very long effect." See Slavery's long effects on Africa: http://news.bbc.co.uk/2/hi/africa/6504141.stm accessed April 7, 2012.

[25] Several development paradigms have attempted to explain underdevelopment, i.e. the Lewis model; Harrod-Domar model; the theory of balanced growth; the theory of circular causation; Modernization; and Dependency. Of all the aforementioned theories, the modernization and dependency theories seem to have interested African studies scholars the most. For instance, according to modernization theory, internal factors, such as illiteracy, traditional agrarian structure, the traditional attitude of the population, the low division of labor, the lack of communication and infrastructure, etc., are responsible for underdevelopment. The modernization theory erroneously assumes that traditional societies needed to go through a set of stages in order to reach economic progress. Dependencia basically asserts that that poor countries exiled to the periphery of the world economy could not develop as long as they remained enslaved by the rich nations at the center of the global economic system.

[26] The ASA was founded in 1957, with the primary goal of promoting the study of the continent in all academic disciplines. There are currently 1700 due paying members and institutions subscribing to the ASA. The organization convened its 54th annual conference from November 16th through the 19th at the Marriott Wardman Park Hotel, Washington DC. A multitude of people, including researchers, ivory-tower based scholars, public intellectuals, and students and various organizations, partook in the intellectual pursuit.

[27] See Olayiwola Abegunrin, *Africa in Global Politics in the Twenty-First Century: A Pan-African Perspective*, New York: Palgrave Macmillan, 2009.

[28] African Studies Association,"50 Years of African Liberation," 54th Annual Meeting of the African Studies Association, held in Washington, D.C., November 17-19, 2011.

[29] Over the years, there have been several works done on military intervention in Africa's politics. However, three notable works in this regard are: Claude E. Welch, Jr., *Soldier and State in Africa*. Northwestern University Press, Evanston, IL: 1970. Also see Ruth First *The Barrel of a Gun: Political Power in Africa and the Coup d'Etat,* London: Allen Lane Penguin Press; 1970, and Samuel Decalo, *Coups and Army Rule in Africa*, New Haven, CT: Yale University Press, 1976.

[30] Margaret Vogt, *The Liberian Crisis and ECOMOG: A Bold Attempt at Regional Peacekeeping*, Lagos: Gabumo Press, 1993. Also see Funmi Olonisakin, *Reinventing Peacekeeping in Africa: Conceptual and Legal Issues in ECOMOG Operations*, The Hague: Kluwer Law International, 2000.

[31] See Adekeye Adebajo, op. cit.

[32] "The Hopeful Continent: Africa Rising." *The Economist*, Print Edition, December 3, 2011.

[33] Ibid, p. 82.

[34] Ibid, p. 15.

[35] Ibid.

[36] The longer version of this quote—which has been attributed to Chinua Achebe and which has been cited by several books and reputable websites—reads: "People go to Africa and confirm what they already have in their heads and so they fail to see what is there in front of them. This is what people have come to expect. It's not viewed as a serious continent. It's a place of strange, bizarre, and illogical things, where people don't do what common sense demands." See for instance, Ama

Biney's Resisting hegemony: 10 years of Pambazuka News at: http://www.pambazuka.org/en/category/features/67669/print See also *Exploring African Life and Literature: Novel Guides to Promote Socially Responsive Learning* by Jacqueline N. Glasgow and Linda J. Rice, Newark, Delaware, June 28, 2007.

[37] According to official statement, the "2012 Seoul Nuclear Security Summit", which was held in Seoul, South Korea, from March 26 to 27, is the largest summit in the security field that discusses international cooperative measures to protect nuclear materials and facilities from terrorist groups, with participation from more than 53 heads of state and international organizations. The main issues discussed at the Summit were as follows: Cooperative measures to combat the threat of nuclear terrorism; Protection of nuclear materials and related facilities; and Prevention of illicit trafficking of nuclear materials.

[38] In economic and development parlance, the Asian Tigers refers to the highly developed economies of South Korea, Taiwan, Hong Kong and Singapore. From the early 1960s through the 1990s, these countries experienced super-growth: their economies grew around 9% every year during those decades. By the tail end of the twentieth century, these four economies had bridged the gulf with Canada, the US, Britain, France and other industrialized economies of the world.

[39] See Sabella Abidde, "Jonathan promises to replicate Asian Tigers economy in Nigeria," *The Punch newspaper*, Lagos, March 27, 2012.

In: Africa
Editor: Olayiwola Abegunrin
ISBN: 978-1-62948-561-4

Chapter 2

REEXAMINING THE VICTORY OF THE BATTLE OF ADWA: A PAN-AFRICAN AND POST-INDEPENDENCE AFRICAN PERSPECTIVES

Getachew Metaferia
Professor of International Studies, Department of Political Science,
Morgan State University, Baltimore, Maryland, US

INTRODUCTION

Historically, the great North African warrior and military genius, Hannibal, waged a war against Rome in 218 B.C. Since then, during the period of European Imperialism, African leaders such as the 17th century Queen Nzenga of [Angola] and the 18th century Shaka Zulu of South Africa have fought against slavery and resisted European imperialism. The Battle of Adwa was a military confrontation between Ethiopia and Italy in 1896 at Adwa, a small town in Northern Ethiopia. The battle heralded the first victory by an African country over a European [p]ower in recent history. Emperor Menelik of Ethiopia rendered a devastating defeat to a well-armed Italian force that ventured to colonize Ethiopia. The defeat of a European power by an African leader sent a mixed wave of fear and admiration for Menelik in European capitals. The Battle of Adwa demonstrated the African ability to withstand a European military advance and bolstered the African psyche both in Africa and among Africans in the diaspora. Furthermore, the successful battle invigorated the Pan-African struggle against colonialism, imperialism, Euro-based domination, and slavery. The Ethiopian success at the Battle of Adwa, therefore, is an epic achievement in the modern history of Africa. This chapter reexamines and analyzes the significance of the victory of the Battle of Adwa to the Pan-African movement and to the post-independence Africa.

PAN-AFRICANISM

Pan-Africanism is a global racial identity that transcends territorial political boundaries and is a belief in the common historical, racial, and experiential background that all blacks share [1]. The early emphasis of pan-Africanism was to recapture the racial identity and pride of black people that was lost because of slavery, colonialism, and social oppression [2]. The idea of Pan-Africanism was born in the West, especially in the United States. It is a global racial identity that transcends territorial political boundaries [3] and is a belief that the destiny of all Blacks is intertwined.

The genesis of Pan-Africanism, as a movement, can be traced back to the different political and religious movements called Ethiopianism or the Ethiopian movement. Ethiopianism, or the concept of Ethiopia, was a generic reference to the black race or to the continent of Africa. Later, the name Ethiopia came to refer to the specific geographical area of what was at one time called Abyssinia. Ethiopianism was a messianic and quasi-religious movement that was inspired by the reference to Ethiopia in the Old Testament; a prophesy that: "Ethiopia shall soon stretch out her hands unto God" [Psalm 68, verse 31].

The core value of Ethiopianism or Black Nationalism was to rid Blacks from the dehumanizing situation under colonialism and slavery, to which Blacks are subjected. The total liberation of Africa, the emancipation of all Blacks of the diaspora, and the unity of Black people remained at the core of the movement [4]. Ethiopia symbolized the Pan-African movement --- a belief in the borderless racial unity of all Blacks who face the same form of subjugation, oppression, and dehumanizing experience. In order to reverse the situation, the unity of blacks, the level of consciousness, and the resolve to alter the situation had a paramount importance.

The messianic message, as expressed above in the Old Testament, was interpreted that God will deliver all Black people from the social, economic, and political oppression and dehumanizing situations heaped on Black people by some European countries, especially by the propagators of racism and colonialism. Ethiopianism, therefore, was a confidence-builder, an uplifting message. Its influence and impact resonated in literary and economic spheres. It was embraced by persons who came from a wide and diverse range of backgrounds and geographic locations. Hence, "Ethiopianism [was] not only a trans-Atlantic political movement, but a literary movement well-known among all black people from the Congo basin to the mountains of Jamaica to the sidewalks of New York city" [5].

The Pan-African movement, inspired by Ethiopianism, was conceived and brought to the fore by westerners: US and Caribbean intellectuals, such as William Edward Burghardt Dubois, an intellectual and Henry Sylvester Williams, a lawyer, from Trinidad. Henry Sylvester Williams coined the word "Pan-Africa" and convened the first Pan-African conference in 1900. W. E. B. Dubois convened the Pan-African conference of 1919, held in Paris, France, and the 1945 Pan- African Congress in Manchester, Britain. Both personalities were instrumental not only in convening conferences but also in crystallizing the vision of the movement [6].

It should be noted that the initial Pan-African movement was among Anglophone Africans and people of African heritage. Francophone and Lusophone Africans in Africa and Afro-Hispanics in Latin America were not part of this movement; not by design but because of language, historical background, geographic proximity [in the case of Afro-Hispanics], and close relationship of the early leaders who were mainly English speakers.

African countries, with the exception of Ethiopia and Liberia, were under colonial rules and were not in a position to participate in this movement. Eventually they waged anti-colonial wars, declared their independence, and their leaders joined their fellow Pan-Africanists. As indicated above the first Pan-African conference took place in London in 1900. Subsequent Pan-African conferences were held in Paris, 1919, London 1921, Lisbon 1923, and New York City 1927, and Manchester, England 1945. At the dawn of independence, African leaders, such as Kwame Nkrumah of Ghana and Jomo Kenyatta of Kenya, who lived abroad, were active participants in the Pan-African movement and conferences. After the independence of African countries, the venues of the meetings were shifted to Africa and African countries convened Pan-African conferences. Thus, after the dawn of independence, Pan-African conferences were hosted --- in Dar es-Salam, Tanzania [1974] and in Uganda [1994]. The Pan-African movement climaxed when Ethiopia hosted a conference of thirty two heads of independent African countries which gave birth to the Organization of African Unity in May 1963.

In this process, it is obvious that Pan-Africanism was invigorated by the result of the Battle of Adwa. Africans in Africa and those in the diaspora were emboldened in their struggle to liberate themselves from the grip of colonialism, imperialism, slavery and servitude. Hence the Battle of Adwa is an important chapter in the Pan-African struggle for liberation.

The Battle of Adwa

The Berlin conference of the European leaders of November 1884 to February 1885, and the General Act of Berlin (signed in February 1885) encouraged European countries to partition and divide Africa among themselves. The partitioning of Africa was to advance European interests at the expense of Africa --- a zero-sum strategy. Hence, artificial boundaries were drawn, ethnic groups and families separated, and Africans lost their identities and cultures. It was along this line that Italy aimed at colonizing Ethiopia.

In order to fulfill its colonial desire, Italy assembled heavy weapons of the time and a well trained military to colonize Ethiopia. Using Eritrea, a historical part of Ethiopia, as a launching pad, Italy systematically worked to encroach on Ethiopia's northern territory and tried to intimidate her. Italy also used another ploy to gain sovereignty over Ethiopia. It signed an accord, the infamous Treaty of Wuchale, with Ethiopia on May 2, 1889 [7].

The treaty had all the dubious traits of trickery that some colonial powers used to deceive African leaders during the advent of colonialism. Article XVII of the treaty was written with a deliberate inconsistency. The Italian version made Ethiopia an Italian protectorate; a country that would not independently chart its own foreign policy and pursue its national interest. The Amharic version, on the other hand, did not restrict Ethiopia from contacting foreign powers as a sovereign state. Once the inconsistency between the Amharic and the Italian version came to light, Emperor Menelik informed European powers --- Britain, Germany, as well as Italy --- of Ethiopia's unquestionable sovereignty and denounced Article XVII of the treaty. That became the major source of conflict between Ethiopia and Italy -- a conflict that led to the Battle of Adwa.

Deceptive "treaties" between European powers and African leaders were not exceptional. Historically other Africans had faced such duplicity when Europeans came in contact with African leaders. In the Ethiopian case, some European powers gave Italy their diplomatic support and gave overt approval to impose colonialism on Ethiopia. Queen Victoria, for example, informed Emperor Menelik that her government accepted the Italian interpretation of Article XVII of the Wuchale Treaty. Hence the British government proclaimed its recognition of Ethiopia as an Italian protectorate and communicated with "our Friend His Majesty the King of Italy" [8] to that effect. Furthermore, Queen Victoria notified Emperor Menelik that he "need not bother to communicate with her and her government directly, not to send his envoy to London" [9]. Emperor Menelik, however, undertook his own diplomatic measures through formal and informal correspondence and communications with European powers. He also appealed to the imperialist Italian King Umberto I about their common Christian values and to avoid bloodshed, and repudiated his false claim of Ethiopia being Italy's protectorate [10]. After four years of unfruitful efforts to diplomatically resolve the impasse between the two countries, Emperor Menelik unilaterally abrogated the doctored Wuchale Treaty. That course of action amounted to a direct affront to a European power by an African country, an unusual challenge to the arrogance of some Europeans. That episode invited the Battle of Adwa.

Having European powers of the time on its side, the Italian government was confident it could defeat the poorly armed and trained Ethiopian conscripts. In fact the war had a racist incline as the Italians believed to represent European whites and Ethiopia, black Africa. During the battle, Ethiopian forces brought forth the experience they had in fighting the other foreign forces such as the Egyptians, the Ottomans, the Dervishes and the Italians themselves at Dogali (1887), Coatit (1895), and Senafe (1895) [11]. The Ethiopians withstood the Italian superior force by using their own indigenous fighting tactics such as *Afena* [12] --- envelopment of the enemy force, similar to the Zulu military's "pincer" strategy. Ethiopians were motivated to defend themselves by a love for country and the *Negus* (king) and a strong belief that God was on their side. Women and men, under the leadership of Empress Taitu, played a significant role as they boosted the fighter's morale and tilted the scale in favor of Ethiopian fighters. Women attended to the wounded and encouraged them not to give up but to push forward during the fierce fight. Empress Taitu, therefore, garnered admiration and contributed mightily to the outcome of the war. Acknowledging Taitu's astute leadership, Dejazmach Zewde Gabre Selassie, compared her to her "illustrious predecessors [such as] Empress Elleni and Empress Seble Wongel of the 15th and 16th centuries .... [that she was] the animating spirit and the driving force during all the negotiations and an active participant in the war arena leading her own army under the command of Azaj Zamanuel" [13].

Consequently, Italy suffered a great disaster that had never occurred to Europeans in Africa in modern time [14].

The Battle was costly to both sides, especially to the Italian force, as thousands lost their lives. Italy assembled 17,700 solders, of which 10,600 were White and the rest [7,100] were *askaris* or natives from Italian colonies, mainly from Eritrea. The Italian army was said to be the largest when compared to other colonial powers that faced an African army [15]. Ethiopia assembled a massive 100,000 men. At the end of that decisive battle, almost 8,000 Italians were killed. On the Ethiopian side, the casualty numbered 7,000 dead and 10,000 wounded.

The Battle also had a wider political implication. The decisive victory of Ethiopia against Italy forced some European countries to alter their views of Ethiopia. They were grudgingly forced to respect this African country and saw her as a power to be reckoned with. For example, *The Times* of London referred to Ethiopia as a "barbarous foe" and deeply regretted the defeat of a European army by a "native" force. It could not help but declare that the Ethiopians were a "civilized power both in the way they made war and in the way they conducted their diplomacy" [16]. The French newspaper, *La Liberte'*, declared that "All European countries will be obliged to make a place for this new brother who steps forth ready to play in the Dark Continent the role of Japan in the Far East" [17]. In general, racist discourse was penned about Ethiopia by some writers; but it was soon to be put in a "positive" light. That was not lost on the mind of diaspora Africans. As the late Ethiopianist, Harold Marcus, aptly put it, for the Black diaspora the success of Ethiopia at Adwa was "… the shining … triumph [that] signified present dignity and future possibilities" [18] It was obvious that European discourse on Ethiopia, prior to Adwa, was racist and manifested sheer paternalism.

The Battle of Adwa, therefore, cannot be side-stepped by students of history and most importantly by Africans and their descendants in the diaspora. As the late Ethiopian historian, Knife Abraham, acknowledged, ignoring Adwa is "overlooking a crucial cogwheel of black history and an almost indispensible lubricant of the protracted decolonization struggle"[19].

Thus, the Battle of Adwa remained a testament to Ethiopia's astute leadership, fighting zeal, diplomatic skills, and loyalty to king and country by the nobility in the face of a well armed and trained European power [20]. As indicated earlier, Emperor Menelik appealed to European powers, especially to Italy, that it was not his intention to see the blood of Christians, on both sides, spilled. Apparently his words fell on deaf ears. Unbeknown to Emperor Menelik was that moralized diplomatic relations, then and now, is not in the scheme of international relations but pursuing and protecting vital national interest at any cost persists.

Adwa has a major implication to Africans in Africa and to diaspora Africans. Adwa was a psychological liberator for Africans. While it was a debacle to those who espoused European racial superiority, it bolstered Africans in the continent and those in the diaspora. Adwa challenged the racial supremacy of some. It spared at least one African country from European domination and provided Ethiopia the opportunity to inspire others, and provided a psychological, spiritual, and political base for anti-colonial and anti-slavery movements.

Post-Adwa and the Pan-African Movement

The victory at Adwa ensured that only one sovereign African country remained independent by defeating a European colonial power. In the post-Adwa period, Ethiopia had a comparatively peaceful time and was not openly antagonized by European countries for four decades. Hence, Ethiopia became a symbol of independence and hope for Blacks in the continent and those in the diaspora. The victory at Adwa enhanced the symbolism which Ethiopia represented. It strengthened the messianic belief in it and that a European power could be challenged by an independent African nation [21]. Ethiopia remained the torch bearer of independence for the struggle against colonialism and imperialism in Africa, and a symbol of resistance for pre-civil rights movement in the US and anti-colonial struggle in the Caribbean. Haiti was the only Black country in the Caribbean to proclaim its independence from France in 1804. Its struggle, however, failed to inspire others who were enslaved and subjugated.

After the successful victory at Adwa, Ethiopia earned recognition and respect by European powers. For Africans both in the continent and in the diaspora, Ethiopia became a glimmer of hope in their struggle against colonialism and domination. In short, a Pan-African North Star. Also, Adwa had an overwhelming impact on the psyche of the "civilized" Europe: one of their folds was devastatingly defeated by a "barbarian" African [22].

That symbolism also manifested during WWII when Ethiopia, once again, was attacked by fascist Italy in 1935 and poison gas, a weapon of mass destruction [WMD], was rained on defenseless Ethiopians. Africans in the continent and those in the diaspora rallied in support of Ethiopia so that "the sole remaining pride of Africans and Negros in all parts of the world" [23] remained independent. An American historian, John Hope Franklin, also observed that "Ethiopia was a black nation, and its destruction would symbolize the final victory of whites over blacks" [24]. Such was the general view on Ethiopia, a symbol of Black Nationalism for Africans in Africa and those in the diaspora.

ADWA AND ITS IMPLICATIONS TO PAN-AFRICANSIM

The defeat of Ethiopia at Adwa could have rendered Africa a total capitulation of the continent to European colonial grips (except for Liberia, a mere US appendage). That would have possibly denied Africans on the continent and in the diaspora, Pan-Africanism, a symbol of their struggle against colonialism and racial oppression.

The Battle of Adwa was a psychologically liberating force for all Blacks. It demystified the superiority and invincibility of the White race, as Italy was portrayed to represent European whiteness and Ethiopia was portrayed to represent Africa or the Black race. The devastating defeat of Italy debunked the feeling of superiority by most whites. Both were viewed by some as poll bearers of their respective races. Actually some European powers blindly supported Italy only because of their racial affinity.

Ethiopia continued to be "celebrated" by Africans in Africa and in the diaspora. Writers and artists evoked the country. Thus, Post-Adwa, during the Italian occupation of Ethiopia [1936-1941], the African national anthem of Universal Negro Improvement Association (UNIA), founded by Marcus Garvey, took Ethiopia as a symbol of Black Nationalism. The Declaration of Rights of the Negro Peoples of the World stated that the anthem *Ethiopia, Thou Land of Our Fathers,* shall be the national anthem of the Negro race. The anthem includes the following:

Ethiopia, thou land of our fathers, though land where the gods loved to be. As storm cloud at night suddenly gathers; our armies come rushing to thee. Ethiopia shall stretch forth her hands. By thee shall all fetters be broken. And Haven bless our dear fatherland [25].

Two observations can be made here. One is the mentioning of Ethiopia in the Old Testament which indicated to the faithful that Ethiopians (a reference to Black people) are the children of God and will be saved by their Creator. The second reference is country specific, the current Ethiopia, which has defeated an imperialist European power, Italy, at the Battle of Adwa. The two events, especially the Battle of Adwa, has stimulated and invigorated Pan-

Africanism. Hence the symbolic importance of Ethiopia in both the Pan-African movement and in the struggle against colonialism, slavery, and the dehumanizing system heaped on people of color worldwide.

REEXAMINING ADWA: IMPLICATIONS TO 21ST CENTURY AFRICA

As indicated above, the glory of the Battle of Adwa epitomized Ethiopia as a bulwark against European imperialism. While such gallantry is laudable, yet countries should consider not to completely relying on their past laurels. Knowing and remembering one's history is very important. But they also have to prepare themselves for the most complicated situation of the 21st century. Their sovereignty is challenged assiduously by internal and external forces. Internally, dictators, corruption, and absence of human security, poverty, the persistent erosion of human rights, and environmental crises all have devastating impacts on African countries. African leaders have failed to empower their citizens to greatness. Externally, in pursuit of their vital national interest, foreign powers, in collaboration with authoritarian regimes and the forces of globalization, are challenging the very sovereignty of African countries and the dignity of their citizens left tarnished.

Ethiopia's post-Adwa situation, especially after the second attempt of Italy to colonize Ethiopia in 1935, must be reexamined and analyzed in light of the glory of the Battle of Adwa. Italy tried once again to colonize Ethiopia in order to avenge its defeat at Adwa. Furthermore, the fascist head of Italy, Benito Mussolini, during the reign of King Emmanuel, wanted to avenge the disgrace of Adwa. King Emanuel was the son of King Umberto I, the instigator of the Battle of Adwa. Mussolini also wanted to demonstrate his racial superiority and chauvinism, and address the economic depression Italy had faced by starting a war, employing the jobless, deploying them to the front, and settling them in conquered and colonized countries. The attack on Ethiopia by Italy (both were members of the League of Nations) heralded the impending Second World War. Ethiopia became the first country to be attacked by a member of the Axis power, Italy. It also became the first to be liberated by the assistance of the Allied power, Britain, after five years of occupation and persistent fighting by Ethiopian patriots. Emperor Haile Selassie returned from exile in Britain and established a modern government;

modeled after the British system. Eventually, Emperor Haile Selassie shifted to the United States, an emerging superpower [26].

Emperor Haile Selassie's reign lasted for fifty years but his government was overthrown by a military coup d'état in 1974. The feudal system, the devastating long period of drought, the ensuing famine that claimed thousands of lives, and the general unhappiness in the country, especially by the educated young Ethiopians, led to the overthrow of the monarchy. The aging [octogenarian] emperor Haile Selassie also lost touch with his people. His government was rendered dysfunctional by internal rivalry, squabbling among his cabinet ministers and the royalty. Employment opportunities got bleak and frustration gripped all segments of the society. An emperor referred to as the Father of Africa, for his role in realizing the first continental organization, the Organization of African Unity [OAU], and because of his support for the decolonization struggle and anti-apartheid movement, fell from power in disgrace. The emperor failed to build strong democratic institutions and organizations such as political parties and civic organizations, an independent judiciary and legislature. When his government was overthrown, a power vacuum was created which was filled by the military, the sole organized modern institution with power of coercion.

The Military regime that ruled the country for 17 years [1974-1991] introduced socialism, as the national ideology, nationalized land and nascent business enterprises, and was responsible for gross human rights abuses. In most cases the record of the military rule was worse than the government it overthrew and replaced. It was during the military regime and because of its gross human rights abuses that Ethiopians started fleeing their country en mass; unparalleled in the country's recent history. Thus Ethiopia witnessed the exodus of its burgeoning educated and trained human resources that has remained unabated ever since [27]. Gross human rights abuses and the bleak economic and political situations in the country forced young Ethiopians to leave their country in droves. Some were engaged in forceful removal, albeit unsuccessfully, of the military regime. Others were technocrats and educated people who saw no hope for themselves and for the country. Once again, Ethiopians were brutalized and cowed by their own indigenous government. As indicated above, Ethiopia succeeded in repelling foreign aggression. Nonetheless, fell prey to a home grown and internal colonizing power, the military dictatorship.

The Military was overthrown in 1991 by a coalition of ethnic-based guerilla forces, the Ethiopian People's Revolutionary Democratic Forces [EPRDF.] There was a general optimism and hope in the country that any government that replaced the military regime was an improvement and lent the new force the benefit of the doubt. Still others were doubtful about the new force as its track record was replete with human rights abuses, and it had a divisive, rather than national agenda, -- a divide and rule stratagem based on ethnic, religion, and region. It is the antithesis of Ethiopia during the Battle of Adwa. Ethiopians marched to Adwa in unison, notwithstanding the country's religious diversity and ethnic pluralism.

The new fighting force, EPRDF, introduced ethnic politics and alienated most Ethiopians. The country's provinces were redistributed and divided based on ethnicity and not on administrative rationality. The core of the EPRDF, the Tigre People's Liberation Front [TPLF], initially a secessionist organization, tried to ensure the hegemony of a minority Tigre ethnic group by employing a divide-and-rule stratagem, controlling the economy, the bureaucracy, the security apparatus, and the military. In short, while a new authoritarian rule emerged which was not a stark improvement from the previous regime. Once again, the TPLF-controlled government has a complete monopoly over all aspects of life. It violates human rights and is accused of corruption and nepotism. It has failed to empower citizens, address poverty while aggrandizing itself and ensuring and benefitting from crony capitalism. Despite the mushrooming of high rise buildings in Addis Ababa, the quality of life in the city is wanting. The governing process lacks transparency and is replete with corruption. While a well coordinated, organic, and democratic system is lacking, a few people who are close to the regime remain the beneficiaries of the situation while the majority are still condemned to poverty.

Unlike the period of Pan-African movement of the 19th century, Ethiopia has lost its symbolism. Ethiopia and other post-independence African countries are subjugated by their own corrupt and disempowering leaders. The sacrifice paid at Adwa and in the struggle against foreign domination and colonialism seems to have not borne fruit for the vast majority of citizens and the post-independence optimism has failed to be sustained. Africans, by and large, are now disempowered, marginalized, brutalized by their own leaders who are akin to European colonizers.

Reexamining the victory of the battle of Adwa and post-independence Africa will not leave one with great optimism. Both endogenous and exogenous forces have left Ethiopia and other African countries marginalized. Sustainable quality environment, food security, quality of health and educational services, poverty mitigation and political and economic empowerment remain perplexing issues. The heroes of the Battle of Adwa and leaders of the Pan-African movement and African liberation would be very proud if these burning concerns and issues are addressed and solved. That will make their dream and aspirations for their people come true. As it stands today, they won the battle but their descendants are losing the war.

GENERAL OBSERVATION

Post-Adwa and Post-Independence Africa can draw some lessons from the Battle of Adwa. Though Ethiopians have successfully resisted foreign domination and imperialistic onslaught, they have not succeeded yet in seriously challenging indigenous and home-grown dictators, adequately addressing dehumanizing poverty, protecting human rights, and ensuring human dignity. Furthermore, Ethiopia and other African countries have not succeeded in withstanding the forces of globalization that has marginalized them. Although this force is inevitable and unavoidable, Africa is unable to call the shots and so it dances to the tune that is orchestrated by the Washington and Beijing Consensus. These are the two endogenous and exogenous forces that challenge Ethiopians and others in the 21st century.

The other lesson that Post-Independence Africa can draw from the Battle of Adwa is that Ethiopia resisted colonialism and retained its sovereignty while other African countries gained their independence through bloody wars of liberation or through peaceful negotiations. Post-Adwa Ethiopia and Post-Independence Africa came under indigenous "colonial rulers" whose modes operandi of rule somewhat resembles that of the colonial system which was long ejected from Africa. Similarly, Post-Independence African leaders look and speak like the citizens they rule. Nevertheless, the corruption, subjugation, and arrogance of the leaders are tantamount to the discarded colonial system. Furthermore, the Post-independence African countries have not yet charted a new development theory or a new paradigm that reflects African persona, aspirations, and vision. They have continued operating based on foreign ideologies, economic strategies and a mindset that has failed to adequately improve the lives of their citizens or contribute to a meaningful national development. Africa has a leadership crisis.

In its recent annual Economic Report on Africa [ERA], the Economic Commission for Africa [ECA] indicated a shift in its economic policy and rejected both free-market fundamentalism of the "Western Consensus" and exclusively state-controlled development as failed models [28]. Latin American countries such as Brazil and Chile registered economic development and poverty reduction after they reconsidered neoliberal reforms and charted their own policy of reducing poverty and addressing income and social inequalities. Because of the fact that Africa is still marginalized and situations in most cases continue to be grim, there is a call from different quarters for African leaders to come up with their own development strategies, democratize themselves, and truly serve their own citizens. Most people remain marginalized, are disease-ridden, and lack the necessary knowledge and training that will help them improve the status quo and contribute to a vibrant, organic, and self-sustaining national development in order for African countries to compete globally. In the political discourse, the track record indicates that citizens are increasingly disenfranchised, their vote stolen, and deprived of their rights to choose their leaders without being arm-twisted, bribed, intimidated or harassed by the incumbent leadership and party.

A new foreign onslaught, that amounts to colonialism, …"land grabs" … has taken yet another twist in Africa as exercised by the newly emerging economies such as China, India, Indonesia, South Korea, and Saudi Arabia. Africa's farmland is producing food for export from countries that experience widespread food insecurity. The situation reminds one of the colonial period when Africa's fertile lands were annexed and distributed among the colonizers and tropical products looted and exported to Europe to propel European industries and build their economies. That led to unequal development and an exploitative relationship. Today, the underdeveloped regions, inhabited by minority ethnic groups, remain the most exploited areas. Rather than supporting and enhancing the productivity of farmers through sound agricultural policies and supportive measures, governments are waging war on their own voiceless and marginalized small-scale farmers and ethnic groups. It seems that there is no government that stands for the rights and aspirations of small farmers and poor citizens who are the majority.

A farmer in Bako, a small farming town in Ethiopia, compared British colonialism in neighboring Kenya to the new land grabbers in Ethiopia. He commented: "Now we see Indians coming. Before, we were just Ethiopians. What do they want here? The same as the British in Kenya; to steal everything? Our government is selling our country to the Asians so they can make money for themselves" [29]. The money from land grabbers has not trickled down to benefit the uprooted rural farmers. The situation, therefore, could lead to instability and xenophobia.

It was also reported that a river designated for cornfields and rice paddies for foreign farmers "is no longer open for locals to water their cows" [30]. The Ethiopian farmer has succinctly captured the sorry situation in other African countries who are also victims of land grabbers. Ethiopia and other African countries are not facing a well armed and mechanized foreign troop but brief case totting, well financed entrepreneurs who are indirectly colonizing Africa in collaboration with corrupt African leaders in the guise of "feeding the world", introducing mechanized farming to "unused" agricultural land, and raising GNP that camouflages the reality. Economic growth is not necessarily indicative of development as people are increasingly marginalized and wallow in poverty. Quite a disheartening experience!

Small scale farmers are uprooted and end up underpaid, exploited and overworked manual workers laboring on their own land that no more belongs to them but to foreign farmers --- the land grabbers. As one report indicated, "... the government in Addis Ababa is snatching some of Ethiopia's most productive farmland from local farmers and leasing it to foreign companies to grow and export food" [31], This is in light of famine 2011 that has revisited the Horn of Africa, the worst in six decades. Some people survive on food aid, yet governments are committing the worst human rights abuses by letting citizens starve and even denying that it exists. That had been the sorry situation of Ethiopia's past two governments, a prelude to their disgrace and ultimate fall. The current EPRDF government, not learning from the recent past history, seems to be on the same slippery slope. Draught might be caused by nature but famine is the epitome of political crisis in a country.

In another similar case, in the fertile region along the Omo River of Ethiopia, fertile land is leased out to Malaysian, Indians, Italian, and Korean companies to harvest what is called "green gold." Lower Omo Valley is acknowledged by UNESCO as World Heritage site. Vast stretches of land are also cleared for huge state-run plantations producing export crops, forcefully uprooting 90,000 peoples who depend on the land for sheer survival. This human rights violation, social disintegration, and destruction of the ecology and rich biodiversity is carried out by the government in the false claim of "civilizing" a backward people in order to "modernize" them [32]. It sounds like the voice of the colonial powers. When Benito Mussolini's army trudged in Ethiopia in 1936, he boisterously claimed to "civilize the country" and "Christianize" its people --- a country with a long history and civilization where Christianity was introduced in the 4th century.

Once again, the future of Post-Independence Africa is determined by other countries and foreign entities in the face of a growing population, water and food insecurity, environmental degradation because of climatic vagaries, poor health, and a general feeling of alienation by the people. Indeed Ethiopia won the Battle of Adwa and other African countries gained the upper hand in the struggle for national liberation. Yet it is debatable as to how most of them may win the 21st century onslaught that is directed against their very sovereignty, a battle far different from what they once faced.

Because of water shortages, increasing desertification, population growth, and dwindling resources in other affluent countries, Ethiopia and other African countries are letting themselves once again be colonized by leasing land dirt cheap for a long period of time. The world population is projected to reach a record high of 9.5 billion by 2050. In this equation, developing countries are expected to register substantial population gain in the face of the current undernourished population. If these situations are not reversed, one cannot be optimistic about the future.

Similar to the colonial era, Africans are once again evicted from their lands so that commercial agriculture can be introduced to feed other countries while Africans are facing food insecurity which is a manifestation of short-sighted policies of African leaders who have failed to craft policies that address environmental sustainability, poverty mitigation and high level inequality. Along this line, some Latin American countries such as Brazil, Chile and, to some extent, Peru are impacting millions of lives [although they have a long way to go and face complex issues such as the prevalence of illicit drug and the exploitation of minerals by foreign companies and uprooting the indigenes people] because of policies that improve the situation of their citizens [33].

Meanwhile, UN agencies, NGOs, and governments at different times call for food assistance in order to ameliorate food shortages in Africa. Countries are experiencing deepening draught and environmental crises, ground water depletion in populated regions of the world, such as Northern India and Northeastern China, and politically sensitive and unstable regions of the world --- such as North Africa, Indo-Pakistan region, and the Middle Eastern countries, including Israel and its neighbors. Food, environmental, and hydro insecurity will lead to human insecurity and political instability. East African countries (Ethiopia, Eritrea, Djibouti, Kenya, and Somalia) are once again severely affected by draught that has resulted in famine in summer 2011. As a result Somalis are flocking to neighboring countries in search of shelter and food. Lack of effective and good governance is to blame; especially in the case of Somalia, a failed state. Africa is not free from these general insecurities and it might have to wage another peaceful and democratic freedom struggle against its own corrupt and insensitive leaders and their foreign benefactors. Some are contributing to increased insecurity, general hopelessness of the peoples, environmental degradation, dumping of toxic materials in streams and rivers, and polluting the environment of African countries.

Countries such as China and India are competing for Africa's economy. Indeed they provide economic assistance and arrive in Africa with aid packages. Generally, there is no altruism in foreign assistance as vital national interest remains at the core of any foreign assistance. China's involvement in Africa, for example, is to assure its long-term access to strategic resources; it employs cheap Chinese labor and uses cheap goods in its projects. Furthermore, China establishes a special economic zone [SEZ] that will serve as a dynamo to spur and sustain its own economic growth and industrialization. If the collaboration brings about a win-win and not a zero-sum situation for Africa and China, it would be most preferred. Past experience and the current situation, however, seems not to lead one to be too optimistic about the situation.

The overall state of affairs seems to have placed countries on crossroads. National and global situations seem to be in flux. China, itself is facing crisis at different levels, despite its ostensible economic rise. It is facing labor crisis where by its work force is not only aging but is in decline, and environmental crises also remain a threat to its food security. The Gobi Desert, for example, is inching south. The Yellow River is polluted. Rapid urbanization and the growth of megacities are all putting pressure on the land, the underground aquifers, and the farmlands. Hence, China's land grab and monopoly of sources of raw material is to ensure its own national interest at the expense of African countries. African land grab is also putting pressure on countries such as Egypt and Kenya as the flow of the Nile and the Omo Rivers affects them respectively. This is because of large-scale mechanized farming by Ethiopia's land grabbers and a government bent on building dams for selling electricity and not for irrigating farms to feed its own citizens. A misplaced priority!

Food and water shortages, population growth, environmental degradation in light of corrupt leaders, and exploitative external forces will remain Africa's litany of problems in the post-independence era of globalization. It was because of this gloomy situation that one African posed this question … When would colonialism return to Africa? That states the nature of despair and frustration with the post-independence situation and a leadership whose style of governance remains no different from that of the colonial rulers of the past. Ironically, the person was yearning for a colonialism that promised so little and delivered nothing. In the post-colonial era, however, governments promise much and deliver so little.

In such a perplexing situation, post-independence Africa could lose the game unless its leaders are farsighted. The farsightedness and selflessness of African leaders remains pivotal in propelling post-independence Africa in a complex 21st century towards the vision of pan-Africanism provided in the 19th century.

Africa is urged not to lose the 21st century and bring upon itself a new form of colonialism that could probably remain for a longer period, a colonialism which Pan-Africanism and Pan-Ethiopianism vehemently resisted and fought against. The Battle of Adwa also epitomizes African struggle against foreign domination. Based on the past experience and knowledge, the current African leaders are urged to show leadership and protect the interest of their respective countries and fellow compatriots. Under democratic leadership and the resilience of Africans, I am confident that Africa will once again rebound and claim its proper place on the world stage.

REFERENCES

[1] Lockseley Edmondson. "Pan Africanism and the International System: Challenges and Opportunities," in W. Ofuatey-Kodjoe (ed.), *Pan-Africanism*. Lanham, MD: University Press of America, pp. 285-316. Also refer to Getachew Metaferia, "The Ethiopian Connection to the Pan-African Movement," *Journal o Third World Studies*, vol. XII, no. 2, all, 1995, p. 300.

[2] St. Clair Drake, "Pan-Africanism, Negritude, and the African Personality" in William John Hanna (ed.), [*Independent Black Africa: The Politics of Freedom*]. Chicago: Rand McNally & Co., 1964, pp. 530-541. Getachew Metaferia, "Ethiopia: A bulwark against European colonialism and its role in the Pan-African movement," in Paulos Milkias and Getachew Metaferia. *The Battle of Adwa: Reflections on Ethiopia's Historic Victory Against European Colonialism*, New York: Agora Publishing, p. 191.

[3] Edmondson, Lockseley. "Pan Africanism and the International System: Challenges and Opportunities" in W. Ofuatey Kodjoe (ed.), *Pan-Africanism*. Lanham: University Press of America, pp. 285-316.

[4] Getachew Metaferia, Ibid. p. 191.

[5] Wilson Jeremiah Moses, *The Golden Age of Black Nationalism 1850-1925*. Hamden, CT: Archon Brooks, 1978, pp. 158-159 as quoted from David Walker, Walker's Appeal in Four Articles [1829] and Henry Highland Garnet, *An Address to the Slaves of the United States of America*. Troy, NY, 1848.

[6] Shepperson, George, "Notes on Negro American Influences on the Emergence of African Nationalism," *Journal of African History*, Chicago: Rand McNally& Co., 1964, pp. 530-541. Also Getachew Metaferia, Ibid. p. 191.

[7] Refer to Sven Rubenson, [*Wuchale XVII*,] Addis Ababa, 1964].

[8] Negussay Ayele, "Adwa 1896: Who was Civilized and who was Savage?" in Paulos Milkias and Getachew Metaferia, as quoted from Paulos Gnogno "Ate Menelik. Also refer to Sven Rubenson, Wuchale XVII …" Addis Ababa, 1964, p. 150.

[9] Negussay Ayele, Ibid. p. 150.

[10] Ibid. p. 152.

[11] Paulos Milkias, 2005. "The Battle of Adwa: The Historic Victory of Ethiopia over European Colonialism," in Paulos Milkias and Getachew Metaferia, Ibid. p. 57.

[12] Ibid.

[13] Zewed Gabra Selassie, "Continuity and Discontinuity in Menelik's Foreign Policy," in Paulos Milkias and Getachew Metaferia, Ibid. p. 131

[14] Paulos, p. 87, quoted from *The Spectator,* March 7, 1986.

[15] Getachew Metaferia in Ibid, p. 188.

[16] Richard Pankhurst, "Diplomatic Relations with Europe, 1861-1896." *Ethiopia Observer*, vol. I, no. II, p. 359.

[17] Pankhurst, *Ibid,* p. 366. Also Getachew Metaferia, Ibid. p. 188.

[18] Harold Marcus, "Racist Discourse about Ethiopia and Ethiopians before and after the Battle of Adwa," in Paulos Milkias and Getachew Metaferia, p. 229.

[19] Knife Abraham, "The Impact of the Adowa Victory on the Pan-African and Pan-Black Anti-Colonial Struggle." A paper delivered at The Institute of Ethiopian Studies [IES], Addis Ababa University, February 8, 2006.

[20] For the general history of the battle of Adwa, refer to Paulos Milkias and Getachew Metaferia, Ibid. Also refer to Abdussamad Ahmad and Richard Pankhurst, Adwa Victory Centenary Celebration Proceeding Conference [1998], Adwa centenary celebration Conference proceedings, 26 February- 2 March 1996, Institute of Ethiopian Studies, Addis Ababa.

[21] Getachew Metaferia, "The Ethiopian connection to the Pan-African movement," *Journal of Third World Studies*, Fall, 1995, Vol. XII, no. 2, p. 303.

[22] Negussie Ayele in Paulos Milkias and Getachew Metaferia, Ibid, pp. 150-152.

[23] Jomo Kenyatta, “Hands off Abyssinia,” *Labor Monthly*. London, XVII, 9 September 1935, p. 536.

[24] John Hope Franklin and Alfred A. Moss, Jr. 1994. *From Slavery to Freedom*, New York: McGraw Hill, Inc, pp. 433-434.

[25] “Though land where gods loved to be” seems to be a reference to Illiad authored by Homer. This stated that Greek gods rested in Ethiopia every night to be in the company of the blameless Ethiopians. Also see Amy Jacques Garvey, *Garvey and Garveyism*, London: Collier-Macmillan, 1970, pp. 31-32.

[26] Refer to Getachew Metaferia, *Ethiopia and the United States: History, Diplomacy, and Analysis,* 2009, Algora Publishing: New York.

[27] On the topic of brain drain from Ethiopia, refer to Getachew Metaferia and Maigenet Shifferraw, 1991, *The Ethiopian Revolution 1974 and the Exodus of its Trained Human Resources*, New York: Edwin Mellon.

[28] The report can be accessed at http://www.uneca.org/era2011.

[29] Barry Malone, Reporter for Reuters, “Is Africa Selling out its farmers?” http://www.ethiomedia.com/course/4475.html. Also refer to Stephanie McCrummen, “The ultimate crop rotation: Lured by a new business model, wealthy nations flock to farmland in Ethiopia, locking in food supplies grown half a world away,” *The Washington Post*, November 23, 2009, pp.1 and 12.

[30] Stephanie McCrummen, Ibid, p. A12.

[31] Jerome Mwanda, “Ethiopia’s World Heritage Site tribes threatened,” August 1, 2011, as reported in http://www.ethiomedia.com/andenet /2753.html.

[32] Ibid.

[33] Refer to an article by Mark Loyka, “Decline of Inequality and Poverty in Latin America,” July 28, 2011, in *Worldpress.org*. http://www. worldpress.org/print_article.cfm?article_id=4084&dont=yesresulting.

In: Africa
Editor: Olayiwola Abegunrin
ISBN: 978-1-62948-561-4

Chapter 3

HALF A CENTURY OF PRO-DEMOCRACY UPRISINGS IN AFRICA'S EXPERIENCE: FROM SHARPEVILLE TO BENGHAZI

Ali A. Mazrui
Albert Schweitzer Professor, Humanities
and Director, Institute of Global Cultural Studies, Binghamton University,
State University of New York, Binghamton, New York, US

THE DEATH OF PASSIVE RESISTANCE

Among the intriguing paradoxes of South Africa's history is the fact that this land is the last country on the African continent to be liberated, and yet it is also among the first to be truly democratized.

In our context here, liberation is either from racial minority rule or from colonialism in the imperial sense. On the other hand, democratization is either the quest for, or the consolidation of a system which combines government's accountability, with popular participation and links the pursuit of social justice with the open Society.

Almost every other African country which attained liberation from European colonial rule in the 20th century was unable to maintain its democratic order beyond its first decade of independence. Within that first decade either the military captured power or the elected president became a dictator, or a civil war broke out, or the ruling party outlawed any rival political party and turned the country into a single-party state [1].

The Republic of South Africa, on the other hand, liberated Nelson Mandela in 1990 after 27 years in prison, held its first democratic election in 1994, and is now with its third president [2]. Nearly two decades after apartheid South Africa has not outlawed opposition parties, or experienced a military coup, or permitted the Head of State to govern the country as a dictator.

But what role have pro-democracy uprisings played in South Africa's transition from racial liberation to genuine democratization?

In 1960 black people of South Africa focused on the pass-laws of apartheid as the main instruments of control. Both the African National Congress and the newly-formed Pan-African Congress started planning for a possible series of protests as part of a general anti-pass uprising in 1960 to commemorate the anniversary of the anti-pass-laws campaign of 1919 [3].

The height of the drama occurred in Sharpeville when five thousand protesters confronted three hundred policemen in March 1960. These so-called security forces in Sharpeville went to the extent of using live ammunition. To add insult to injury, armored vehicles and air force jets were used to deepen the atmosphere of intimidation.

The protesters were unarmed and had been using Gandhian methods of non-violent disobedience and passive resistance.

Official figures of casualties claimed that 69 were killed and 180 were seriously injured. Unofficial calculations estimated casualties in their hundreds, including many people shot in the back as they were trying to run away from the indiscriminate violence. Sharpeville and its memory became iconic in the struggle against apartheid. The killings, beatings and large scale imprisonment of hundreds of people virtually destroyed the dream of ending apartheid by non-violent means and passive resistance. Both the African National Congress and the Pan-African Congress started seriously considering armed struggle in pursuit of a more democratic order in South Africa. And yet Sharpeville continued to be an inspiration for collective protests elsewhere in Africa. While Sharpeville coincided with the liberation from colonialism of 17 other African countries in the same year of 1960, the Soweto uprising in 1976 coincided with the 200th anniversary of the outbreak of the American war of independence in 1776. But while in the case of America's independence the relevant month of celebration was July 1776, the relevant month of celebration for the Soweto uprising was June 1976.* However, a big difference between both Sharpeville and the American war of independence, on one side, and the uprising in Soweto, on the other, was generational. Soweto was a rebellion of young people – while the two earlier historic eruptions were inter-generational.

Approximately 20,000 African students exploded into the Soweto uprising on June 16, 1976, protesting the marginalization of indigenous languages in black schools, and the imposition of Afrikaans and English as media of instruction in most of the syllabus. Particularly offensive to the young people was the imposition of Afrikaans, which black people in those days widely regarded as a language of oppression. While the American Boston Tea Party in 1776 used "taxation with_representation" as a symbol of liberation, and Sharpeville used abolition of "the pass laws", the youth of Soweto believed in "no choice of communication without choice of representation". Language policy in education was at the center of the Soweto uprising. It was reinforced by the support of the Black Consciousness Movement. Language was allied to Black Nationalism. We mentioned that 20,000 students revolted in Soweto. Nearly 180 of the students paid with their lives. Particularly moving was young Hector Pieterson who was fatally wounded, and was carried by Mbuyisa Makhubo in a dramatic photograph which captured the imagination of the world. Pieterson arrived dead at the local clinic. June 16, 1976 continues to be celebrated in post-apartheid South Africa as a milestone in the history of the struggle for liberation. This last country on the African continent to be racially liberated became one of the first to be truly democratized. The formerly oppressed of Sharpeville, Soweto and elsewhere in South Africa were much later to be followed by the pro-democracy protesters of Tunisia and Egypt early in 2011, and by the armed rebels against Muammar Gaddafi's Libya soon after the fall of Egypt's Hosni Mubarak. North Africa in 2011, like Soweto in 1976, was led by the youth. The young not only read history in the classroom; they made history in the streets of destiny. Let us look more closely at the different intermediate stages between Sharpeville in 1960 and Tahrir Square in 2011 and between the Soweto uprising in 1976 and Benghazi after Gaddafi's 42 years in power in Libya.

Phase I: The Anti-Colonial Phase of Africa's Struggle

The Second World War triggered new waves of anti-colonial struggle. Leaders like Kwame Nkrumah of Ghana and Kenneth Kaunda of Zambia considered Gandhian methods of passive resistance and non-violent strikes. Albert Luthuli became Africa's first Nobel Laureate for Peace in 1960 for championing peaceful struggle. Leaders like Julius K. Nyerere of Tanzania and Leopold Senghor of Senegal adopted non-confrontational agitation for decolonization. Movements like Mau Mau in Kenya and the National Liberation Front in Algeria engaged in armed struggle against colonial rule. Ghana became independent in 1957, but it was preceded by Sudan and Tunisia who attained sovereignty in 1956. In 1960 seventeen additional African countries became independent in a single year, as we indicated earlier.

Phase II: The Struggle Against Racial Minority Governments

In Rhodesia (Zimbabwe) the target was Ian Smith's white regime in rebellion against Great Britain, the world community and the aspirations of African peoples. Smith's Unilateral Declaration of Independence (U.D.I.) on November 11, 1965 plunged Zimbabwe into 15 years of bloodletting [4]. Robert Mugabe was successful in gaining independence for Zimbabwe but has had a hard time creating a post-racial society.

In the first two years there was a lot of anti-black racism in Harare, the newly renamed capital of Zimbabwe. When I complained to him in 1982 of white racism in the restaurants of independent Zimbabwe, Mugabe enumerated three methods of teaching one's citizens to become non-racist: by non-racist example, by anti-racist persuasion and education, and thirdly, by the use of force to promote a post-racial society.

In 1960 South Africa witnessed the massacre of Sharpeville, and in 1976 the revolt of Soweto erupted. In South Africa the struggle continued longer than in Zimbabwe, but achieved positive results more fully than did the smaller country like Zimbabwe. In South Africa the pace of change speeded up when Nelson Mandela was released after twenty-seven years of imprisonment.

The African National Congress had been banned for decades. A deal was struck in the early 1990s. The whites agreed to give blacks the crown if whites could retain the jewels. In 1994 Nelson Mandela was able to wear the political crown, while white South Africans still enjoyed the economic jewels.

PHASE III: THE STRUGGLE FOR A MORE PLURALISTIC CONSTITUTIONAL ORDER

Large scale uprising occurred from time to time. Black Africa was partly inspired by anti-communist movements in Eastern Europe, partly by the First Palestinian intifadah against Israel, and partly by the agitation in China's Tiananmen Square in Beijing when the young were in revolt. Pro-democracy aspirations were contagious.

Africans were demanding a multiparty system, the elimination of detention without trial, the minimization of corruption, and new steps against military coups from the 1980s to the end of the 20th century. Africa witnessed widespread abolition of single-party systems, drastic reduction of military coups, and legitimation of rival political parties. South Africa was later spared some of these lapses and arrested democratization.

PHASE IV: THE STRUGGLE FOR FULL DEMOCRACY BY POPULAR UPRISING

Sudan set the precedent of civilian non-violent demonstrations against military rule. Sharpeville was fresh in Sudanese memories in the mid-1960s. Non-violent popular eruptions occurred against General Ibrahim Abboud in the Sudan in 1964 against General Jaafar Nimeiry in 1985. The two Sudanese uprisings did not trigger imitation either in sub-Saharan Africa or in the Arab world – in spite of the fact that the old Sudan shared borders with nine other countries.

But there was another reason why Sudanese women were less evident in the uprising against General Ibrahim Abboud in 1964 than in the uprising against General Jaafar Nimeiry in 1985. The trend was towards greater political awareness among women. South Africa had led the way with female protesters in both Sharpeville and Soweto.

Women in Khartoum were outraged by Nimeiry's decision to execute Mahmoud Muhammad Taha, an old man who was radically re-interpreting Islam in a more liberal direction. Taha's book in the English language was published under the title of *The Second Message of Islam* [5].

But there was another reason why Sudanese women were less evident in the uprising against General Ibrahim Abboud in 1964 than in the uprising against General Jaafar Nimeiry in 1985. Sudanese Universities had far fewer women students in the 1960s than they did in the 1980s. Female students enhanced the numbers of those who protested against Nimeiry in 1985 more noticeably than they did in the outburst against Aboud twenty years earlier.

In the 2011 uprising in the Arab world women have had a pronounced presence in situations in which the opposition has engaged in *protest* but not in situations when the opposition has resorted to *rebellion*. Tunisia and Egypt were cases when the opposition had consisted of *protesters*, but in Libya the opposition rapidly turned into *rebels*.

But what is the difference between *protest* and *rebellion*? The difference is when the opposition is *armed*. The Libyan opposition turned to weapons and transformed the conflict into a civil war in less than a week. The Tunisian and Egyptian opposition tried to be non-violent throughout the struggle. So were the protesters in Sharpeville in 1960 and in Soweto in 1976.

THE TUNISIAN STYLE

What has now been called "the Arab awakening" or "the Arab Spring" was triggered by the uprising in Tunisia in January 2011 against the regime of Zeinal Abideen Ben Ali. Was it merely a coincidence that Tunisia as a country led in the twentieth century the whole of the Arab world in women's liberation? The seed of Tunisia's liberation of women goes back to the early years of the twentieth century.

By the 1920s Tunisia had produced an outstanding Islamic reformer who belonged to the Great Mosque of the Zaitouna. The man's name was Tahar Haddad who championed the liberation of women from the shackles of what he regarded as un-Islamic customs and taboos. In 1930 he published his influential book *Our Women in the Sharia and Society* – arguing that Islamic teachings had been distorted to the disadvantage of women [6].

Tunisian women were inspired by Haddad but initially decided to join the national struggle against French colonialism rather than fight feminist battles. Women patriots started being arrested by French colonialists as early as 1938. By 1950 the leading Neo-Destour party opened its first women's section. Many women agitators against France were from time to time arrested and imprisoned.

On attainment of independence on March 20, 1956, women's credentials as Tunisian patriots were so strong that the first postcolonial Tunisian President, Habib Bourguiba, leader of the Neo-Destour Party, declared within months of independence [August 13, 1956] that Tunisia owed its women a debt of gratitude not only for their roles as mothers, wives, daughters, and sisters, but also for their roles as nationalists and patriots.

Tunisia led the Arab world by promulgating a Code of Personal Status "removing all injustices against women and conferring upon women their full rights" [7]. Such ideas were echoed by both the African National Congress and the Pan-African Congress in South Africa.

Tunisia was the first Arab country to outlaw polygamy – but not the first Muslim country. Turkey under Mustafa Kemal Ataturk had led the way in improving the status of women in marriage, inheritance, and dress culture. Much later Turkey became the first Muslim country in the Middle East to elect a female Prime Minister – Tansu Çiller.

In Tunisia women in the year 2011 were significant participants in the pro-democracy uprising. They were protestors rather than rebels. It remains to be seen if Tunisia will become the first Arab country to elect a woman Prime Minister or a woman President.

Although there have already been at least *four* Muslim countries (Pakistan, Bangladesh, Indonesia as well as Turkey) which have produced women Prime Ministers and one President (Indonesia), none of them was an Arab country. If Tunisia in 2011 led the Arab pro-democratic awakening, was it partly because it had led the Arabs half a century earlier in women's liberation? The immediate trigger of the Tunisian uprising was the self-immolation of a young trader who was victimized by bureaucrats at the expense of his livelihood. Muhammad Bouazizi set himself aflame in protest [8]. Although politically inspired self-immolation is much rare in Muslim countries than among Hindus and Buddhists elsewhere, the Tunisian suicide of a food cart vendor in January 2011 was widely regarded by Tunisians as a case of heroic martyrdom. The physical flames which consumed the young man became a political flame which helped to light a revolution. Tunisian mothers were reportedly particularly moved by the young man's rage. So were South African mothers in 1976 when nearly 180 students rose and were killed in Soweto [9].

The Egyptian Precedents

The Egyptian uprising of 2011 against Hosni Mubarak finally succeeded in ousting Mubarak on February 11, 2011. Women were very visible participants in the protests of Tahrir Square. Egyptian women, though among the best educated in Africa and the Muslim world, were not as liberated as the women of Tunisia and Turkey. But historically Egypt has led the way in female empowerment in other ways. The first great female ruler in recorded history was probably the Egyptian Hatshepsut who reigned from 1479 to 1458 before Christ [10]. Because Pharaohs were supposed to be male, Hatshepsut was represented in statues with a false beard! But she was a strong ruler – and is widely regarded as a forerunner of such tough future female rulers as Catherine the Great, Elizabeth I and Indira Gandhi.

Other great women rulers of Egypt itself included Pharaoh Akhenaton's co-Regent, Queen Nefertiti and Cleopatra VII, arguably the last Pharaoh of ancient Egypt, though less indigenous than either Hatshepsut or Nefertiti. Cleopatra was North Africa's great woman ruler. Her life was from 69 BCE to 30 BCE. Her reign was from 51 BCE to 30 BCE [11]. Egypt has always been the northern extension of sub-Sahara Africa, the Southern extension of Mediterranean Europe, and later became the Eastern extension of Arabia. These influences probably eventually have helped the relative liberation of Egyptian women. They have been much freer than the women of the Arabian Peninsula. Did this empower them in Tahrir Square as protestors in February 2011?

THE LIBYAN LEGACY

Muammar Gaddafi has ruled Libya since the military coup of 1969. He has been less important as a social or religious reformer domestically than in his efforts to be a political player globally. On the gender question Gaddafi used symbolism. Far from regarding women as unsuited for military roles, or incapable of using firearms efficiently, Gaddafi theoretically entrusted his life to female bodyguards. These were often referred to as "the Amazons".

The Pope in history has had the physical protection of the Swiss guards and the spiritual protection of the Virgin Mary. Gaddafi had women body guards who were spiritually required to be virgins. On the link between virginity and military effectiveness, Gaddafi in North Africa in the twenty-first century had shared a characteristic with Shaka Zulu of South Africa in the eighteenth century. Shaka wanted his male soldiers to be celibate, totally denying them-selves sex. Gaddafi had wanted his female guards as virgins from the start – and committed to celibacy until military retirement.

But since the current uprising erupted in the second half of February 2011, there has been no evidence of female soldiers protecting Gaddafi. Actually, there have been more female warriors in the opposition in Benghazi than among Gaddafi's forces in Tripoli. Much more interesting was Gaddafi's decision from the 1990s that he was an African first and an Arab second [12]. He got disenchanted with fellow Arabs – having first begun as a Pan-Arabist. But in his last twenty years in office he had put his money more in Pan-African ventures than in Pan-Arabist projects. He saw himself less and less as heir to Gamal Abdel Nasser of Egypt and more and more as heir to Kwame Nkrumah of Ghana.

Dual Africanity: Of the Blood and of the Soil

There are two broad types of Africans on our continent – Africans of the blood and Africans of the soil. Africans of the blood are primarily products of the black race; Africans of the soil are primarily of the African land. Egyptians or Tunisians who are not racially mixed are Africans of the soil, but not of the blood. Similarly, white South Africans or white Zimbabweans are, like Egyptians and Tunisians, Africans of the soil, but not of the blood.

On the other hand, African Americans, Afro-Jamaicans and Afro-Brazilians are Africans of the blood, but not of the soil. When Boutros-Boutros Ghali was elected Secretary-General of the United Nations, he was supposed to be a candidate for Africa and not for the Middle East or the Arab world. But Boutros-Ghali was an African of the soil (i.e. Egyptian) and not a black African.

Boutros-Ghali's second term as Secretary-General of the United Nations was filled by the Ghanaian, Kofi Annan. This West African diplomat was both an African of the soil (because he was born in Ghana) and an African of the blood (because he was a black African).

Being an African of the soil but not of the blood does not necessarily mean the person is an immigrant or descended from immigrants. Boutros-Ghali was a Coptic Christian whose African ancestry went back centuries. I would not be surprised if Boutros-Ghali's ancestry was Pharaonic – going back thousands of years to the building of the pyramids. Although he was not an African of the blood, his Africanity went deep into the soil of Pharaonic Egypt. He was profoundly an African of the soil.

Complications arise when a person is descended from racial mixture like so many of the so-called Coloreds of the South African Cape. The majority of them may be Africans of the blood as well as of the soil. Similarly, Egypt since the 1952 revolution has had two presidents who were racially mixed –

President Muhammad Neguib and President Anwar Sadat. The two Egyptian presidents were Africans of the blood as well as of the soil.

It is possible that Muammar Gaddafi himself is ethnically mixed as an African. But in Arab terms he is basically an Arab. In spite of being culturally and linguistically Arab, he did prefer to see himself as African first and an Arab second. On the whole Gaddafi in the last two or three decades in office had been a good African but a bad Libyan. He had been a bad Libyan by being intolerant of dissent, and being too long in power. Although he rejected titles like President or His Excellency, and preferred to live in a tent, he did suppress critics uncompromisingly.

But if he was a bad Libyan, in what sense was he a good African? He had invested heavily in African countries often at great loss and on limited returns for himself. He had financed expensive African conferences from his own resources. He supported the very expensive Arabic translation of the eight volumes UNESCO General History of Africa.

Black Africans had jobs in Libya when they were rejected elsewhere. Young Malians who recently enlisted to go and fight for Gaddafi did so out of sentimental attachment to the Libyan leader. Black faces fighting for Gaddafi were not mercenaries necessarily. Gaddafi's money could have bought better skilled mercenaries than the peasants of Mali and Burkina Faso. East European mercenaries would have been better trained.

Over dinner in Gaddafi's tent as his guest some years ago I found myself defending the Arabs against Gaddafi's hostility. I was also astonished when Gaddafi asked me to send him a copy of my father's book, *The Mazrui Dynasty of Mombasa*. It was part of his fascination with *Afrabia*. The book was published by Oxford University Press in the 1990s.

In the present situation Gaddafi has paid a price for preferring his African identity. He has alienated fellow Arabs to a disastrous extent. The Arab League virtually gave the green light to the Security Council and the Western powers to bomb Gaddafi's Libya. His fellow Arabs threw him under the bus and consequently, his assassination on October 20, 2011.

YEARNINGS OF YEMEN

An Arab country outside Africa which may also be drifting towards a civil war has been YEMEN under President Ali Abdullah Saleh. Yemen's links to Africa include their own settlements in East Africa and the Horn of Africa – especially from the Yemeni sub-region of Hadhramount. Such Hadhrami settlers were highly visible in Mombasa as shopkeepers, merchants, intellectuals and Muslim missionaries. Many became assimilated and Swahilized.

On the gender question this is partly neutralized by the Yemeni equivalent of "the right to bear arms". Yemen is the most heavily armed of all Arab countries at the level of individuals and families. It has been estimated that most adult males not only *own*, but often *wear* arms in Yemen. Some families even own a tank or two, often marked "Private," though this may be a hyperbole.

This culture of militarized manhood (macho) has contributed to the extra marginalization of women. Yemen is also the poorest Arab country. However, it is worth remembering the more eminent of Yemeni's female leaders, such as the Executive Editor of *The Yemeni Times*.

The most famous woman in the history of Yemen is the Queen of Sheba. Jewish, Biblical and Qur'anic versions of the Queen of Sheba place her in a kingdom called Sarba in Yemen instead of in Ethiopia. So Yemen competes with Ethiopia in claiming Sheba. But Ethiopia is taking the legacy of Sheba much more energetically than do the Yemenis. Emperor Menelik I was supposed to have been the offspring of Solomon and Sheba. Indeed, Ethiopians believe that King Solomon's Ark of the Covenant is protected today in St. Mary's Church in Aksum [13]. The divine right of the Emperor is traced to the Covenant [14].

To top it all, modern Ethiopia produced the first Empress of today's history of Black Africa. This was Queen Zewditu, daughter of Menelik II (1844-1913) [15]. Zewditu reigned from 1916 to 1930 [16]. More than half a century later Liberia produced Africa's first elected female Head of State – Ellen Johnson-Sirleaf.

CONCLUSION

For the first time in the history of the Middle East at least ten Arab countries have witnessed pro-democracy demonstrations in varying degrees of intensity. The uprisings in Tunisia and Egypt have already resulted in ousting dictators who had been entrenched in power for decades. In Libya a third dictator's future has also been sealed. Other Arab countries may have to avert political collapse with pre-emptive reforms. Never in the history of the Arabs have there been so many popular uprisings which seem to be inspired neither by Islam nor by anti-imperialism but in the quest for liberal reforms. Half a century earlier in Sharpeville and Soweto South Africans experienced their own political awakening.

Researchers in the Western world should join the scholarly effort to try and understand both the probable causes and the likely consequences of the most remarkable democratizing political contagion since the collapse of the Soviet Union and of communism in Eastern Europe in the final decade of the twentieth century. In recent years political scientists have increasingly examined the hypothesis that mature democracies do not go to war against each other. The question therefore arises whether successful democratization in Southern Africa and the Middle East would reduce the propensity for warfare in these volatile regions of the world in future decades. Political scientists now regard a war between Germany and France or between Britain and Italy as inconceivable [17]. Would a democratized Middle East become similarly pacified?

In the 1920s and 1930s Mustafa Kemal Ataturk embarked on a long term project of democratizing a Muslim society (post-Ottoman Turkey) *from above*. What the Arab world in the year 2011 is struggling to achieve is the goal of democratizing Muslim societies *from below*. The long-term consequences may be of vital importance in relations between Israel and the Arabs, between the Muslim world and the United States, and between Islam and Western civilization. However, a grand precedent had been set by South Africa—the last country on the African continent to be liberated but the first to democratize itself credibly. South Africa had combined democratization both from below and from above.

Think-tanks in the Western world are well-placed to participate in the relevant research and scholarship. Such a Western tradition has produced not only authors of relevant books and articles. It has also produced leaders in the Study of Islam and Democracy in the world, Presidents of Associations of Muslim Social Studies worldwide and scholars who have been to almost every Arab country and met some of their leaders. The West had also analyzed the lessons of Sharpeville in 1960 and the courage of the youth of Soweto in 1976 [18].

New England's credentials are strong in the effort to promote greater understanding between the United States and the Muslim World in this new phase in Arab history. Initiatives from liberal arts colleges are likely to be an important step forward.

What must not be forgotten are the different roles of women – articulate when the opposition consists of protestors, but more cautious when protestors become rebels. The story of powerful women in North Africa goes back to

Hatshepsut and Cleopatra. In more modern times the range is from Madame Beheira Ben Mrad of Tunisia in the twentieth century to Queen Zewditu of Ethiopia before the Second World War.

More recently Liberia bestowed upon Africa the electoral credentials of Ellen Johnson-Sirleaf as Africa's first elected female Head of State. And South Africa has produced women-liberators like Winnie Mandela, Albertina Sisulu (Africans of the blood) and women-democratizers like the first female speaker of post-apartheid Parliament in Cape Town, Dr. Frene Ginwala (African of the soil).

The struggle continues, as the politics of identity embrace Africanity in all its diverse forms.

REFERENCES

[1] Samuel Decalo, *Coups and Army* Rule in Africa: Studies in Military Style, New Haven, CT: Yale University Press, 1977.

[2] Heather Deegan, The Politics of New South Africa: Apartheid and After, New York, Longman, 2001.

[3] G.M. Carter and Patrick O'Meara (eds.), Southern Africa: The Coming Crisis. Bloomington, IN: Indiana University Press, 1979, pp. 89-128.

[4] Kees Maxey, The Fight for Zimbabwe: The Armed Conflict in Southern Rhodesia Since the UDI, New York: Africana Publishing Company, 1975.

[5] Abdullahi Ahmed An-Na'M, The Second Message of Islam: Mahmoud Muhammad Taha, Evanston, IL: Northwestern University Press, 1996

[6] Chris Jones-Pauly and Abir Dajani Tuqan, Women under Islam: Gender, Justice and the Politics of Islamic Law, New York: Palgrave Macmillan, 2011.

[7] Ibid.

[8] James L. Gelvin, The Arab Uprisings: What Everyone Needs to Know, New York: Oxford University Press, 2012.

[9] P. Eric Louw, The Rise, Fall and Legacy of Apartheid. Westport, CT: Praeger Publishers, 2004, pp. 128-130.

[10] Ellen Galford, World History Biographies: Hatshepsut; The Princess Who Became King, Washington, D.C.: National Geographic World History Biographies, 2007.

[11] Stacy Schiff, Cleopatra: A Life: Boston, MA: Little, Brown and Company, 2009.

[12] Muammar Gaddafi, The Green Book: The Solution to Problem of Democracy, The Social Basis of the Third Universal Theory, Tripoli: 2005. Also see Mohamed A. El-Khawas, Qaddafi: His Ideology in Theory and Practice, Battleboro, VT: Amana Books, 1986.

[13] Linda Tarry and Avi Katz, King Solomom and The Queen of Sheba, New York: Pits Popany, 1997.

[14] Wilson Jeremiah Moses, The Golden Age of Black Nationalism 1850-1925. Hamden, CT: Archon Books, 1978, 148-159.

[15] Harold G. Marcus, The Life and Times of Menelik II of Ethiopia, 1844-1913, 1995. Also see Sylviane Anna Diouf, Kings and Queens of East Africa, New York: Watts Library, 2000.

[16] Getachew Metaferia, Ethiopia and the United States: History, Diplomacy, and Analysis, New York: Algora Publishing, 2009, pp. 31-32.

[17] S.K.B. Asante, Pan-African Protest: West Africa and Italo-Ethiopian Crisis, 1934-1941. London: Longman, 1977.

[18] Sheridan Johns and R. Hunt Davis, Jr., Mandela, Tambo and the African National Congress: The Struggle Against Apartheid 1948-1990, Also see The Rise and Possible Demise of Afrikaans as a Public Language. http://web.uct.ac.za/depts./praesa/opaper14.PDF.

In: Africa
Editor: Olayiwola Abegunrin
ISBN: 978-1-62948-561-4

Chapter 4

LIBERIA AND AFRICA SINCE DECOLONIZATION, 1950S TO 2012

D. Elwood Dunn
The Alfred Walter Negley Professor of Political Science Emeritus
The University of the South, Sewanee, TN, US

INTRODUCTION

As the century of African independence ended, Liberia was consumed by a vicious civil war. Modern Africa's first republic in 2012 began to show signs of recovery.

Liberia twice elected as president Africa's first female president and she together with Liberian peace activist Leymah Gbowee was among the awardees of the 2011 Nobel Peace Prize. The country was also beginning to resume key positions and activity in the continent's regional organizations. [1]

Liberia is an African country unlike the others. It was founded as a black settler state in early 19th century Africa with a mission to enlighten and Christianize indigenous Africans.

The experience of cultural encounters is leading slowly to a shift toward building an African nationality inclusive of the entire population.

THE TUBMAN ADMINISTRATION AND AFRICA

As the Second World War drew to a close and African nationalism began consolidating in the decades that followed, Liberia, one of then only four independent African states, was challenged to consider a clearer Africa policy. Because the wave of decolonization would soon replace Liberia's European colonial neighbors with free states under African leadership, the administration of President William V.S. Tubman (1944-1971) deemed it necessary to formulate policies toward these new states within the broader framework of the challenge that loomed of creating a new African political order.

Over time, Tubman's Africa policy developed along two lines: one domestic, the other international, or more precisely the development of a domestic base for an external policy.

Domestically, Tubman proffered a National Unification and Integration policy designed to address a historic divide between New World settlers and indigenous peoples. Internationally, Tubman shared America's apprehension toward radical nationalism and its Pan-African derivative. [2]

He consequently joined the United States to contain what both parties perceived as radicalism tending toward socialism. Tubman aspired toward a moderate African political order and probably understood that his American Cold War partner would assist him achieve that end.

As regards the domestic dimension, Tubman attempted to formalize a process of gradual assimilation of the indigenous population into what remained largely a settler state employing constitutional amendments and other measures. He once proclaimed with near finality that his National Unification policy had "bound up the wounds of the nation, healed them and drawn us firmly together. It has brought to our doors national solidarity, national prosperity and a new sense of direction." [3]

The Liberian leader wanted the extension of the same "spirit of unification" to Liberia's new African neighbors.

The essential message was that as gradual unification had brought together "twenty-eight tribes of varying dialects, traditions, cultures and customs," so too was this approach being commended as foundation for "the pattern of African unity which we of this nation have advanced for the achievement of closer relations with the independent nations and freedom-emerging peoples of this continent." [4]

Liberia was thus attuned to African developments both as witness and participant in a period of birth, growth, and profound changes in the immediate post-Second World War period.

As an early advocate of the rights of African peoples to self-determination and independence, Liberia availed herself of the arenas of the United Nations (UN). The status of non-self-governing territories and Trust Territories were not only reflected in UN Charter articles 11 and 12, but specific issues emanating from them soon claimed the attention of UN organs. In 1950, at the General Assembly's Fourth Committee on the Trusteeship Council Report, Liberian Ambassador Henry Ford Cooper regretted that he could not associate himself with the congratulations which had been extended to the Administering Authorities on their achievements in the Trust Territories; he had been impressed, rather, with the aspirations of the indigenous populations, which had occasionally made themselves felt through violence, and had, in some instances, compelled the Administering Authorities to accede to the demands of the people.

The small measure of self-government, advanced education and social and economic improvement won by the indigenous population had been achieved through great sacrifice". "History has shown" he averred, "that no people had attained independence except through its own express will to be master of its own destiny." [5]

Cooper further said that Liberia was in favor of amalgamating Non-self-governing and Trust Territories "since conditions in both types of territories were virtually the same, the indigenous inhabitants must have a common desire for political freedom, and the administrative union of the territories could, therefore, only result in a strengthening of that desire." [6] In this he presaged the 1960 UN General Assembly *Declaration on the Granting of Independence to Colonial Countries and Peoples* that eventually removed the distinction between the two categories of non-sovereign and independent territories.

Liberia remained vocally engaged as the UN went on to address such colonial issues as the disposal of the former Italian colonies of Libya, Somaliland and Eritrea; the question of Algeria, the question of South West Africa (Namibia); and the policy of Apartheid of the government of South Africa. On the South West African question the Liberian role was large as she joined Ethiopia in filing before the International Court of Justice in 1960 application instituting contentious proceeding against South Africa for attempting to relinquish its international obligations by introducing Apartheid into the territory.

Moreover, the diplomatic activities of Liberia's first female Ambassador Angie Brooks-Randolph enhanced Liberia's engagement with a decolonizing Africa during this early period.

She saw service as president of the 24th regular session of the General Assembly though her 1969 election came amidst reticence about her candidacy as she followed in the trails of only two other African diplomats – Tunisia's Mongi Slim and Ghana's Alex Quaison-Sackey. Her time at the UN spans two decades during which she served in a variety of capacities in furtherance of the anti-colonial struggle. She chaired the General Assembly's Fourth Committee, Special Committee on the issue of Ruanda-Urundi (the Belgium Trust Territory that was divided in 1962 into Rwanda and Burundi), and the Trusteeship Council in 1966 – the first African woman to serve in that capacity.

In 1951, as Kwame Nkrumah bursts on to the African scene as first "leader of government business" in the former Gold Coast (Ghana), he was invited by President Tubman to discuss options available for obtaining full independence. The visit took on the character of a full-fledged state event with the attendant pomp and circumstance.

Both Tubman and Nkrumah in their respective remarks spoke of the imperative for accelerated African independence. This Liberian invitation triggered a *Time Magazine* feature story on the Gold Coast march to independence and may have added momentum to the African independence movement.

Meanwhile, Liberia made other gestures towards African nationalists during this early period and beyond. Herbert W. Chitepo of the Zimbabwe African National Union (ZANU) thanked Tubman in 1961 for a $10,000 contribution. Chuime of Nyasaland received a similar amount on behalf of Hastings Kamuzu Banda, as did Thomas Karua of the same territory. Karume of Zanzibar and Holden Roberto of the National Liberation Front of Angola (FNLA) were among beneficiaries of Liberian assistance. Nelson Mandela himself reports a 1962 visit to Monrovia where he received $5,000 for weapons and training in the armed struggle, as well as "pocket money." [7]

Consider as well a meeting of African foreign ministers in Monrovia in August 1959 to address the Algerian war of independence. With representatives of the rebel Provisional Government of Algeria (GPS) in tow and the rebel Flag of Algeria hoisted perhaps for the first time in a sovereign state, Tubman's identification of Liberia with the Algerian cause was unmistakable: He declared as he opened the conference, "my brothers, my friends one can fight an army of a million men, but independence is a million ideas, and one cannot fight a million ideas." [8] Such strong expression of support for African liberation notwithstanding, Tubman's approach to liberation contrasted sharply with Nkrumah's.

The independence of Ghana in 1957 with its promise of radical nationalism as reflected in Nkrumah's remarks that "The independence of Ghana is meaningless if not linked to the total liberation of Africa," [9] while welcomed, did not go un-noticed by Tubman. Rather than radical political transformations Tubman envisaged formal, legal sovereignty with pragmatic ties to the Western world. He thought Guinea's Sekou Toure's confrontation with France ill advised, and later said as much in terms of Congo's Patrice Lumumba's strained relations with Belgium.

Only months following Ghana's independence and in view of the radical rhetoric that emanated from Accra, Tubman addressed the question of the leadership of Africa and the form unity might take: He declared in his 1957 Independence Day Message, "I have observed that there seem to be three schools of thought on the leadership question." [10] There are those who feel that Liberia should assume leadership based on the fact that she is the oldest African Republic and is riper in political experience; but it will require more than age and political experience to assume leadership of Africa. There are others who hold that Ghana should assume that role because she is physically more developed and embraces larger territories. It will require more than development and larger territory to assume leadership of Africa. And there are yet those who opine that Egypt with its rich traditions dating back to the remotest antiquity should do so. It will require more than rich traditions of antiquity. It will require, in my opinion, the aggregate of all three of these and more besides. It will require the aggregate of the best of all that Liberia, Ghana, Egypt, Tunisia, Ethiopia, the Sudan, Morocco, and all other African Territories and States possess, molded together, to assume the leadership of Africa, compounded in such a manner as to represent the divisibility of Africa indivisible. [11] Ghana seemed to be persuaded neither by what was seen as Liberia's, and perhaps Ethiopia's lack of African leadership initiative in the immediate post war decade of the 1940s, nor Tubman's later attempt to wax philosophical in a situation that demanded "positive action." Nkrumah therefore took the initiative in inviting to Accra the first conference of independent African states in April 1958. All of the eight independent states were represented, but Tubman was the only head of state and government other than the host. The polite exchange of views and vague communiqué was disappointing to Nkrumah, but consistent with Tubman's approach to African affairs. Nkrumah decided to compensate for this setback by attempting to reach "progressive" thinkers and organizations across African borders. The All-Africa Peoples' Conference was consequently convened in Accra in December 1958.

The ruling True Whig Party and government-sponsored youth and labor organizations represented Liberia at the All African Peoples' Conference. The Liberian delegation soon discovered their isolation from the rhetorical bombast that seemed the order of the day in Accra. Ambassador T. Ernest Eastman who was on the delegation has reported on the anti-Liberian atmosphere that filled the assembly hall, spilling into the corridors as nationalists such as Tom Mboya of Kenya, Patrice Lumumba of Congo joined H. Kamuzu Banda of Malawi in the threatening question: "Where shall Liberia be ten years from now when we are free? You must ask yourself that question a thousand times." [12]

Until the independence in October 1960 of the populous Nigeria, Liberia appeared the leader of African moderation. Nkrumah was riding a crest of radical nationalism as the situations in such disparate places as Guinea, the Congo, and apartheid South Africa, and elsewhere on the continent tended to lend credence to this approach. Tubman consequently initiated, in reaction to the unstoppable developments, a crucial consultation in Sanniquellie, Liberia in July 1959 involving Nkrumah and Toure. The substance of the Sanniquellie Declaration was that consultation and the patient hammering out of a consensus should be the African modus operandi. A fuller African consultation to involve a larger number of states whose independence was pending was slated for Ethiopia the following year.

At the 1960 gathering in Addis, free Africa had grown from 8 to 15 states, including populous Nigeria and a host of moderate Francophone states. Liberia was now in its comfort zone. And when African differences split the continent into three ways – the so-called Brazzaville, Casablanca, and "uncommitted" (Monrovia Group) groups, Liberia felt it had positioned itself precisely where it wanted to be, a potential moderator, a facilitator of African affairs. According to Tubman's Secretary of State, J. Rudolph Grimes, Liberia was soon urged by "quite a few" African leaders to take some initiative to bridge the existing African divisions. [13]

Tubman's response to the suggestions that he convene a bridging conference was to propose that such a conference be sponsored by a number of carefully chosen states. He proposed two representatives each from the Brazzaville and Casablanca groups, and three from the "uncommitted." Through consultations, Guinea and Mali represented Casablanca, Ghana having refused the invitation to serve a sponsor. Ivory Coast and Cameroon represented Brazzaville. And Nigeria, Togo, and Liberia represented the uncommitted. It was therefore these seven African states that issued invitations to all independent African states to meet in Monrovia May 8-12, 1961.

After the invitations had been issued and many had indicated acceptance, a meeting was held in Accra of the Casablanca group. Guinea and Mali soon announced withdrawal of their sponsorship. Tubman was not dissuaded. By May 7, fourteen delegations had arrived Monrovia. Some six others would soon follow as the conference convened on schedule. Though Tubman held a commanding role at informal preconference exchange of views, a participant, Liberian economist Charles Dunbar Sherman relates this interesting anecdote: "It was interesting to observe the attending Heads of States meet around the Conference table as equals, many for the first time. I recall distinctly a rather sharp exchange between Abubakar Tafawa Balewa, who was at that particular session said to President Tubman: 'You are wrong!' Mr. Tubman, forgetting who Balewa was, for a moment, shouted back at him and said: 'What did you say?' Alhaji Balewa calmly repeated: 'I said, Mr. President, you are wrong.' Tubman smiled and the tension was broken." [14]

The 20 states attending the conference marked the largest single gathering of African countries ever to that date. They reviewed the issues on the continental agenda, regretted the absence of the Casablanca powers, and expressed the hope that these powers would soon join the African consultative process. Awarded the chairmanship of the conference by his colleagues, Tubman stated that the objective was "to bring all African leaders to reason together." Only tolerance, good faith, honor, good neighborliness" could lead Africa to the desired unity and solidarity. [15]

In an overwhelming endorsement of Tubman's approach to unity and cooperation, the conference's communiqué faithfully reflected his views. Participants agreed that a summit meeting would convene in Nigeria in 1962 to develop processes for technical and cultural cooperation and carry forward the "unity of aspirations and action" of African states. While a majority of the African and Western press hailed the Monrovia gathering as a success, the Ghanaian press issued scathing attacks on "the Monrovia slave-mentality." Tubman remained quiet. He had won a major battle. The Inter-African and Malagasy Union emerged from the January 1962 Lagos conference. It fixed a date of May 1963 for a summit conference in Ethiopia that would usher in what became the Organization of African Unity (OAU).

All seemed in order for a conference designed to organize African unity when on January 13, 1963 the congenial Togolese President, Sylvanus Olympio was assassinated under circumstances that evoked considerable concern among African leaders. The concern was acute for Liberia for several reasons. Olympio had attended Tubman's January 1960 Inauguration and the two leaders seemed to have much in common.

They had both closely collaborated as sponsors at the crucial 1961 Monrovia conference. Even more, the assassination had occurred only a day before Olympio's scheduled departure for a state visit to Liberia. The slain president's widow's January 29, 1963 letter to Tubman recounting the events leading to her husband's death and characterizing the brutal murder "as sinister non-Togolese design" fueled the concerns. [16]

Shortly following the Olympio assassination, a dramatic meeting of the council of ministers of the Inter-African and Malagasy Organization (IAMO) convened in Lagos January 24-26, 1963. Two rival Togolese delegations, one from the provisional Nicholas Grunitzky government and the other composed of members of Olympio's cabinet were present. The IAMO recognized that the murder of Olympio could not be condoned by automatic recognition of a successor government, thus establishing a dangerous precedent. The ministers called for an investigating mission of neighboring states to visit Togo, the prosecution of those responsible for the murder and free elections at an early date. The group also agreed a draft Mutual Security Treaty for submission to the May meeting of African Heads of State in Addis.

The Addis summit convened under the cloud of this assassination, as well as against the backdrop of the still outstanding differences between the two African political tendencies. At one early session President Toure of Guinea openly accused President Nkrumah of complicity in the Olympio assassination. This accusation of one member of the erstwhile Casablanca group by another placed Nkrumah squarely on the defensive and weakened his moral authority, and therefore his effectiveness in making the case for political union. Continuing what must have been a moment of personal delight, Tubman calmly implored his fellow conferees to "think like men of action and act like men of thought." The OAU that emerged from the 1963 Addis conference was precisely the traditional state-centric body Tubman had hoped for and Nkrumah had feared would materialize.

The functionalist imperative or the approach of socio-economic, as opposed to exclusive political, development was advanced with consistency especially following Nkrumah's positing of his united states of Africa thesis. In a series of well-staged diplomatic offensives directed from Monrovia, a steady stream of working papers and strategic conversations were held across and beyond the continent. Some of these efforts culminated eventually in the establishment of such staple African institutions as the West African Rice Development Association (WARDA), the African Development Bank, the Mano River Union (MRU), and the Economic Community of West African States (ECOWAS). [17]

Implicit in Tubman's association of African States idea has always been what he described as the need for Africans, long estranged from one another, to come to know each other through a variety of social and economic measures, not the least of which the need to promote intra-African trade and other forms of economic cooperation. Beyond the memoranda of conversations with African and Africa-interested players, Tubman underscored economic cooperation in all of his landmark statements including the July 1959 Independence Day remarks, and speeches at the Sanniquellie conference, and at the 1962 Monrovia conference.

In pursuit of African economic regionalism, Liberia joined Sierra Leone, Guinea and Ivory Coast in February 1965 in initiating an interim West African Free Zone Area. In August of the same year the West African Iron and Steel conference ended in Liberia with agreement in principle to establish an Iron and Steel Authority to coordinate industrial development in West Africa. [18] The OAU and the UN Economic Commission for Africa endorsed this important initiative. In attendance were Diallo Telli, first Secretary General of the OAU and Robert Gardiner, first Executive Secretary of the UN Economic Commission for Africa (UNECA). Crucial conferences prior to the 1975 establishment of ECOWAS occurred in Monrovia in November 1967 (14 countries and a draft Articles of Association) and in April 1968. The latter conference brought together 9 of the 15 West African Heads of State with the object of evolving what they called appropriate measures to remove obstacles to economic cooperation in the sub-region. These efforts awaited more propitious circumstances in the early 1970s to begin bearing fruit.

One organizational effort, however, the African Development Bank (ADB), was actually realized in 1962 with the organization's establishment of its first headquarters in Abidjan, the first presidency to Sudan, and Liberia serving on the first board of directors. This was result of a tortuous series of events that began with an idea from the Liberian banker A. Romeo Horton. Possibly in reaction to President Tubman's earlier advocacy for African economic cooperation, Horton presented the President a concept paper for an African development bank that he conceived of as contributing to African unity "by financing and investing in multinational enterprises and projects." Horton has insisted that the original idea was not for financing national projects as has actually happened but trans-national ones. At Tubman's behest, and following extensive consultations with African leaders, Horton and the Liberian economist P. Clarence Parker prepared a draft charter. An implementation committee of nine countries (Cameroon, Ethiopia, Guinea, Liberia, Mali, Nigeria, Sudan, Tanganyika, and Tunisia) was constituted and the committee held its first meeting in Monrovia June 18-22, 1962. [19] It was this committee that husbanded the organization into existence following intensive and extensive consultations with African leaders. The multilateral agreement that brought the ADB into existence was signed by 25 African states in Khartoum in September 1964.

There were multiple motives for this Liberian advocacy of African regionalism. They included a desire to blunt Nkrumah's idea of an African union government, a practical alternative for cooperation among African states, as well as a concomitant Liberian desire to show solidarity with the US in the midst of the Cold War. Whatever the primary motive, what followed was the majority acceptance of the furtherance of African cooperation in all domains, with any possible union government in the distant future. Until then, Liberia wanted the territorial integrity of Nigeria maintained, as she became a part of the OAU mediation committee on the Nigerian civil war of 1967-1970, even engaging Vice President William R. Tolbert, Jr. in dangerous shuttle diplomacy in the Biafra war zone. [20]

Tubman died in July 1971 and Africa paid homage. Ten heads of state attended his funeral, the Nigerian military leader Yakubu Gowon among them. Gowon called Tubman "one of Africa's greatest sons of all times, a true servant of God who had served his people, humanity and the world at large with great devotion and honesty." [21]

THE TOLBERT ADMINISTRATION AND AFRICA

The transfer of the mantle of leadership from Tubman to his vice president, William R. Tolbert, Jr. in July 1971 promised some significant changes, while building on Tubman's legacy of a moderate African political order. The challenge at home of a more thorough Africanization of Liberia would move in tandem with Tolbert's engagement of solidarity with African "progressives" who were in the vanguard of completing African liberation, including terminating white minority rule on the continent. Crucially, the new administration endeavored to carry decidedly forward the measure of economic regionalism earlier initiated.

As Liberia hosted, at much sacrifice, the sixteenth OAU summit in 1979, the contours of its Africa policy were clearly in evidence given the country's now legendary advocacy for ending the vestiges of colonialism over the preceding years. Considering Liberia's role in the founding of the organization some saw the OAU "returning home."

Yet, one cannot escape observing that the OAU of 1979 was unlike the OAU of the founders. Where Tubman wished to heal the "wound of loneliness since [Liberia's] 1847 independence" and stamp on the organization a conservative imprimatur "with some Casablanca [representing African radical nationalism] coloring," Tolbert saw his task as one of deepening the dye of the Casablanca coloring. [22]

An early signal of Tolbert's regionalist thrust was the start of his presidency with a series of one-day visits to neighboring Guinea, Ivory Coast, and Sierra Leone. An activist policy was pursued with frequent messages to African colleagues as well as the frequent dispatch of special envoys. Africa was clearly on Liberia's radar screen. A 1979 defense pact with Guinea signaled less dependence on the United States. At accelerated pace, African freedom fighters made their way to Liberia for material and moral support. Peace efforts were undertaken as Liberia served on the OAU mediating committee on the Ethiopia-Somalia dispute. In addition, Tolbert's efforts resulted in the "miracle of Monrovia" when in March 1978, along with the presidents of Togo and The Gambia, Tolbert facilitated an end to a longstanding acid relationship between President Toure of Guinea, and his colleagues, Presidents Houphouet-Boigny of Ivory Coast, and Senghor of Senegal. Tolbert had used his lightening shuttle to good effect. The result was a solemn undertaking "to finally end all dissensions which have affected their relations." and to establish full diplomatic relations with the exchange of ambassadors. [23]

Economic emancipation was Tolbert's way of advocating for and carrying forward the earlier OAU economic cooperation schemes. Such schemes took the form of specific cooperation agreements with Ivory Coast, Guinea, and Sierra Leone, respectively. These agreements culminated in the 1973 creation of the Mano River Union (MRU) and the 1975 establishment of the ECOWAS. In early 1979, Liberia hosted another "Monrovia conference," with OAU and ECA joint sponsorship of a colloquium. Its purpose was to suggest common patterns for African economic development up to the year 2000. A number of African experts assembled in Monrovia. They agreed to tackle the problem of first creating joint institutions toward an African common market and the development of a center to promote the continent's technological potentials. [24] The sixteenth Summit built its economic resolutions on these foundations.

A series of other progressive resolutions emerged from the Summit, among them the Monrovia Strategy for the Development of Africa and a resolution to establish an Africa expert group to study and prepare a treaty for an African Economic Community; the first-of-its-kind resolution on human rights that called for a committee of experts to draft an African charter on human rights, an initiative that subsequently became the African Charter on Human and Peoples' Rights (Supreme Court Associate Justice and former Ambassador Angie Brooks Randolph contributed significantly); the renewal of the OAU Committee of Twelve on Afro-Arab Cooperation, which included Liberia; the unequivocal resolutions on southern Africa including support for OAU-recognized liberation movements in Namibia and South Africa and the Lancaster House peace negotiations for Zimbabwe; as well as a prescient proposal for OAU charter amendment to create an ad hoc action machinery to include a Pan-African force that would enable the organization to "respond at all times to problems of varying dimensions." [25] The OAU chairmanship, which traditionally went to the host head of state, was to give Tolbert a platform to demonstrate Liberia's African commitments, as well as a challenge to convince a majority of African leaders about the needed new path.

Despite Zambian President Kenneth Kaunda's experience of duplicity with South African Prime Minister John Vorster as revealed in an April 1971 Zambian publication of "Details of exchange between President Kaunda of Zambia and Prime Minister Vorster of South Africa," [26] Tolbert decided to engage in dialogue with the apartheid regime and to do so publicly, where such countries as Ivory Coast, Malawi, Madagascar, Ghana, Gabon, Kenya, Senegal, and Congo-Kinshasa had all conducted dialogue in secret with the apartheid regime.

Accordingly, at Tolbert's invitation John Vorster and his foreign minister arrived in Liberia in secret on February 11, 1975 and departed the next day; no sooner had they departed than the *Times of London* headlined "Mr. Vorster Pays Secret Visit to Liberian leader." [27] Stunned by the revelation, Liberian officials initially attempted to deny the story, but then they soon issued a statement of explanation. Such an explanation was necessary because of the widespread internal and external suspicion generated by the visit.

In the wake of the revelation the Liberian press headlined "Tolbert in Trouble with the OAU," the opposition movement Progressive Alliance of Liberia (PAL) pointed out "how seriously embarrassed the people of Liberia [felt] before the entire world," and the Tanzanian press exclaimed: "Liberia Welcomes Africa's Enemy!"

To address the public relations implications of the revelation, Tolbert dispatched his foreign minister on expensive briefing shuttles to 15 African states. While the Liberian minister reported general African understanding of the initiative, there was some African outrage.

For example, Guinea's Sekou Toure tried unsuccessfully to contain his anger as he rejected any rationale for dialogue. Toure exclaimed twice to the Liberian envoy: "I am scared… scare not of Tolbert being bought, but of making moral mistakes because as leaders of our people our only true strength is our moral stature before our people and world opinion." And then, in what must have irked Tolbert, Toure added, "If (former President W.V.S.] Tubman was not dynamic leader as far as his internal policies for social development [were concerned], at the African level he was always an honest man, and all African leaders knew this and had confidence in him." [28]

This occurrence notwithstanding, Liberia remained faithful to what had become a tradition of solid support for African liberation. African freedom fighters continued the tradition of beating their path to Monrovia for support and assistance. Union for the Total Independence of Angola (UNITA's) Jonas Savimbi met with Tolbert in October 1975, receiving Liberian diplomatic passport and $3,000 in cash. A year later, the Pan Africanist Congress's (PAC) of South Africa Potlako Lebello received travel documents and $25,000. SWAPO's Sam Njoma was supported with a check of $10,000 dated April 19, 1978. Others making the journey to Liberia included National Cultural Liberation Movements' (INKATHA's) Mangosuthu Buthelezi, ANC/ Zimbabwe's N.G. Nukumo, and PAC's David Sibokwe. [29] PAC's Vusumzi Make resided in Liberia, lecturing at the University of Liberia while freely engaging in his liberation activities, often briefing government officials about the progress of the struggle in southern Africa.

In furtherance of economic regionalism, three landmark regional organizations emerged in the 1970s. The first was the West African Rice Development Association (WARDA), an agricultural research center constituted by 11 West African states including Liberia. Its constitution was signed in Dakar in 1970, with the first meeting in Liberia in September 1971 at which time the secretariat was established there as Liberia made the first financial contribution to the organization. This was the product of OAU/ECA cooperation in agriculture research. First headquarters was located in Liberia, and Liberian agriculturist Nah Doe Bropleh became deputy executive secretary. In the 1980s WARDA became The Africa Rice Center (Africa Rice) with eventual expansion to 24 states of West, Central, East and North Africa. Now headquartered in Republic of Benin, the center is one of 15 specialized research outfits under the Future Harvest Centers of the Consultative Group on International Agricultural Research (CGIAR).

The Mano River Union (MRU), a customs union, originates from a series of bilateral cooperation arrangements – Ivory Coast/Liberia, Guinea/Liberia, and Sierra Leone/Liberia. At a September 12, 1973 joint ministerial meeting on Liberian-Sierra Leone cooperation emerged the text of a document, The Mano River Declaration that in October was signed in Malema (Sierra Leone) by Sierra Leone's Siaka Stevens and Liberia's William R. Tolbert, Jr. Guinea and Ivory Coast subsequently acceded to the treaty. Headquartered in Freetown, three Liberians have served as Secretary General, first the economist Cyril Bright, followed by the diplomat Ernest Eastman, and then the sociologist Augustus F. Caine.

As regards the Economic Community of West African States (ECOWAS), efforts were initiated in the early 1960s and credited to Liberian President Tubman who was an early advocate for a West African economic community. The idea was re-launched by Togo and Nigeria in 1972, following which a series of technical meetings culminated in a ministerial meeting in Monrovia, January 27-31, 1975. The Treaty of Lagos that brought into existence the organization was signed in Nigeria by 15 West African states, including Liberia, on May 28, 1975. ECOWAS' initial mission was to promote economic integration across the sub-region, but since expanded to address political and security issues as well. ECOWAS has been designated one of five regional pillars of the African Economic Community (AEC) that grew out of the preparations for the 16th OAU summit in Liberia and has since become a part of the continent's development architecture. Among institutions under which it functions are a Secretariat and a Fund for Cooperation, now the ECOWAS Bank for Investment and Development. Liberians Romeo Horton and Robert Tubman have served as executive directors of the bank. Another Liberian, Toga McIntosh, joined the staff as Vice President of the ECOWAS Commission in early 2012.

THE DOE ADMINISTRATION AND AFRICA

A few months into the Liberia-hosted sixteenth summit of the OAU and while serving as the Current Chairman of the organization President Tolbert was assassinated and overthrown in a bloody military coup d'état. Ten days following the April 12, 1980 event, 13 senior officials of the regime, including his foreign minister, C. Cecil Dennis, Jr. who was well known across the continent, were publicly executed. Africa's immediate reaction to the bloody events was to twice rebuff the military regime that emerged from the coup, first at the second extraordinary session of the Heads of State and Government of the OAU on the Economic Development of Africa in Lagos, April 28, 1980, and then at the ECOWAS summit in Lome, Togo on May 28, 1980. In reaction to these rebuffs, the size of the Nigerian mission in Liberia was reduced, and Liberian ambassadors were recalled from neighboring Sierra Leone, Ivory Coast, and Nigeria.

Guinea opted to play a mediatory role, and communication channels were gradually opened enabling Head of State Samuel K. Doe to attend arranged summits in Yamoussoukro and Monrovia with four other West African leaders – Houphouet-Boigny of the Ivory Coast, Sekou Toure of Guinea, Siaka Stevens of Sierra Leone, and Gnassingbe Eyadema of Togo. Houphouet's abrupt departure from the June 1980 one-day visit to Liberia during which he reportedly said that he would return only when Liberians were smiling again, did not bode well for the Ivory Coast-Liberia relationship. Though normalcy was returned over time, it does not appear that the traditional relationship of mutual trust among regional neighbors was ever fully restored. A war of words, several months later, ensued between Liberia and Sierra Leone. Then came the November 1985 foiled coup during which former Commanding General Thomas Quiwonkpa attempted to overthrow the Doe regime. Under the circumstances, Houphouet never returned to Liberia. Rather, he allowed liberal use of his territory when the Liberian insurgents, under the National Patriotic Front of Liberia (NPFL), led by Charles Taylor, initiated the Liberian civil war in December 1989.

At this point Liberia quickly became a negative force on the continent rekindling such cleavages as the Francophone and Anglophone divide, including Nigeria and a neo-colonial France. In addition to the Ivory Coast from whence the Liberian insurgency had been launched, Libya and Burkina Faso were early allies of Taylor's NPFL.

Too, the powerful Nigerian military leader, Ibrahim Babangida, remained faithful to his Liberian counterpart, Samuel Doe. As the standoff between Taylor and Doe spiraled out of control, and the OAU seemed unable to do more than issue appeals seemingly paralyzed by its Charter provision of non-interference in members' domestic matters, ECOWAS deemed it necessary to attempt robust mediation.

Authorized by a five-member mediation committee an ECOWAS-created Economic Community of West African States Monitoring Observer Group (ECOMOG) force of some 3500 troops from Gambia, Guinea, Ghana, Nigeria, and Sierra Leone entered Liberia on August 24, 1990 in an attempt to enforce a ceasefire and otherwise facilitate resolution of the conflict through an "ECOWAS Peace Plan." ECOWAS had first taken note of the Liberian conflict at its annual summit in Gambia May 28-30, 1990.

A Standing Mediation Committee was established and the organization soon endorsed a Liberia-derived peace plan that essentially called for a ceasefire and the installation of interim political arrangements pending elections.

Once the mediation committee established ECOMOG in August, and following the establishment of an interim government by Liberian politicians and civil society organizations, the committee decided to deploy to Liberia.

Given the context of the deployment or intervention, not to speak of the motives of the various internal and external players, Liberia soon found itself the proverbial cloth between the scissors. All of this was played out in seven years of war and mayhem amidst international conferences that finally culminated in a reluctant UN Security Council involvement in 1992 with the imposition of an arms embargo on the warring factions and the posting of a UN Secretary General Special Representative to monitor the situation in Liberia.

Preceding UN action was widespread foreign involvement in the crisis. First came the African provision of training facilities for the rebellion. NPFL rebel recruited in the Ivory Coast were taken to Libya and Burkina Faso for training and in time military personnel from both countries fought alongside NPFL rebels in Liberia. [30]

In addition to the original ECOMOG contingent, Senegalese, and East African soldiers saw service in the West African-led intervention force. There was yet another dimension to the foreign involvement. As the conflict escalated as result of Sierra Leone and Gambia dissidents aiding the NPFL in expectation of reciprocal assistance in future launching of similar rebellion in their respective countries, the NPFL invaded Sierra Leone on March 23, 1991 and initiated there a brutal war. The Liberian involvement in the war in Sierra Leone led to Taylor's indictment for war crimes and crimes against humanity. [31]

The civil war changed the character of Liberia's relations with her fellow Africans.

There were many negative, but also some positive consequences. Among the negatives was the war itself, and the staggering human toll. In addition to the high casualties, it produced thousands of refugees and internally displaced persons as Liberians were forced to take to bush trails as they poured into neighboring countries. Makeshift refugee camps mushroomed in many towns in the region. Ghana and Nigeria also became refugee destinations. Danane camp in the Ivory Coast and the Buduburam camp in Ghana will remain seared in the memory of many Liberians.

As will the Bulk Challenger saga when more than 2,000 Liberians packed and exposed to the elements in an un-sea worthy Nigerian vessel were turned away repeatedly from West African ports.

Some of the positive effects of the war include long and sustained Liberian exposure to life away from home in fellow African countries, though also in a host of other countries around the world. The sort of "let's get to know each other before we consider uniting into one African nation" plea of Tubman in the 1960s was in some curious way being realized. Old worldviews were exposed to challenge. Liberians in their numbers found their voices perhaps in ways never before. The war may have facilitated regional integration in ways few other occurrences could. For good or ill, or despite the atrocities of war, Liberians have come intimately to know their African neighbors. The leaderships and peoples of organizations such as the AU, the MRU and ECOWAS may find few circumstances more propitious for carrying forward the missions of those organizations. The region has become interlocked at the economic, security, cultural and political levels. Perhaps at no other time has Liberia been ripe for thoroughgoing Africanization of its very ethos.

THE TAYLOR ADMINISTRATION AND AFRICA

Charles Taylor has given Liberia and Africa the dubious distinction of being the first African president to be indicted by an international tribunal. The route to this position has been long and bloody. What perhaps set the stage was the predecessor regime of President Samuel Doe. Doe's difficulties as his regime unraveled in 1990 became Taylor's opportunities, soon to be squandered.

In the wake of the hotly contested elections of October 1985, Doe erstwhile military colleague, General Thomas Quiwonkpa attempted a coup to remove Doe from power. Failure of the attempt led Doe to institute a pogrom against the people of Nimba County, Quiwonkpa's home region. Some of the survivors of the foiled coup escaped across the border into neighboring Ivory Coast. They became in time the nucleus of the insurgency of the NPFL led by Charles Taylor.

Following a daring and improbable *escape* from prison in the US in 1985, Taylor found his way to West Africa, first arriving in Ghana. There with the help of fellow Liberian dissidents he was introduced to officials of the regime of President Jerry Rawlings. In Ghana he acquired contacts for Burkina Faso.

Soon an organization of dissidents began to take shape, later to be styled the National Patriotic Front of Liberia (NPFL), ostensibly dedicated to removing from power the regime of Samuel Doe, revenging the death of Quiwonkpa, and facilitating democratization in Liberia. NPFL operatives in Burkina Faso found themselves caught in a local power struggle between President Thomas Sankara and his deputy, Blaise Campaore. They reportedly joined what became the winning side as Sankara was killed and Campaore came to power. One of the operatives, Prince Y. Johnson said the following in October 2008 during a Truth and Reconciliation Commission hearing: "Our only option for remaining in Burkina Faso was to respond positively to the appeal from Blaise Campaore to get rid of Sankara, who was against our presence." [32]

Blaise Campaore introduced Taylor and colleagues to Colonel Gaddafi, the Libyan leader, whose own interest then focused on a revolutionary anti-Western movement in West Africa. The NPFL men soon found themselves as part of Libya's training for African anti-colonial rebels. To this Taylor took advantage of a network in Ivory Coast of disaffected Liberians and Lebanese businessmen willing to help his cause.

By late 1989, the NPFL was well equipped with arms and men and the vital support of immediate neighbors. They were supplemented by hundreds of Burkinabe troops provided by Campaore's government as well as fighters from Gambia, Sierra Leone, and Ghana. Mixed motives explain the involvement of the latter group that consisted of idealists in a Pan-African revolutionary cause, migrant workers finding themselves behind the frontline, as well as mercenaries.

The first phase of the civil war was waged to a stalemate. Doe's disastrous response to the insurgency led to his death in September 1990. The NPFL factionalized, and in time some seven warring factions were in the field struggling for power. Neighboring Sierra Leone's sister revolution was given a boost when Taylor saw reason both to go after his Liberian opponents in Sierra Leone, as well as assist the Revolutionary United Front (RUF) in its rebellion against the Sierra Leone government. Respite in the Liberian conflict made possible general elections on July 19, 1997.

Taylor's NPFL converted party, the National Patriotic Party (NPP), won 75.3 percent of the presidential vote, 49 of 64 legislative seats, and 21 of 26 senatorial seats. Where the principal regional player, ECOWAS and its ECOMOG forces were expected to help transition the country to peace in collaboration with the new Taylor administration, Taylor's war-time difficulties with Nigeria and ECOMOG led him to resist attempts by the international community to address Liberia's immediate security needs, often referencing the Liberian constitutional prerogatives to determine its own security priorities. "Just as Tolbert had paid the price for cultivating African allies at the expense of allegiance to Washington, so Taylor failed to cultivate regional allies whilst still believing in a US that no longer believed in him." [33] Soon a cash-strapped regime that had squandered its democratic opportunity found itself embattled. War alliance with Sierra Leone and its revolutionaries and what appeared as a sub-regional network of a shadow state took precedence over the responsibilities of stable and purposeful governance in Liberia. As the international community tried to rein in Taylors continued participation in Sierra Leone, Taylor grew intransigent. The international community responded first with persuasion, and then coercion.

After a return to bloodshed in Sierra Leone in 1999, the US appeared determined to remove what was seen as Taylor's fueling of the Sierra Leone war. "The continued connection between Taylor's involvement with the RUF, the illegal export of diamonds from Sierra Leone's mines, and the shipment of weapons to the RUF rebels was increasingly at top of Washington's agenda in the region, and US diplomacy soon turned to curtailing the assumed Liberian government role in the situation." [34]

A controversial UN report on the Mano River Union's regional war of March 2001 ultimately became the basis of a Security Council resolution of March 7, 2001, which renewed an arms ban, placed an embargo on export of diamonds from Liberia, and a travel ban on Taylor was expanded to include 130 persons. Taylor himself was only permitted to attend international conferences of the UN, the OAU or ECOWAS.

This was the context in which was born in 1999 the rebel groups, Liberians United for Reconciliation and Democracy (LURD), and in early 2003 the Movement for Democracy in Liberia (MODEL).

Guinea became the proxy US support to LURD while Ivory Coast's Laurent Gbagbo's disaffection for Taylor led to Gbabgo's support for MODEL. By mid-2001 the combined forces of LURD and MODEL controlled 70 per cent of Liberia, and had Taylor, in a twist of irony, hemmed into a Monrovia enclave, defending the Capital against well-armed and well-backed invaders.

A 2002-establised UN-sponsored Special Court for Sierra Leone moved into action as it targeted Taylor's involvement in the atrocities committed in the Sierra Leone war. In March 2003 the judges of the Court approved Taylor's indictment on 17 counts of war crimes and crimes against humanity. Events then transpired in rapid succession.

While Taylor was in Ghana for peace talks in June 2003 the indictment was unsealed and a warrant for his arrest was issued, but the government of Ghana did not cooperate, and Taylor returned home.

Military and diplomatic pressures for Taylor to relinquish the presidency mounted. The African Union delegates in Mozambique added their voices to the US and unanimously called for Taylor to leave, he finally succumbed on August 11, 2003, going into Nigerian exile. The tranquility of this exile was rudely disturbed some two years later following elections in Liberia and the installation of Ellen Johnson Sirleaf as President of Liberia.

Johnson Sirleaf Administration and Africa

Given Ellen Johnson Sirleaf's intense engagement with Liberian and African affairs since the 1970s, it may be useful to capture a Sirleaf profile on the African scene prior to her ascendency to the Liberian presidency. She began service in the Liberian Finance Ministry, moving up the ranks from assistant to full minister in 1979. Two stints at the World Bank followed between 1972-1977, and again 1980-1981. During the latter period she was loan officer for Kenya, Tanzania and Uganda. She commented in my presence at the time that inclusion of Uganda in her responsibilities could come in handy particularly as post-Idi Amin Uganda could prove a good training ground for future reconstruction work in post-Doe Liberia.

Sirleaf moved on to the international private sector with Citibank/Citicorp at the Africa regional office in Kenya where as vice president she was coordinator of African country risk assessment and responsibility for business in 11 East and Southern African countries. Equator Bank/Equator Holdings then followed. Here she was vice president responsible for business in East Africa. This was followed by her 1992-1997 services as UNDP assistant administrator and regional director for Africa. The responsibility entailed the management of country programs in 32 sub-Saharan African states.

Sirleaf thus came to the Liberian presidency in 2006 with strong African credentials and appeared to have fitted almost seamlessly into her role as an African leader. It is important, however, to frame her government's ties with Africa both in terms of building upon some solid historical foundations as well as responding to the positive and negative impact of the civil war on Liberia-Africa relations. The three major regional organizations, the African Union, ECOWAS, and the Mano River Union were established in large measure thanks to the astute diplomacy of her post-World War II predecessors notably

Presidents Tubman and Tolbert. (See details above). In terms of the nature of Liberia's ties to individual African countries, the past is also instructive, for, as we have seen difficult relations with neighbors experienced by both the administrations of President Doe and President Taylor played no small part in the circumstances that brought their respective regimes to grief.

A phalanx of African leaders attended Sirleaf's January 2006 inauguration, as they did again for the January 2012 inauguration. This included all immediate neighbors as well as Nigeria, Burkina Faso, Senegal, Togo, testimony to esteem and signal of Liberia having returned to the African fold. As president-elect in 2005, Sirleaf followed President Tolbert in making brief visits to immediate neighbors. The Taylor saga followed in short order. She reported to the nation on March 30, 2006 that Taylor was in custody of the UN and had been transferred to Sierra Leone to the Special Court to face charges. She added the expectations of a UN resolution for a change of venue to a "more conducive environment" of the facilities of the International Court of Justice (ICJ) in The Hague. This announcement came following a harrowing saga that involved the former Liberian president's escape from his Calabar guesthouse and attempt to leave Nigeria for an unknown destination on the continent. With international intervention, including the US and Nigerian authorities, Taylor was apprehended, placed on a plane and delivered to the custody of the Liberian government. Upon his arrival at the airport in Liberia, he was quickly transferred to UN authorities that then whisked him off to Freetown. The stay in Freedom was brief as he was soon transferred to The Hague where the Special Court has been engaged in proceedings against Taylor since 2006. He was sentenced to 50 year in prison on May 3, 2012. [35]

Otherwise Sirleaf engaged a hectic travel agenda, logging many flying miles in her first term of office with emphasis on *our neighbors*. There was important symbolism to some of the visits as she sought to deepen historic and neighborly ties with fellow Africans, but also importantly, to express, as she did in her 2006 Annual Message to the Liberian Legislature "our country's deep gratitude and appreciation to our fellow African leaders and their people for their invaluable and sustained support of the Liberian peace process." In the same year there was the customary engagement with the AU, ECOWAS, and MRU "to promote a common agenda of collective security, peace, collaboration, consultation, and development." [36]

Excluded during the war years because of non-compliance with financial obligations to regional organizations, Liberia resumed active involvement in 2007 with the AU following apparent negotiation of arrears of some $2, 172, 984.26. [37]

Liberia became the third vice chair of the Bureau of the AU Assembly in the same year, and chaired the working group on staff rules and regulations of the AU Commission.

Highlighted as well was African support for raising anew an army for Liberia. Though the US was in the lead role, the training was supplemented in specific areas by support from Nigeria, Ghana and Benin. Hundreds of new Liberian soldiers received training at the Nigerian Command Staff College and Nigeria provided leadership for the army pending training of Liberian men and women for the leadership. General Luka Yusuf served as the first Army Chief of Staff, and upon his reassignment another Nigerian, General Suraj Abdurrahman, replaced him.

In 2007 Sirleaf continued to serve as current chair of the MRU, attempting to reactivate by reorganizing the Sierra Leone-based Secretariat of the organization. At a MRU summit in Monrovia in 2008, Ivory Coast acceded to the Union, ending its observer status since 2004. Other developments of note included establishment of a MRU Joint Border Security and Confidence-Building Units (JBSCBU) in all four MRU member states in the areas of defense, immigration, intelligence, customs, and other security-related areas.

Manifestations of deeper Liberian engagement in Africa included restoration in 2008 of The Roberts Flight Information Region (FIR), an arrangement instituted by Liberia, Guinea, and Sierra Leone under MRU auspices. It is relocated in Liberia while the leadership rotates between Liberia and Sierra Leone. In 2007 Liberia and Sierra Leone entered into a non-aggression pact, an interesting move in light of the Liberian-Guinean pact of 1970s vintage. The umbrella African Union Non-Aggression and Common Defense Pact may obviate the need for security bilateralism. [38]

It is of some significance that as of July 2008, a total of 5,900 Namibia Defense Force troops had been rotated in Liberia as part of UNMIL contingent in the country. Considering Liberia's historic engagement with, and support for, Namibia during the liberation struggle, it seems fitting that Namibia was in the position to return a national favor. Other African countries contributing to UNMIL's military arm include Benin, Egypt, Ethiopia, Gambia, Ghana, Mali, Niger, Nigeria, Senegal, Togo, Zambia and Zimbabwe. For the international police personnel the following African countries have participated: Egypt, Gambia, Ghana, Kenya, Namibia, Nigeria Rwanda, Uganda, Zambia and Zimbabwe. There were other vital areas of regional cooperation. West Africans collaborated through the West African Power Pool (WAPP), a coordinated cross-border power supply project where power from Ivory Coast will be supplied to Liberia.

In 2009 President Sirleaf headed a high-level ECOWAS mission to Niger to mediate in a constitutional crisis there. As chair of MRU, Liberia participated in all seven sessions of the International Contact Group on Guinea (ICGG) promoting constructive engagement while supporting the positions of the AU, ECOWAS and the ICGG. Such activities provided Liberia opportunity to mediate in efforts that resulted in placing neighboring Guinea on the path to democracy.

Conclusion

Since President Ellen Johnson Sirleaf's re-election and installation in January 2012 for a second term, Liberia is moving forward a national project dubbed Liberia Rising 2030, a structured exercise in nation-wide consultations designed for national introspection and reflection involving the entire populace. The objective is to determine a national vision to guide the country's future course of development. This may be the first of its kind since the establishment of the Liberian state in 1847. Doubtless, Liberia's African vocation will figure prominently. Also likely to be highlighted is the relationship between Liberia's unique role in the making of the post-World War II African political order and Liberia's post-civil war aspirations. Is continuity envisaged? How much of the new aspirations are likely to represent a break with the past? Beyond the social, political, security, environmental, and economic circumstances imposed by war, how might the role and place of Liberia in a twenty-first century Africa be articulated – change *or* continuity, or rather change and continuity?

References

[1] For a good account of the war, see A. Adebajo, *Liberia's Civil War*, Lynne Reiner, 2002. The Nobel Peace Prize was awarded to three women, among them President Ellen Johnson Sirleaf and Leymah Gbowee. Former Foreign Minister Toga McIntosh became in early 2012 vice president of the ECOWAS Commission, while Professor Amos Sawyer assumed the chairmanship of the Africa Peer Review Mechanism.

[2] Other Liberians who have served in regional organizations include Ambassador Carlton Karpeh as deputy chief of protocol of the OAU, Dr. Edward Clinton as head of both the environment and human settlement department, as well as human resources of the AU. I would like to acknowledge an interview with Dr. Clinton in Monrovia on 3/5/12. Clinton served as Liberian Ambassador to Ethiopia January 2006 to July 2011.

[3] See Dunn, D. Elwood, *Liberia and the United States*, London: Palgrave, 2009, chapter 2.

[4] Smith, Robert A. *The Emancipation of The Hinterland*, The Star Magazine and Advertising Services, Monrovia, 1964, Appendix IX, pp. 117-124.

[5] Ibid.

[6] As quoted in Dunn, D. Elwood, *The Foreign Policy of Liberia*, London: Hutchinson Benham, 1979, pp. 66-67.

[7] Ibid.

[8] Mandela, Nelson, *Long Walk to Freedom*, Back Bay Books, 1995, p. 300; D. Elwood Dunn and S. Byron Tarr, Liberia: *A National Polity in Transition,* Scarecrow Press, 1988, pp. 178-190.

[9] See *New York Times*, "Flag of Algeria Flies at Parley," 8/5/59.

[10] Quoted in Dunn, *Liberia and the United States*, p.60.

[11] Ibid.

[12] See Liberia, Department of Information, "President Tubman on African Unity," 1959.

[13] Eastman, Ernest, *"The Road to Addis,"* 1973 (author's file).

[14] Liberia, "Dr. J. Rudolph Grimes Talks About the Foundation of the OAU," FORUM, numbers 1 and 2, ELTV, July 1979. (Transcript in author's files).

[15] Unpublished Memoir of Charles Dunbar Sherman, Former Secretary of the Treasury and former Liberian Senator, p. 114 (author's files).

[16] Dunn and Tarr, p. 186.

[17] Letter of Mrs. Olympio to President Tubman, 1963 (author's files). The following documents (author's file) provide evidence of pioneering Liberian advocacy for African regionalism: Draft documents for Ernest Eastman, Edward Moore, and David Neal on West African Cooperation, 1960, 46 pp. *"The Foundation of West Africa, An Examination"*, 4th draft, Part I by Mr. XYZ, 6 pp., draft Charter (4 pp.), 14 pp. total. *"The Rationale for West African Cooperation in Selected Fields,"* 10 pp. + appendix, 1960. *Conference of Heads of African and Malagasy States,*

25-30 June 1962. Proposed Charter of the Inter-African and Malagasy States Organization (adopted in principle), 1962, 10 pp. CEI/HSWA/ Doc. 8 (4 pp.) "*First Conference of West African Heads of State and Government.*" Draft General Resolution, "Decide to establish the West African Group." – Toward a draft treaty, December 1968. Appended is President Tubman's 8-page address, Monrovia, April 22, 1968.

[18] That this desire did not become reality is much discussed in the literature comparing the South Korean growth experience with those of West Africa, notably Ghana.

[19] *Memoir of A. Romeo Horton*, Ghana Universities Press, 2005, p. 84. See also the unpublished Memoir of Charles Dunbar Sherman, pp. 97-100.

[20] See Sankawulo, Wilton, *Tolbert of Liberia, A Biography of Dr. William R. Tolbert,* Jr., London: The Ardon Press, 1979, p. 90. See also series of letters dated 2/26/67 from President Tubman to the following Nigerian leaders in reference to Liberia's mediation efforts in the Nigerian civil war: Lt. Col Yakubu Gowon, Head of the Federal Military Government of Nigeria; Lt Col David Ejoor, Military Governor of Mid-Western Nigeria; Lt. Col. Hassan Usman Katsina, Military Governor of Northern Nigeria; Lt. Col. Robert A. Adebayo, Military Governor of Western Nigeria. Though the OAU that emerged from Addis in 1963 was not compatible with Nkrumah's union government idea, it is interesting to note invocation of his memory years later with a golden statute at entry to recently completed Chinese constructed African Union building in Addis.

[21] See Funeral Rites Programs For President Tubman (author's files).

[22] Dunn, *Liberia and the United States*, chapter 3.

[23] Ibid, p. 128.

[24] Organization of African Unity, "What Kind of Africa by the year 2000, Final Report of the Monrovia Symposium on the Future Development Prospects of Africa Toward the Year 2000," Monrovia, Liberia, 12-16 February 1979, 129 pp.

[25] Opening Address by William R. Tolbert, Jr. President of Liberia to the Assembly of Heads of States of the OAU, Monrovia, Liberia, July 17-21, 1979.

[26] Details of exchange between President Kaunda and Prime Minister Vorster of South Africa, Zambia Information Services, Lusaka, 1971, See also Kaunda to Tubman, 4/29/71 p. 7 (author's files).

[27] Author's Files.

[28] Report of Foreign Minister Dennis on his mission to President Sekou Toure, Nov. 28-Dec. 1, 1975, p. 22 (author's files).
[29] Dunn, *Liberia and the United States*, p. 132.
[30] Waugh, Colin M. *Ambition and Atrocity In Africa's Lone Star State: Charles Taylor and Liberia*, London: Zed Books, 2011, p. 119. See also J Saabaato-Wai, "Resolving the Liberian Crisis," in *The Guardian*, June 13, 1990.
[31] See website of The United Nations Special Court For Sierra Leone, "The Prosecutor vs. Charles G. Taylor, and The Special Court for Sierra Leone, Case No SCSL-03-1, and The Indictment.
[32] Ibid, pp. 247-248.
[33] Ibid, p. 261.
[34] See Waugh, *Ambition and Atrocity*, p. 261.
[35] Mike Corder, "Liberia's Charles Taylor Gets 50Years in Prison," *The Washington Post*, May 31, 2012.
[36] Annual Message of the President of Liberia to the Legislature, Monrovia, Liberia, 2006.
[37] See Annual Report of the Ministry of Foreign Affairs, 2006.
[38] For the Pact with Guinea, see Dunn, 2009, pp. 119-120. For Pact with Sierra Leone, See Annual Report of the Ministry of Foreign Affairs, 2007.

In: Africa
Editor: Olayiwola Abegunrin
ISBN: 978-1-62948-561-4

Chapter 5

THE POLITICS OF LAND REFORM IN ZIMBABWE: PROBLEMS AND PROSPECTS

Charity Manyeruke
Department of Politics and Administrative Studies,
Faculty of Social Studies, University of Zimbabwe, Harare, Zimbabwe

THE BACKGROUND

The land question has not only been topical and controversial in Zimbabwe but also to other Southern African countries. Conflicts over land and other natural resources in Zimbabwe are both a pre- and post-independence phenomenon. The conflicts have been evident in the country between individuals and other communities even before the arrival of British settlers in 1890. The colonial era, however, introduced new dimensions that exacerbated the conflicts. Conquest and series of oppressive legislations, for example the Land Apportionment Act of 1931, [1] affected a racially discriminatory settlement pattern. Grievances over the racially skewed distribution of land stood as one among the major mobilizing factors in the struggle for political independence [2]. The liberation struggles (First and Second Chimurengas) and subsequent political independence was expected to resolve Zimbabwe's land problems. However, the problem was not resolved which later led to the waging of the Third Chimurenga. Much attention in this chapter shall be focus on the 2000 period (2000-2010) when the problems of land redistribution became well pronounced on the socio-economic, political as well as the environmental scene of the country.

Though problems arose as a result of the implementation of the Fast Track Land Reform Program was an inevitable and necessary undertaking whose major aim was to redress the historical injustices that resulted from colonialism [3]. Thus in the eyes of the black majority it has been viewed as a necessary evil. It is of importance to note that as from 2010 there is a positive drive towards addressing the challenges of land reform which will be discussed in this chapter. Such redress should result in full utilization and equitable distribution of land in Zimbabwe.

The year 1979 marked the beginning of land redistribution problems under the Lancaster House Agreement. According to Tendi, there was a disagreement on how to redistribute land equitably between the blacks and whites [4]. The agreement was signed by the Patriotic Front and the British government without resolving the land issue. The British government with the support of the United States of America had agreed to settle the land question under the willing buyer willing seller condition where compensation was to be paid for the land taken from the white farmers for a period of 10 years. This arrangement was moving at a slow pace which led to the landless peasants and war veterans becoming too impatient with the willing buyer willing seller Agreement. President Jacob Zuma of South Africa also agrees with the view that Britain is also responsible for the land crisis in Zimbabwe because it reneged on funding commitments made at Lancaster House Conference in 1979. The Conservative Government of Margret Thatcher made commitments in 1979 to fund Zimbabwe's land reform program. Unfortunately Tony Blair's Labor Government disowned commitments made by the Conservative Government. According to Marongwe "the Lancaster House Constitution presented many constraints that hindered the speedy distribution of land in independent Zimbabwe, including emphasis on the supremacy of market forces in the land acquisition process, a factor that has haunted the land reform program since 1980." [5] As such the constitution was designed to further defend the white interest on the land issue.

Apart from the Lancaster House Agreement, 1990 was an important turning point that gave birth to some of the problems around the land reform. The Lancaster House Agreement had stated that the issue of land will not be dealt with within the constitution until after ten years. This led to the enactment of the Land Acquisition Act (LAA) of 1992 which transferred authority over property rights from the judiciary to the executive presidency with the purpose of facilitating expeditious land redistribution.

The 1992 LAA was designed to remove the willing buyer willing seller system, limiting the size of farms and introducing a land tax (although the tax was never implemented) [6]. The act empowered the government to buy land compulsorily for redistribution and a fair compensation was to be paid for land acquired. Landowners could challenge in court the price set by the acquiring authority hence the Act gave a room for landowners to challenge the process and lack of proper implementation by the government led to the slowing down of land redistribution. In 2001, Edison Zvobgo (ZANU-PF legal Chief Adviser) confessed that he had made a huge mistake in drafting the 1992 Land Acquisition Act, making it far too esoteric, complex and quite overlooking that Government lacked the capacity to acquire land in the way prescribed [7].

The cracks on the land reform were also caused by the division in Zimbabwean African National Union- Patriotic Front (ZANU-PF) in the late 1980s on the process of redistribution between the radical elements, demanding rapid state-led land redistribution and technocratic elements who were in favor of the structural adjustment. Tendi notes that technocratic elements triumphed in the struggle in the 1990s [8]. As Economic Structural Adjustment Program (ESAP) was seen as the best alternative approach to accelerate economic growth through improved fiscal management, and market liberalization, thereby lead to the ZANU PF adopting the ESAP. This is another key factor that contributed to the slowdown of land reform. Market-based land reform was adopted, but the World Bank did not raise adequate resources to support this new policy approach [9].

According to Tendi ESAP failed to integrate land reform into other economic reforms that took place, thereby aggravating market failures in land acquisition [10].

As such the liberal land and agricultural policy reforms in the late 1990s had failed to address the land question. In addition, ESAP adversely affected peasant farmers who lost state subsidies and other forms of support. Moyo is of the view that ESAP resulted in a declining capacity of the state to regulate access to land and natural resources, given its commitment to the implementation of neoliberal policies [11]. Lack of consistent government policies hampered the land redistribution process.

Moyo observes that there was growing demand for land by the indigenous black farmers, [12] peasants and retrenched workers during the ESAP era which led to the redefinition of the land reform policy framework. Accordingly the economic difficulties under ESAP led to different social groups, including war veterans demanding increased access to state finances to offset the erosion of their standards of living.

Within these conditions of economic decline, Moyo notes that there was worker agitation and increasing "*illegal*" land occupations in 1997. The veterans of the liberation war challenged the state to pursue radical land redistribution based on land expropriation. [13]

According to Moyo, until 1997 that the government land policy had done little to address the broader needs of the landless and land-poor in communal areas, while the population of these areas was expanding as they increasingly absorbed the tens of thousands of urban laid off during the adjustment process [14]. Rukuni notes that sporadic illegal land occupation in 1998 set the tone for massive land occupations in 2000 which were largely backed by the state in view of collapsed negotiations for land reform financing with the United Kingdom and other donors [15]. The 2000 referendum and the elections that proceeded thereafter triggered the Third Chimurenga. According to Marongwe the land occupations started in February 2000 soon after a referendum rejected the government's proposed Draft constitution [16]. Marongwe further notes that the main opposition, the Movement for Democratic Change (MDC) together with a host of civic organizations had campaigned against the draft constitution. These two events however, shaped the dynamics of the land occupations in that it forced an immediate and dramatic shift in the strategies of ZANU PF in which veterans and the land took center stage. Rukuni and Jensen note that the violence directed towards white farmers and black farm workers as part of the political campaign for the June 2000 parliamentary elections led to the freezing of donor support for a proposed new Land Reform; and Resettlement Program that had been widely welcomed at a large donor conference in Harare in September 1998 [17]. This resulted in further problems mounting on the government as it lacked financial and institutional capacity to support the program. Rukuni et al observe that this lack of resources created further problems, not least a threat to the legitimacy of government in terms of fulfilling its political promises of redistributing land to benefit the black majority who were grossly disadvantaged by colonialism and its preceding problems [18].

POLITICIZATION OF THE LAND REFORM AND PARTY CONFLICTS

According to Marongwe the farm occupations in 2000 were precipitated more by politically motivated intentions than by social, moral or economic considerations. [19] Marongwe notes that faced with possible electoral defeat in 2000 the ZANU PF government backed the land occupations. The ruling party ZANU PF used farm occupations as their official campaigning strategy for wooing voters in the June 2000 parliamentary elections. In Manicaland, veteran leaders of an unofficial "land committee" reportedly threatened to evict occupiers they accused of voting MDC [20]. This resulted in what Alexander describes as chaotic and partisan nature of land redistribution [21]. Apparently the perspective by Marongwe and Alexander shows that it was the ZANU PF party which spearheaded land reform in Zimbabwe. Whereas the MDC party thought largely supporting land reform would cause conflict of interest as their sponsors from United States of America and Europe were totally against the Fast Track Land Reform program (FTLRP) in Zimbabwe. Supporting MDC was therefore regarded as being anti-land reform and working against the wishes of the people and the objectives of the liberation struggle.

The politicization of the land by the state had brewed great consequences on the distribution of the land. Some people see the land issue as a class issue. Sachikonye describes the land process as "a competitive scramble for commercial farms by members of the ruling elite" [22]. He contends that in early 2003 the extent of abuses was revealed in an official audit. The audit showed, in Raftopoulos and Phimister's words, "the displacement of resettled people by the party elite; elite struggles over prime land; the use of *hired thugs* by sections of ZANU-PF leadership to press their demands; and the problem of multiple ownership amongst prominent members of the ruling elite [23]. There is no doubt that such a revolutionary process would have its own problems which would require mainstreaming but what was important is to be able to kick start the major land reform process.

The distribution of land coupled with competitive scramble by the ruling elite resulted in multiple farm ownership at the expense of the landless. The question of multiple farm ownership did not go away, despite the concerted efforts of Minister Nkomo, and the establishment of a "National Land Inspectorate (NLI)", drawn largely from members of the security forces and veterans, and dedicated to rooting out multiple farm owners. Alexander cites McGregor who said that the land occupations required the state to answer a new logic [24]. Its authority was to be grounded in political loyalty and patronage, not expert knowledge and bureaucracy.

According to the *Zimbabwean Independent* [25] the ministries charged with agrarian policy were marginalized in favor of an alliance led by ZANU-PF and veteran technocrats were left to lament that their painstaking plans produced by the "serious scientific analysis of Zimbabwe's agriculture", were "dead". Arguably technocrats cannot lead political revolutions. They can only assist to a limited extend. The land revolution was an arena for politicians; to demonstrate the power to mobilize masses for a record total transformation. Logic would follow after the success of a revolution.

Marongwe observes that politics had a bigger role to play in the farm occupation of 2000 [26]. In this respect he reasonably concludes that the farms targeted for occupations were suspected to be owned by members or supporters of the main opposition party MDC.

Discussions with the leaders of the occupations at various farms revealed that one was required to produce a ZANU PF party card and a data form if one wanted to be allocated land. In Masvingo, the provincial ZANU PF political commissar said MDC supporters should be bundled off the land and they should go to MDC if they wanted land [27]. The 2000 land occupations shows that the unresolved nature of the land question has meant that the situation can be exploited for political objectives.

In any case land is a political issue. During the liberation struggle, the freedom fighters were referred to as '*vana vevhu'* (sons of the soil). This shows the centrality of land to the liberation struggle of Zimbabwe and the protracted negotiations at Lancaster House in 1979.

Furthermore, Tendi cites that farm invasions and the violence that accompanied them cloaked an agenda to discipline ZANU-PF members perceived as disloyal [28]. In 2000 alleged war veterans raised the ire of Zvobgo when they invaded his farm in Masvingo. Tendi argues that the invasion of Zvobgo's farm was as a result of factional struggles by other means and a manifestation of his supposed "disloyalty" to the land seizures [29].

This trend has also persisted with the recent farm invasions on ZANU-PF Member of Parliament, Mrs. T. Mutinhiri's farm in Mashonaland East who has been accused of wining and dining with Prime Minister Morgan Tsvangirai [30]. Mutinhiri was dismissed from ZANU-PF after a party hearing. She is still however able to appeal against the decision if she wants. These two examples clearly demonstrate the dangers of a loose land tenure system as it is open to abuse and manipulation.

The system can be easily taken advantage of by unruly elements to undermine investment in agriculture. There is therefore a need for Government to ensure better security for the new farmers, like establishing police posts in the farm compounds. ZANU-PF has actually made it clear that the land reform program was non-partisan in the case of Mutinhiri.

ECONOMIC IMPLICATIONS

The politics of land reform resulted in poor economic performance. Alexander notes that the economy contracted significantly every year from the start of the Third Chimurenga, shrinking by record levels of over 13 percent in 2002 and 2003. Approximately half of all Zimbabweans were deemed in need of food aid in 2002 and severe food shortages persisted in subsequent years. These shortages however should be considered in their proper perspective. There was drought during that period coupled with hyperinflation which pushed the cost of inputs beyond what the majority of the new farmers could afford. The interventions by the Government through the Reserve Bank of Zimbabwe (RBZ) support facilities could not cope with the magnitude of the problem. Alexander asserts that the manufacturing and mining sectors reported drastic falls in Production while agriculture output plummeted adding to already severe levels of unemployment [31]. Moyo adds that inflation soared out of control while foreign currency and fuel shortages added to the crisis [32].

Due to the economic crisis and the unstable political environment in the Third Chimurenga era many people were forced to leave the country in search of greener pastures. Moyo [33] posits that millions of Zimbabweans simply left the country, seeking their fortunes in the wider region or further afield. He further argued that amidst an "uprising" ostensibly designed to address the inequitable distribution of resources of the past, most Zimbabweans, including many who were recipients of land, were left considerably worse off than they had been prior to the Third Chimurenga. Rob Davies argues that "What we are seeing in Zimbabwe at present is the destruction of the future by the rhetoric of redress for the past." [34] Whilst the appropriateness of the way the Fast Track Land Reform Program was executed is open to debate, it's however important not to lose sight of the noble objective of redressing inequalities in land ownership that were inherited from the past colonial legacy. Protest measures taken by the international community in particular the European Union, United States of America and Britain made this situation worse by fuelling capital flight and closing access to important lines of credit.

Lack of support to the beneficiaries of the 2001 land occupations had a great impact on the economy's decline. According to Alexander [35] the Zimbabwe Farmers Union condemned the lack of support given to those who had been resettled. Settlers faced severe problems in the 2000/2001 season due to late settlement on the land and a lack of draught power and inputs; the absence of infrastructure and services and in some areas drought.

In the late 2001 a United Nations Development Program (UNDP) mission found that the vast scale of resettlement posed a threat to national agriculture production and food security and made the provision of essential services and infrastructure impossible to achieve within a reasonable time.

The major reason why land reform had a profound effect on the economy and politics of the country is that most of the country's production is dependent on agriculture production.

Over 70 percent of Zimbabweans are dependent upon land and natural resources for their livelihoods. Most observers agree that prospects for poverty reduction are dependent on a significant part of the population gaining access to productive land to meet their food, energy and shelter requirements [36].

As such in Moyo's view Zimbabwe's industrial resource base is largely 66 percent dependent upon the manufacture of agriculture based products, while key sectors (including finance, commerce and tourism) are intricately linked to agriculture. Agriculture contributed to 17 percent of the gross domestic product (GDP) in 2001 in comparison to the rest of Southern Africa where agriculture contributed 8.2 percent to the GDP in 2000.

Raftopoulos cites that agriculture production came to a standstill due to the tensions between the war veterans and the white farmers in the 2000 land reform [37].

A police report from Mvurwi showed that a white farmer at Msonendin farm ploughed the fields of resettled people who had already planted their crops. At Virginia farm in Mazowe, a white farmer was reported to be locking his gates and electrifying the fence to ensure that resettled farmers would not have access to the fields.

Thus resistance to land reform process led to economic slowdown as productive time was lost through such conflicts.

Marongwe [38] points out other unconfirmed reports that have painted a negative picture of farm production, with crop losses significantly threatening food security in the country.

Marongwe adds that seed sales for most crops were reported to have dropped and some large scale farmers have been forced to destock. Livestock thefts increased in general in most parts of Zimbabwe exacerbated by the increased mobility of people associated with land occupations.

According to Moyo a major agriculture shift occurred during the Fast Track Land Reform Program period and this affected the major crops and livestock differently particularly those produced by large scale white farmers [39]. Since 2001 agriculture production has declined by about 50 percent in volume.

For instance food production (maize, wheat and small grains) has declined by over 50 percent in both communal and commercial farm areas while commercial dairy and beef production has declined by the same margin. Besides, the efforts which Government implemented through the Reserve Bank of Zimbabwe of providing the new farmers with capital and inputs; the Government's adoption of the multiple currency system (use of Zimbabwean currency, US dollars and South African rand), has gone a long way in restoring farming as a viable business unlike the losses made during the hyperinflation. In the 2010 to 2011 season the tobacco auction floors were struggling to cope with the increased number of farmers bringing their crop for sale. It is estimated that 129 million kilograms of tobacco were sold with over US$300 million realized. The livelihoods of the new farmers have been tremendously improved.

Whilst the Government's efforts to assist the new farmers are appreciated, during the hyperinflation period superior profits were being made from non-farm investments, particularly in parallel foreign currency and commodity markets where super profits were made. State agriculture subsidies and other interventions were limited by resource constraints, foreign currency shortages and discordant policy management. The allocation of resources to new farmers was allegedly marred by corruption with those well connected benefiting more at the expense of other deserving farmers. The agricultural production decline has led to various degrees of shortages of goods for domestic (consumption) markets and in export earnings both of which contribute significantly to the high levels of inflation which stood at 2200 percent in April 2007 (in addition to the monetary and fiscal policy effects) food insecurity and unemployment. [40]

Impact of International Media on the Land Issue

The land reform had a spillover effect on the tourism sector due to the negative international media publicity. According to Manyeruke the global media joined the bandwagon and became the vehicles of condemnation and negative publicity of the Zimbabwean Government [41]. Raftopoulos cites that tourism is a highly sensitive sector that thrives on politically stable environments [42]. The scale and violence of the 2000 farm occupations was widely publicized around the world and tourist arrivals were very badly affected. Raftopoulos [43] further observes that press reports and discussions with some of the affected farmers have confirmed that tourism was one of the sectors hardest hit by the land occupations. Malilangwe Conservancy Trust and Gonarezhou National Park in Masvingo as well as some farms in the Matabeleland provinces gave an indication of the extent of negative effects of the occupations on tourism in general and on tourist based wildlife farms in particular. Though tourism is more attractable in politically stable environments, negative publicity had an impact on tourist arrival due to lack of international support on the land reform.

Negative media perceptions on land reform had a role to play in limiting foreign direct investment in the country. Moyo [44] cites that the government was however, under strong international pressure to exercise restraint over land expropriation as donors and international financial institutions warned that the proposed takeover programs would inflict severe economic damage by deterring investors and reducing exports. The International Monetary Fund (IMF) delayed balance of payment support disbursement in 1999 primarily because of concerns over the government's land reform policy and its effect on investment, anticipating sanctions imposed since then.

Social Relations (Gender and Class)

According to Moyo, the social facts on the ground regarding the current distributions of land indicate that land redistribution has redressed the imbalanced racial legacy, but has spawned new inequalities which were less sharp [45]. A significant number of poor peasant, women and various other middle class peoples claim to have been excluded from the redistribution. Alexander posits that women groups complained of gender bias in land allocation [46]. Manyeruke is of the view that in Zimbabwe as well as in most African countries women were regarded as minors when it comes to issues to do with land [47]. This has mainly been due to system of tenure, cultural and political practices which unfortunately recognizes and reinforces male domination in all spheres of life.

Lack of transparency in the land reform process led to unequal distribution. Rutherford echoes the same view noted by Women and Land Lobby Group (LLG) that this lack of a transparent process of redistribution has resulted in the denial of community involvement in decision-making processes, and neglect of key groups in the population such as large sections of women and farm workers [48]. This point is supported by the Utete report of 2003 which exposed that the land redistribution at national level was skewed in favor of men.

Manyeruke notes that government led land distribution programs since 1980 failed to eliminate the imbalance between men and women regarding access to land [49].

This exclusion ignores the fact that women constitute about 52 percent of the population and are the most productive in the farming sector. In addition, Manyeruke [50] notes that what is more unacceptable in the Zimbabwean scenario is that women played a very crucial role during the liberation struggle where land was at the center of the struggle. Mgugu cited by Bhatasara notes that 70 percent of agriculture exports come from women in small scale farming [51]. The spaces which are promoted by such patriarchal practices are therefore of the minority and can never result in the development of a nation. Alexander asserts that women groups complained of gender bias in land allocation. Of importance to note is that there is a positive drive by the government towards addressing the women's plights on land reform [52].

The conflicts on land reform are not just about men and women but the farm workers and farm owners too. Marongwe points out that the farm occupations had a negative impact on the social relations between the farm occupiers and the farm workers on the occupied farms [53]. In the land reform process farm workers and their families were especially hard hit by the farm occupations. The disruption of farm operations led to loss of jobs and income. Many farm workers had their homes and properties destroyed and were physically displaced, provisions of services by Non-Governmental Organizations (NGOs) such as the Farm Community Trust of Zimbabwe were interfered with. According to Alexander "farm workers had become an itinerant, poor and unstable class, almost destitute and constantly drifting." [54] Altercation often broke out between farm workers and the occupying communities and war veteran leadership. This is mostly because some farm workers kept resisting the land reform.

Environmental Effect of the Land Reform

The Third Chimurenga had an effect on the environment. Marongwe articulates that there was no particular discretion in deciding on the quality of the land that was occupied. This explains why even marginal land in natural regions four and five was affected. Marongwe attributes this to the lack of control on the part of government on what was happening on the ground.

Factors such as land use were not an important consideration and also the type of land that was to be occupied.

Data from districts including Nyanga, Mutasa, Makoni, Chiredzi and Gwanda revealed that the occupations and subsequent gazetting of farms and fast track resettlement program negatively affected productivity in reaction to almost all land uses.

This includes both agriculture production such as maize, wheat, tobacco, horticulture, cattle ranching and dairy production and non-agriculture sectors such as wildlife, forestry and tourism.

According to Moyo a *negative* environment management process such as uncontrolled gold panning, wildlife poaching and deforestation have emerged in the new resettlement areas [55]. The FTLRP has brought with it a general increase in the activities of gold panners. Gold panning is seen to be more lucrative than farming mainly because of the instant income returns compared to agriculture. Moyo said that in the gold panning areas, serious conflicts and contradictions result between gold panning and farming activities [56].

Wildlife poaching and deforestation also increased during the FTLRP [57]. A survey by the Parks and Wildlife Authority (PWLA) on gazetted game ranches showed that there had been significant wildlife population reductions, largely due to poaching. Moyo notes that in reality the major and immediate effect of the 2000 land reforms has been increased harvesting of wood for building temporary shelters and meeting the fuel-wood needs of new settlers. Moyo et al. [58] assert that deforestation was rampant before settlers knew they were going to remain in the area permanently or not. This environmental damage has been attributed to the capacity by the state to regulate natural resources as it was overstretched, in terms of financial and human resources thus could not fully enforce environmental management laws.

Poor agriculture performance can also be attributed to global climate change. According to Manyeruke climate change is likely to cause additional drawbacks in the country's land reform program which the three main political parties Zimbabwean African National Union-Patriotic Front (ZANU-PF), Movement for Democratic Change (MDC-T) and MDC-M believe should not be reversed [59]. Due to climate change, droughts have been experienced during the 2002 season when the government was not in a position to support adequately cloud seeding programs as a result of international isolation.

LAND REFORM AND THE INTERNATIONAL RESPONSE

The international community particularly the Western countries had shown a lack of support of the land redistribution even after the expiry of the willing buyer willing seller agreement. In 1990 the Commonwealth Secretary General Emeka Anyaoku held a diplomatic parley with the ZANU-PF government in order to dissuade it from engaging in radical land reform, subsequent to the expiry of the Lancaster House constitution's property clause. This drag in the land reform was evident also in the Third Chimurenga as it was received with different responses in the international arena. Rukuni observes that whilst the mainstream African governments came in support of the program, Europe and United States of America were highly critical of the program. As a result the Western countries described smart sanctions which affected Zimbabwe's agriculture performance in a variety of ways [60].

Rukuni further explains that the smart sanctions had a bearing on the economy in that Zimbabwe could only muster foreign currency through the export of both processed and unprocessed agriculture commodities [61]. There was need to mobilize the technology and hardware for agricultural investment from external sources.

In such a situation the country's land reform became handicapped despite the government's mechanization and subsidized inputs support program. Internationally the government was left with the support of the Eastern and Asian countries, China in particular however, this was not adequate.

The land issue had a regional impact economically. According to Cousins Zimbabwe land reform had a profound regional, if not continental negative effect.

Cousins further said that, a recent study estimates that in the three years between 2000 and the end of 2002, Zimbabwe's crisis cut the growth of South Africa 's gross domestic product by 1.3 percent and led to between 20,000 and 30,000 actual and potential job losses [62].

It resulted in the weakening of the rand, higher inflation and higher interest rates [63]. These effects came through reduced exports of goods and services, a drop in tourism, failure by Zimbabwe to service its debt, and reduced foreign direct investment.

Despite these economic disturbances in the region, other regional countries did not stop supporting the land reform in Zimbabwe as it was viewed as restorative justice to the landless. This was evident with the Southern African Development Community (SADC) Heads of State and Government's 2010 Windhoek meeting rejection of the SADC tribunal's ruling and calling for its suspension. The SADC Tribunal had ruled that Zimbabwe had breached its treaty obligations under SADC Treaty and African Union treaty. The ruling was seen as to have been influenced by an invisible hand which supported the dispossessed 79 commercial farmers.

PROSPECTS ON THE LAND ISSUE

Problems of equitable resource distribution amongst the citizens will take time to resolve but what is of importance to the country is the full utilization of the land so as to enhance food security. Though problems have been experienced during the 2000-2008 period but since 2010 the agricultural sector is improving. Zimbabwe's tobacco production is increasing season by season. The 2011 tobacco sales generated US$231 million three months into the season – compared with 123 million kilograms in 2010 that earned the nation US $348 million [64]. Maize output increased by 9 percent, tobacco by 44 percent, finger millet 34 percent, soya bean 20 percent from the 2009/2010 to 2010/2011 season [65]. The improvement has come along with government's support through provision of subsidized inputs schemes. For example a subsidized ammonium nitrate (AN) fertilizer 50 kilogram bag was sold at US$7 against the market price of US$28 [66]. The increase in production has improved the livelihoods of the farmers and the general population as well. Sustainable land utilization requires key land, agricultural and economic policy measures which are necessary to increase agricultural productivity, investment and exports and to bring stability and confidence in the new land property rights and related laws [67]. Such property rights and laws give confidence and security to the new beneficiaries of the land reform and engage in serious farming business which will lead to increased production.

The economy is recovering thereby creating conducive environment for farming to take place. Inflation rate is now stable making agriculture business viable as prices of inputs are also now stable within the country. Finance minister T. Biti said in his midyear budget report that the economy would grow by 9.3 percent in 2011 year, a rate that will make it one of the fastest growth rate of any country in Southern Africa [68]. In addition, more efficient farming methods supported by more people oriented economic policies could lead to significant increases in production on available land, of food and other domestic products, compared to the heavily export oriented land uses achieved in the past.

Land reform has the potential for ensuring sustainable development in Zimbabwe because it can create the necessary conditions for expanded agricultural growth and lively-hoods. If it is coupled with the promotion of environmentally sensitive land use, the degraded communal lands can then recover from more than half a century of overuse.

The current Inclusive (unity) Government in Zimbabwe has also made the political environment stable. The introduction of the multi-currency (the use of

Zimbabwean currency, US Dollar and South African Rand) has made business more viable in terms of buying inputs and selling outputs within and outside the country. This has resulted in attracting back input suppliers and manufacturing companies that had closed down their businesses thus creating employment opportunities.

Another positive sign towards the full utilization of land in Zimbabwe is the contract farming which is going on. These arrangements have made it possible for farmers to engage in farming not only for subsistence but for commercial purposes leading to increased production and economic development. Specialized agriculture companies such as Cottco, Olivine and Seedco have engaged farmers in contract farming which has improved the farmers' knowledge.

Women groups should also take advantage of the drafting of the new constitution to make their voices heard with regards to the land issue. Despite other regional instruments that seek to address the gender disparity, the government needs to be sensitive and empower women with their own land rights as they constitute 52 percent of the population.

Regional programs supporting the agricultural sector are also important in making the land reform successful. Such programs strengthen regional integration which is critical to the sustainable development in the agricultural sector. The Common Market for East and Southern Africa (COMESA) has been training 1100 agro dealers across the country's ten provinces in business skills and use of modern technology at the same time linking them to suppliers of agro products such as seed and fertilizer [69]. This will enable farmers to access inputs easily at reasonable prices which by and large strengthen the food security in the country and region at large. Such programs can take back the country to be the bread basket of the region.

CONCLUSION

The politics of land reform in Zimbabwe's Third Chimurenga has come with its own positives and negatives. The Third Chimurenga however, brought more negative effects on the economy due to the unwarranted response by the international community, especially the Western powers, and the European Union. The process was a necessary evil as it successfully managed to redress the colonial land imbalances between the whites and the black majority. Land redistribution, through redressing historical problems and social justice is a crucial ingredient for sustainable development in Zimbabwe.

REFERENCES

[1] Nelson Marongwe, *"Farm Occupiers in the New Politics of Land in Zimbabwe,"* Harare, Weaver Press, 2003, pp. 155-190.

[2] Ibid.

[3] Manyeruke Charity "The Spaces of Women in Zimbabwe" *SALARN Newsletter*, Volume 1 Issue 4, Harare, SALARN, 2011, p. 8-12.

[4] Tendi M. Blessing, *Making History in Mugabe's Zimbabwe: Politics, Intellectuals and the Media*, Oxford, PETER LANG, 2010, p.73-107.

[5] Nelson Marongwe, op. cit. p. 156.

[6] Schleicer Annie, *Zimbabwe's Land Programme, PBS Backgrounder, Online Newsletter,* posted 14 April 2004.

[7] Zvobgo Edson, quoted in Robin Palmer, *"Zimbabwe in 200: The Land Question, Farm Workers, and the September Conference Season,"* Harare, January 2002.

[8] Tendi M. Blessing, op. cit., p. 83.

[9] Tom Lebert, *"Land and Agrarian Reform in Zimbabwe,"* In: P. Rosset, R. Patel and M. Courville (eds.), Promised Land: Competing Visions of Land Reform, Oakland, Food First/Institute for Food and Development Policy, 2006.

[10] Tendi M. Blessing, op. cit., p. 83.

[11] Sam Moyo, 2000.

[12] For detailed comprehensive on the land reform in Zimbabwe see, Sam Moyo, Kirk Helliker and Tendai Murisa (editors), *Contested Terrain: Land Reform and Civil Society in Contemporary Zimbabwe,* Pietermaritzburg, South Africa: S and S Publishers, 2008, p. 62.

[13] Sam Moyo, *The Land Question in Zimbabwe*, Harare: SAPES, 1995.

[14] Ibid.

[15] Rukuni Mandivamba, *"Challenges of the Agriculture sector from 2000"* Harare, University of Zimbabwe Publications, 2006. p. 13-20.

[16] Marongwe Nelson, *"Farm Occupations and Occupiers in the New Politics of Land in Zimbabwe"*, Harare, Weaver Press, 2003, p. 155-190.

[17] Mandivamba Rukuni and Stig Jensen, *"Land, Growth and Governance: Tenure Reform and Visions of Progress in Zimbabwe"*.

[18] Rukuni et al.

[19] Marongwe.

[20] *Daily News*, Harare, October 10, 2000.

[21] Jocelyn Alexander, *The Unsettled Land: State-making and the Politics of Land in Zimbabwe 1893-2003*, Oxford, James Currey, 2006, p. 180-194.

[22] Sachikonye, (2003), 42. Also see veteran objections in Mail and Guardian (online), 8 December 2003.
[23] Raftopolous and Phimistr, 2004, 370. Also see ICG, 2004, Chapter 7; Crisis in Zimbabwe Coalition, 2002, Annexure 7.
[24] Alexander, 2006, p. 187.
[25] *Zimbabwean Independent*, Harare, 2006.
[26] Marongwe, 2001, p. 156.
[27] *Zimbabwe Independence*, April 27, 2001.
[28] *Financial Gazette*, 30 November-6 December 2000.
[29] Tendi, 2010, p. 100.
[30] *Newsday* 12 July 2011 "Minister's farm invaded".
[31] Alexander, 2006.
[32] Moyo, 2003.
[33] Moyo, 2003.
[34] Rob Davis, 2004.
[35] Alexander, 2006.
[36] Kojo Sebastian Amanor and Sam Moyo, *Land and Sustainable Development in Africa,* London, ZED BOOKS, 2008, p. 57-80.
[37] Brian Raftopoulos *"The State in Crisis: Authoritarian Nationalism, Selective Citizenship and Distortions of Democracy in Zimbabwe".*
[38] Marongwe, 2001, p. 170.
[39] Moyo 2008, p. 70.
[40] Ibid.
[41] Charity Manyeruke, "SADC Tribunal's Ruling on Zimbabwe's case and its Implications on Land Reform in Southern Africa" *SALARN Newsletter*, 2010, Volume 1 Issue 3, p. 7-9.
[42] Raftopoulos 2003, p. 233.
[43] Ibid.
[44] Moyo 2008, p. 76.
[45] Ibid, p. 77.
[46] Alexander 2006, p. 190.
[47] Ibid.
[48] Women and Land Lobby Group, 2001;FCTZ, 2001; Rutherford, 2001.
[49] Charity Manyeruke, *SALARN Newsletter* Volume 2, Issue 4, 2011, 8.
[50] Ibid, p. 10.
[51] Mgugu (2008) cited by Bhatasara, s. (2010) Land Reform and Diminishing Spaces for Women in Zimbabwe: A Gender analysis of the Socio- Economic and Political Consequences of the Fast Track Land Reform Program, M.Sc. Thesis at Maastricht School of Governance,

accessed online@www.maastrichtuniversity.nl/governance-elibrary. 16-11-2010.

[52] Alexander 2006, p. 190.

[53] Marongwe 2001, p.171.

[54] Alexander 2006, p. 190.

[55] Moyo, 2008, 79.

[56] Ibid.

[57] bid.

[58] Ibid.

[59] Manyeruke Charity, "Climate Change A Threat to Zimbabwe's Land Reform" *SALARN Newsletter*, Volume 1, Issue 1, Harare, 2010, p. 4-5.

[60] Rukuni 2006, p. 13.

[61] Ibid.

[62] Ben Cousins 2003, p. 263.

[63] Ben Cousins; *The Zimbabwe Crisis in its Wider Context: The Politics of Land, Democracy and Development in Southern Africa.*

[64] Zimbabwe Online Press- Zimbabwe tobacco sales generate US$231, May 22 2011.

[65] *Newsday*, "Agri-business expo on cards" 16 August 2011, p. 12.

[66] Mid Term Fiscal Review 14 July 2010.

[67] Moyo 2008, p. 81.

[68] *The Washington Times*, "Zimbabwe's Economy showing growth after long time fiscal chaos", 1 August 2011.

[69] *The Times* 07-13 January 2011 COMESA set to train 100 Midlands Agro dealers.

In: Africa
Editor: Olayiwola Abegunrin
ISBN: 978-1-62948-561-4

Chapter 6

THE NEW SOUTH AFRICA AND AFRICA: ALMOST TWO DECADES AFTER LIBERATION

Abiodun Alao[1] ***and Joseph Aihie***[2]
[1]African Leadership Centre, King's College London, London, UK
[2]Department of Political Science, University of Benin, Nigeria

INTRODUCTION

There is no doubt that South Africa occupies a unique space in Africa even during the apartheid period. This was not only because of its dominant economy but also because of its developed infrastructure and the resourcefulness of its population. The struggle against apartheid organized and sustained by African countries was thus not just for the emancipation of the black-man but also the expectation of the emergence of an African nation that would assist in developing the continent and add voice to desire for recognition. Indeed, during the struggle against white minority rule, independent South Africa was widely expected to be the engine of growth that would kick-start development across the continent, with her access to skills, technology, financial services and other key inputs.

Almost two decades after independence, time seems to be ripe for some preliminary stock-taking. Indeed, opinions seem to be divided; while some believe that the country has, within the limits of reality, tried to maintain the delicate balance it has inherited and has managed regional and continental stability, others have argued that the country's output has not been commensurate with its endowment and that its policy towards other African countries has not reflected the policy of a country that is appreciative of the sacrifices that were made to bring about the independence of the country. The objective of this paper is to take a panoramic survey of South Africa's domestic and continental policies since its independence in 1994. There are five sections in the chapter, with the first looking at what the birth of the new country (South Africa) meant for the continent and the second looking at the politics of intergroup relations, especially the issues surrounding land. The third section interrogates the role of South Africa in regional politics, while section four discusses the role of South Africa in Africa. The fifth section concludes discussions in the chapter.

THE DAWN OF A DELAYED GIANT

Although the emergence of F.W. de Klerk and his subsequent introduction of his own version of apartheid *perestroika* gave a clear hint that things were about to change in South Africa, the conduct of the first multiracial elections in April 1994 and the assumption of office of President Nelson Mandela.

Instead, the democratically elected governments led by the African National Congress (ANC) resisted such pressures, even from its own people, and have managed to create a stable, peaceful, and racially balanced political regime with an exemplary record of civil liberties and political freedoms. Economic policy has been conducted in an equally exemplary manner, with South Africa turning itself into one of the emerging markets with the lowest risk spreads. While South Africa has instituted some innovative (and expensive) social transfer programs to address long-standing disparities, it has done so in the context of cautious fiscal and monetary policies which have kept inflation and public debt at low levels. There were no nationalizations or large-scale asset redistributions [1], and the economy and the country was opened to international trade and capital flows [2].

With the reforms, South Africa has become the economic giant of Africa that it was originally meant to be. It is a middle income country with a highly skill manpower and a capital intensive modern sector [3]. As at 2003, its economy constituted about 41 percent of total sub-Saharan Africa's GDP ($160 of a total of $393 billion) and it is responsible for around 40 percent of the continent's industrial output [4].

By 2008, its GDP almost doubled to $276.76 billion [5]. The country is also the only major manufacturer in Sub- Saharan Africa and many African countries turn to its companies and expertise in various sectors to develop their own industries.

Its companies that were hitherto isolated in the continent during the apartheid period got a new lease of life and have since been expanding their reach to all parts of the continent. For instance, South Africa's multinational mobile telecommunications company (MTN) as at 2007 operated in over twenty African and Middle East countries and is reputed to be perhaps, the most profitable company in South Africa's exports to the rest of Africa, and have also been growing steadily [6]. From a shade over R5bn in 1991, the figure peaked at over R43bn in 2002 [7]. Now unlike the rest of Africa that exports mainly primary products or raw materials, South Africa has a high proportion of value-added exports with machinery, mechanical appliances, iron and steel articles, transport goods, chemicals, and plastic and rubber accounting for close to 70 percent of the total export to African countries [8].

These political and economic successes have reflected and South Africans have been *walking tall* [9]. *The rainbow people* have not only worked towards reconciling and uniting its diverse peoples and forming a united and economically prosperous nation, they have also taken their rightful place in the African continent and the world at large.

THE NEW SOUTH AFRICA AND THE MANAGEMENT OF RACIAL RELATIONS

A crucial issue at the independence of South Africa was the management of racial relations. There were concerns that the attainment of black majority rule would bring about retribution on the whites for the crimes of apartheid. It would be one of the most important achievements of post-independence South Africa that it has been able to manage the racial relations very effectively, such that there had not been any major conflict between whites and blacks in the country. Although, the bulk of the commendation here has been given to former President Nelson Mandela who, as the first leader made it clear that there should be no anger against the whites, ordinary black South Africans too deserve some praises for the way they have responded to their President's call for magnanimity. Till date, there has been no clear evidence that white South Africans were targeted for any retribution.

However, a crucial issue that has been testing the extent of racial harmony in South Africa is the land question. As is well known, one of the main issues during apartheid was the inequality in land ownership, with whites South Africans owning the bulk of rich land in the country. Although the situation was not as critical as it was in the neighboring Zimbabwe, it was also profound In South Africa, with about 60,000 white farmers owning more than 200 million acres of land, and 1.2 million black farmers eking out a living on 40 million acres.

However, there are a number of reasons that made the management of land in South Africa better than Zimbabwe. First, the ANC government is determined to ensure that the situation is peacefully managed, especially to protect the racial harmony in the country and safeguard investment and foreign respect it has earned since the peaceful transition from apartheid minority rule to black majority rule. Second, unlike Zimbabwe, South Africa has other natural resource endowments, which reduce the economic and social pressures on land. Third, international interest in South Africa is such that the country is in a better position to obtain external support to address its economic problems, and as such provides a cushioning effect on some social problems that can aggravate land crisis.

But despite these advantages, there were still a number of issues that made things difficult for the government of South Africa. First, it had to satisfy the aspirations of the blacks deprived of their land during apartheid period, especially as some of them fought the war of liberation with such vigor in anticipation that land would be re-distributed after independence. On the other hand, however, the government did not want a situation where whites would be frightened out of the country if their land was acquired. In the end, a balance was thus struck between these two conflicting tendencies, so that while there was a constitutional protection for land ownership, there was also provision for a land reform program.

This land reform program included neutral arbiters of land claims, buyouts of landowners and giving state-owned property to the poor and dispossessed. A Land Claims commission was set up in 1994 to consider the problem of land re-allocation to blacks. This has, however, been bogged down in bureaucracy and in fighting such that, as at April 2000, only 4,000 out of more than 70,000 claims before it had been settled [10].

But there have been a number of challenges to the land issue in South Africa and this has manifested in three contexts. First, there were encroachments on white commercial farms, particularly in the province of Kwazulu Natal.

Second, people dispossessed of land under apartheid re-occupied the land in a desperate bid to force the resolution of their claims and third, people whose houses were destroyed by flood invaded and occupied lands outside Johannesburg and Cape Town [11]. However, more disturbing is another trend of land-related protests, which is the spate of rural murder. A report by the New York-based International Peace Academy (IPA) in February 2002, noted that more than 900 white farmers have been murdered since independence [12]. The report further noted that spatial analysis of the attacks indicates, that "they have been clustered in areas where commercial farms are adjacent to former homelands characterized by overcrowding, landlessness and immense poverty" [13].

The Situation became a bit serious after tension rose in Zimbabwe, with some black South Africans giving implicit support to Mugabe and clamoring their government to embark on similar thing in South Africa. Indeed, by the middle of 2001, some form of land invasion had been attempted in the country [14]. Indeed, in the aftermath of Zimbabwe's land crisis, 54 per cent of black South Africans supported a Zimbabwean-style land invasion. By the middle of 2001, the land crisis in South Africa had become more serious with cases of land invasion in places like Mangete in KwaZulu Natal province and Kloof, just outside Durban. Indeed, the manager of Land-Invasion Control for Durban, Neville Fromberg, confirmed that such land invasion had become a big problem [15]. Also the South African Rand fell by 3 per cent in the period following the crisis in Zimbabwe.

Although all the Black parties were opposed to the land distribution in South Africa during apartheid, only one of the Black movements, the Pan Africanist Congress (PAC) had threatened violence if post-apartheid South Africa fails to address the issue of land redistribution [16]. When the crisis in Zimbabwe began, the PAC acclaimed Mugabe's position and urged Mbeki to follow suit. But while President Thabo Mbeki could afford to ignore the PAC, calls were also coming from the ANC that something should be done to address the land question within South Africa. This, indeed, led to the increase of the PAC activities over land. In July 2001, for example, the party organized an illegal occupation of private land at Bredell, Kempton Park, about 50 kilometers from Johannesburg and sold parcels of the land to squatters for 25 Rands [17]. This sent a message to the government of the politicization of the land problem. There were also local organizations, like Mpumalanga Labor Tenants, the Land Services Organization (LSO) in the Transkei and the Restitution Forum in the Cape, which had undertaken some form of land seizure, even if unsuccessfully.

However, more disturbing, at least initially, was the intra-party division that was apparent within the ANC on the issuc. Some of its members, notably

Mrs. Winnie Madikazala Mandela, appeared to have supported the policy of the Mugabe government [18].

In its management of its land policy, South African government distanced itself particularly diplomatically, from the Zimbabwean government, and this explains why the outcomes in both countries have been different. The South African President, Thabo Mbeki, told the South African Parliament on 11th May 2000 that he would not tolerate a similar land grab [19]. As late as August 2002, the Governor General of the South African Reserve Bank, Tito Mboweni, noted categorically that his country "is not Zimbabwe" and further asserted that South Africa "handle things very different …[believing] in property rights ...[and] in the importance of the Rule of Law" [20]. This was in the wake of the South African Rand hitting its lowest in four months, at R10.95 to the US dollar. Subsequent developments however brought land to the forefront of attention, and the extent to which the government can keep land issue under control will be further tested in the future. There are growing demands among landless blacks and this has not been helped by the brutality of white farmers to their black employees [21]. All this calls for a discussion on the role of South Africa in the Southern African sub-region.

The New South Africa and Regional Politics

Nature and circumstances have combined to make South Africa the most single richest and most endowed country in Southern Africa. It is, by all account, an undisputed regional hegemon and a clear first among equals even during the apartheid days [22]. In 1990 for instance South Africa's GDP was nearly four times the rest of the region, its trade about three times the rest of the region's total; 7 percent of the region's imports went to South Africa, while about 30 percent of its exports came from there [23]. Its neighbors' in Southern Africa were dependent on South Africa's transport infrastructure for their own exports, and it accounted for about 90 percent of the electricity generated in southern Africa [24].

Unfortunately, Apartheid South Africa was never at peace with its South African neighbors. Those Southern African countries offered sanctuary for black South Africans and collaborated with them in fighting apartheid. South Africa on the other hand, assumed an interventionist attitude towards southern Africa, which was viewed by the regime in Pretoria as its backyard or sphere of interest, an exploitable source of cheap labour and an easily penetrable market for its products [25]. Because of this, the apartheid regime in South

Africa in the 1980s, in a deepening paranoia over its security, unleashed a campaign known by the generic term *destabilization policy* that left more than 1.5 million of the region's people dead and is estimated to have cost $62.42 billion [26]. This ruinous policy branded an indelible mark on southern Africa's people and colored all forms of relations between South Africa and its neighbors. Like other regional hegemons, South Africa has not had to worry seriously about the military potential of its neighbors; they were puny beside the power of the apartheid regime-but its own domestic insecurity made it acutely paranoid so much so that it decided to keep the anti-apartheid forces preoccupied with instability in their countries, thus isolating itself from its neighbors. The region's history is littered with examples of promises-most by South Africa-broken, and undertakings-again, by South Africa-unfulfilled [27]. Until the dismantling of apartheid in 1990, regional cooperation in Southern Africa was focused at combating South Africa's apartheid system and its ripple effects on the countries of the region. This was done through the Southern African DevelopmentCo-ordination Conference (SADCC), the forerunner of Southern African Development Community (SADC).

However, with the dismantling of apartheid and the conduct of the first multi-racial elections in 1994, South Africa had turned a new leaf and has now begun to play the role of a ‘benign hegemon’ [28]. The collapse of apartheid means it was accepted and reintegrated into the Southern African community. It made it quite clear that henceforth, its foreign policy will be African centered, and will seek to promote the welfare of the entire continent particularly its southern African neighbors who had borne the brunt of the apartheid regime. At the heart of post-apartheid South Africa’s regional foreign policy has been an effort to facilitate the rejuvenation of the country’s economy through the promotion of regional integration as well as cross-border trade and investment.

This has been informed by, and coupled to, a determination to foster political stability, good governance and sustainable development across the sub region as a prerequisite for general prosperity. This culminated in the transformation of the SADCC established in 1980 with the primary objective of reducing the economic dependence of the region, primarily on South Africa into SADC, and subsequently in South Africa’s accession to the latter in 1994. SADC was established in terms of the SADC Treaty and the Windhoek Declaration of 1992, which affirm the organisation’s intention to establish a framework for cooperation:

> which provides for … deeper economic cooperation and integration, on the basis of balance, equity and mutual benefit, providing for cross-border investment and trade, and freer movement of factors of production, goods and services across national borders [29].

The SADC regional integration process has evolved against a back-drop of gross economic inequalities and imbalances among member states. As in the case of the South African Customs Union (SACU) (whose membership overlaps with SADC), South Africa's economic predominance is underlined by the fact that it produces approximately 80 percent of Southern Africa's GDP. Enormously lopsided trade relationships persist, with South Africa maintaining a massive surplus with its neighbouring trade partners. This is coupled with its active promotion of a neo-liberal blueprint for rehabilitating the sub region to also ensure its continued survival and prosperity [30].

Economic consideration has been at the core of South Africa's relations with its neighbours, the African continent, and indeed, the entire world. It has used its economic powers to gain huge political leverage in the sub-region so much so that it is considered the undisputed regional and continental leader.

But post-apartheid South Africa had been very discreet about its growing powers and has been careful not to demonstrate its powers and leadership position for fear of rejection and the high sensitivity on the part of its neighbours regarding to any behaviour that reminds them of the apartheid regime's aggressive politics of regional hegemony. Besides, participation in United Nations (UN) and African Union peace keeping mission, it has not used its military force outside its territory. Yet South Africa shows the highest defence expenditures in its sub region and on the African continent as well: US$ 3.55 billion. Botswana ranking second in SADC spends US$ 340 million on defence purposes, which is more than ten times less [31]. It has also couched its foreign policy objectives to reflect universal goals such as "to eradicate poverty and under-development in Africa; protect the global environment; promote human rights; resolve conflicts through dialogue and reconciliation; search for peace, security and equity; end xenophobia and intolerance; and pursue global justice through the rules based on international system" presenting itself as a reformed and highly civilised country that will be guided by the principles of the United Nations [32].

Another unspoken South African policy towards its neighbouring countries is the feeling of indebtedness to *fellow African comrades* that helped fight apartheid and seem to have an unwritten commitment to always stand by them.

Since the onset of the Zimbabwean crisis on land reforms program with the attendant global outcry and Mugabe's high-handedness, South Africa has refrained from criticising or castigating Zimbabwe, at least openly. Initially it actively supported Mugabe's programs, but as the situation got worse and Zimbabwe's economy continued to witness a downward slide, and as the western world continued to put pressure on South Africa to get tougher on Mugabe, it based its position on the altruistic motivations to avert a complete 'collapse' of the Zimbabwean economy and prevent any associated domestic and/or regional contagion. With its long and weirdly border with Zimbabwe, an economic collapse will lead to an influx of people into its country. That will exacerbate South Africa's already worsening unemployment problem.

However, with time, the debate has assumed a racial/political economy dimension. The main reason for this racial divide has been the dominant perception amongst South Africans that the land '*reform'* policy of the Mugabe regime, which is an integral component of the contemporary Zimbabwean crisis, is fundamentally defined by issues of race. For President Mbeki's ANC government, and most black South Africans, Mugabe's land policies represent, at their core, a genuine attempt to address what Mbeki calls "one of the enduring legacies of colonialism", namely large-scale white ownership of land at the expense of the black majority.

For the majority of the white population and the predominately white political opposition, Mugabe's land program is viewed as a disingenuous and politically motivated attempt to maintain power at the expense of white Zimbabweans (and, to a much lesser extent, a sizeable portion of black Zimbabweans who do not support Mugabe's ZANU-PF party and government).

This racial divide on the Zimbabwean land question' is also reflected at the international level. The result is that the majority of nations positioning themselves 'against' Mugabe are predominately Northern and white, while most of those siding 'with' Mugabe are predominately Southern and non-white [33].

South Africa's policy towards its neighbours tends to be heavily constrained by its apartheid history and the need to show gratitude to its neighbours for the role they played in the fight against apartheid. As Taylor notes, the new South Africa's foreign policy is a balancing act between interests of the Left and Right [34].

It represents a political compromise, albeit not necessarily an explicit one, that reflects the different visions of South Africa's role and their respective political bases.

THE NEW SOUTH AFRICA AND CONTINENTAL POLITICS

The end of apartheid and acceptance of South Africa into the sub-regional and regional bodies coincided with the collapse of the Soviet Union, the vanquishing of the socialist ideology and the triumph of the capitalist ideology. Leveraging its competitive advantages, abundant investible capital, marketing and technological know-how, advanced public infrastructure, and human resources and its integration into the African and global society; therefore, South African companies used the resultant global push for economic liberalisation and deregulation to exploit business opportunities in Africa [35]. In addition, the northward expansion of South African firms has been actively encouraged by several African leaders who see the country 'as the continent's last best economic hope' [36]. This was in pursuit of its foreign policy which was African centered. As Nelson Mandela said, "South Africa cannot escape its African destiny. If we do not devote our energies to this continent, we too could fall victim to the forces that brought ruin to its various parts." [37] The outstanding feature of foreign policy in the post-apartheid era in deed has been South Africa's identification and engagement with the rest of Africa. This, in retrospect, may be a wise choice. The outward movement of capital of the Post-Cold War era meant South Africa quite correctly located Africa as its primary centre of economic interest rather than competing with long established American and European companies for share of the Western European market.

The country's penetration of the African market has been bolstered by the decision of scores of international companies, such as Rio Tinto to use it as a launch pad for their operations into the continent [38]. Moreover, in recent years, South Africa's investment and trade foray into Africa has been spurred by the country's championing of the New Partnership for Africa's Development (NEPAD), an undertaking by African leaders to eliminate poor governance, corruption and conflicts in their countries in return for increased aid, private investment and a reduction of trade barriers by developed nations. Africa constitutes the highest priority in South Africa's post-apartheid foreign economic policy, as the government regards its long-term political and economic destiny as indissolubly linked with that of the broader African region [39]. To be sure, the Department of Trade and Industry's metaphor '*butterfly strategy*' for South–South cooperation, which placed South Africa at the proverbial head and the African continent the body of the insect, reflects this sensibility. This strategy is designed "to open up South Africa's trading wings from Africa to North and South America and East Asia". [40]

South African companies have succeeded in penetrating even highly complex and lucrative markets like Nigeria and in various sectors like the telecommunications sector and Pay Television industry, have displaced local companies and emerged dominant players in the industry. South African telecommunications giant MTN, for instance, was Nigerian's most profitable company with a total revenue of N749 billion in 2010, 30 percent of the Group's total revenues in 2010 [41]. MTN Nigeria was clearly the jewel of the MTN Group representing 43 percent of group EBITDA and had provided the cash for MTN's expansion into other regions of the world. Despite the intense competition going on in the Nigerian mobile market, MTN Nigeria, as at December 2010, had a market share of 52 percent and a subscriber base of 40.5 million, more than a quarter of MTN's group total subscribers of 141.6 million MTN in 2010. South African corporations have so established themselves through the purchase of privatised assets and outright displacement of local businesses in African countries that it has become a significant foreign investor in Africa and has come to successfully challenge the pre-eminence of the historically dominant corporations from the United States and Europe. As is natural with Africans, not a few countries have raised concerns as to the aggressiveness of South African businesses and whether it will not replace the neo-colonial West in the exploitation of African countries. A Kenyan legislator and businessman captured this sentiment in 2002 when he lamented:

> If we continue doing this we'll end up owning nothing in Kenya. They are looking for control and that's where the conflict is coming in. They bulldoze their way around. It seems like they still have the old attitudes of the old South Africa [42].

This economic dominance of Africa has given South Africa the leverage to claim leadership of Africa. The realist school argues that the military strength of a state is the key factor for power over outcomes in international politics, [43] being based on its economic and demographic resources. The South African example seems to underline the importance of a comparatively high GDP that can be converted into military power. Because on one hand South Africa is outnumbered by far by its sub regional neighbours in terms of inhabitants and military personnel, for example, Angola alone has more troops than South Africa. But on the other hand it can spend much more on military capabilities than its sub regional neighbours put together for the simple reason that it's GDP is twice as large as that of the rest of the SADC members countries combined.

Pretoria shows the highest defence expenditures in its sub region and on the African continent as well: US$ 3, 55 billion. Botswana – ranking second in SADC – spends US$ 340 million on defence purposes, which is more than ten times less. On the continental level only the defence expenditures of Algeria, Egypt and Morocco – between US$ 2 billion and US$ 3 billion – are comparable to South Africa's. Globally South Africa's defence expenditure ranks on place 34. The US spends US$518 billion and Germany US$ 35 billion. South Africa's peers and cooperation partners India (US$ 19 billion) and Brazil (US$ 10 billion) publish considerably higher defence expenditures as well. Considering that in modern conflicts high tech arm systems are much more important than the strength of military personnel. South Africa's superior defence expenditure leads to military supremacy in its sub region and still a dominant role on the continental level. This military power is projected mainly through multilateral peacekeeping missions on the African continent. In global terms however Pretoria's military power is marginal.

This economic power has unwittingly given it leverage to contest for the leadership of Africa with a burly but economically dysfunctional Nigeria. In the debate on the likely candidate for a United Nations Security Council Permanent Membership, the two countries have been locked in a cold rivalry and competition for the leadership of the continent and by extension, an automatic choice for the permanent seat that is being proposed for the continent. Nigerian, of course, often flaunts its large population (the largest concentration of black peoples in the world), its commendable roles in fighting apartheid and colonialism, its visible role in restoration of peace and democracy to some African countries and its active participation in United Nations peacekeeping efforts across the globe as entitling it to the undisputed leadership and spokesperson of Africa. But its heavily ruined economy, its exceptionally bad and kleptocratic leadership, and the deteriorating security situation in the country has increasingly portrayed it as undeserving of leadership of the African continent. South Africa, on the other hand, had often flaunted its economic strength, its success in uniting its once heavily divided people into a United Nation, and its unassailable position in investing in Africa. In deciding the African country to support for the eventual permanent membership of the Security Council, the United State's Department of Defense (DOD) ranked South Africa top on the list. The fact that South Africa is the only country in the continent seriously capable of projecting power beyond its borders (including the provision of airlift during humanitarian crisis) was a key factor in DOD's logic. America's preference for South Africa is only logical considering the argument put forward by Chase et al.:

> An ability to rely upon regional powers relieves the US of some of its global security and disaster response responsibilities. South Africa is indeed the linchpin of security and prosperity in its region, and is therefore important to US national security interests [44].

South Africa's quest for a leadership role in Africa is most visible in what was originally known as the Mbeki doctrine embodied in the idea of an African Renaissance, which has since found expression in the New Partnership for Africa's Development championed by the former President Mbeki and Nigeria's president Obasanjo [45]. It is however, very careful not to portray itself as power hungry so as not to arouse the suspicions of other African countries which are still hunted by the ghost of the apartheid period. South Africa has also being instrumental to the formation of, and a key player in the African Union, which it had the privileged of heading in 2002.

However, critics have carpeted South Africa over its unwillingness to promote democracy and human rights in other African countries as it promotes at home. It appears due to its apartheid history and the strong connection and relationship the ruling African National Congress had with countries in the continent. The South African government is unwilling to publicly criticise mis-governance, dictatorship and abuse of human rights in other African countries. The only exception to date was the case of Nigeria during the late General Sani Abacha when South African first black President Nelson Mandela came down hard on it and championed its expulsion from the commonwealth for human right abuses including the execution of the Ogoni nine led by Ken Saro Wiwa in November 1995 [46]. In Zimbabwe, Sudan, Cote D'Ivoire and recently, Libya, South Africa has dithered in condemning the flagrant disregard for the constitution of these countries or the great human right abuses going on there in the name of African solidarity.

The latest in the series of South Africa's involvement in African affairs is the controversy over the Chair of the African Union. The background of the story here is worth recording. At the expiration of his four year term, there was the need to elect a replacement for Jean Ping as the chair of the African Union. Although Ping is re-contesting, he faces opposition from the South African Minister of Home Affairs and the former wife of President Jacob Zuma, Ms. Nkosazana Dlamini-Zuma. The entrance of Nkosazana Dlamini-Zuma into the race has raised a lot of dust for at least two reasons. First, the announcement was made somewhat late as it was not made until the end of 2011, even though South African diplomats were to confirm that the decision for her to contest had been made since August 2011.

It is believed in some circles that if the intention had been made open since this date, it would have been possible to address some of the key issues that later raised controversy. Second, and perhaps more importantly, is the fact that there exists and unwritten by widely held assumption that South Africa, along with the other four key countries in the African Union (Nigeria, Algeria, Egypt and Libya) would not occupy the office of the Chairperson of the Union. This is like the informally held assumption that the 5 permanent members of the UN Security Council would not occupy the seat of the UN Secretary General. It is against the background of the latter assumption that Nigeria opposed the candidacy of South Africa and the country voted for incumbent Jean Ping, even though he had really not been pro-Nigeria in his policies whilst he was the Chair. The elections ended in stalemate, even after three rounds of voting. Even during the fourth round of voting where Ping was the only candidate, he still failed to secure the necessary two-third majority as stipulated by the Charter of the AU, thanks largely to the block voting position of the SADC countries. It was against this background that the AU agreed to re-attend to the issue when the organisation meets again in June 2012 in Malawi.

The politics of the AU chair has now opened a number of issues in Nigeria-South African relations. In the last two years, two issues have been at the fore of disagreements. These were over Cote d'Ivoire and Libya. In the former, South Africa was against French intervention, which Nigeria implicitly supported after the blatant recalcitrance of former President Laurent Gbagbo, while in the latter, Nigeria, a known critic of late President Muhammar Ghadaffi, endorsed the forceful removal of the Libyan leader, a venture the government in Pretoria found repugnantly disgraceful to the African continent. On Libya, Nigeria was particularly surprised at South Africa's position after Pretoria had endorsed Resolution 1973 of the UN Security Council that authorised the "*No Fly Zone*", only for the country to object to the North Atlantic Treaty Organization (NATO) military intervention.

Moving back to the Chair of the African Union, Nigeria's position is based more on an informal agreement, rather than on a strict legal position. There is nothing within the African Union Charter that excludes any country from contesting for the position of Chairperson, so South Africa, "technically" has the right to contest for the position. However, Nigeria is also right to stand against South Africa's candidature because of the gentle-man agreement that excludes some countries from contesting for the position. Now where does the situation take us?

First, it has to be established that any disagreement between Nigeria and South Africa is not in the best interest of the African continent. While, of course, it is recognised the respective national interests will sometimes dictate the pursuit of divergent policies, there must remain a threshold that must be maintained to ensure that such disagreements do not result affecting wider continental interests.

Second, it has to be pointed out that the South African candidate Nkosazana Dlamini-Zuma, is an extremely strong candidate whose qualification for the position is not in doubt.

Consequently, regardless of her country's style and approach, she would have served the office credibly well, so are many other illustrious children of the continent. In conclusion, it may be appropriate for the two key candidates: Jean Ping and Nkosazana Dlamini-Zuma may be asked to step down during the next round of competition in Malawi in June.

As noted earlier, the continent is not in short of credible individuals who can serve the Africa in that capacity. There can be no doubt that continental interest will not be served if the two African powers fight over the Chair of the Commissions.

CONCLUSION: THE FUTURE OF SOUTH AFRICA

South Africa has made significant progress since independence and it seems almost certain that the years ahead will be fruitful. Internally, having established racial and ethnic harmony since independence, it can be safely said that some form of national stability has now been put in place and the country can now go further to consolidate this.

Within the region, South Africa continues to play an important role and has been able to contain some of the major challenges that have confronted the region, including the situation in Zimbabwe.

It is most likely that regional challenges, especially the unfolding developments in Zimbabwe, will continue to be the main issue facing South Africa.

On the continental plain, Pretoria's attention is likely to be focused on how to continue championing African cause, especially against the on-going desire to secure a permanent seat at the United Nations.

References

[1] D. Rodrik, *"Understanding South Africa's Economic Puzzles," Centre for International Development Working Paper, No. 130*, Harvard University, 2006, 1.

[2] Alan Hirsch, *Season of Hope: Economic Reform under Mandela and Mbeki*, University of KwaZulu-Natal Press/IDRC. 2005.

[3] World Bank, Washington, D.C: 2004.

[4] E. Leslie et al., "Issues of Economic Integration in Southern Africa," *Konrad-Adenau Stirftung, Occasional Papers*, Johannesburg, 2001: 71.

[5] I. Friedman and L. Bhengu, Fifteen Years of Income Poverty Alleviation Programmes in the Social and Related Sectors, South Africa: Health System Trust, 2008, 71.

[6] Nigeria, *Businessday*, 10/3/2011).

[7] South African Foundation, *"South Africa's Business Presence in Africa," Occasional Paper No. 3*, 2004: 11.

[8] Ibid.

[9] V. Moller et al., "South Africa's Rainbow People: National Pride and Happiness," *Social Indicators Research*, Volume 47, No. 3, 1999: 1.

[10] *Daily Telegraph*, London, April 25 2000 p. 16.

[11] Democracy and Land Reform in Zimbabwe, *New York: International Peace Academy (IPA) Workshop Report,* February 2002, p. 6.

[12] Ibid. p. 6.

[13] Ibid.

[14] "South Africa: Space Invaders", *The Economist*, July 14 2001, p. 62.

[15] *Newsweek*, 13 July 2001.

[16] Of all the South African movements during the war of liberation, the PAC was the most militant in its position against the whites. Its slogan was "one-settler, one bullet". Its decision to make land an issue was predicated, to a large extent, on the importance of land to the settler community. It, however, did not have a wide appeal and no military might to pursue any radical anti-white policies even during the apartheid regime.

[17] *African Research Bulletin* July 2001, p. 14494.

[18] Mrs. Mandela had a widely publicized meeting with Chenjerai Humzi, the leader of the War Veterans, during the peak of the occupation of farms in Zimbabwe.

[19] "Zimbabwe Land Grabs are a Wake-up Call for South Africa", *Monitor*, Kampala: May 17, 2000.

[20] *South African Times*, London, August 28, 2002.
[21] In 2005, there was a celebrated case of a white farmer who threw the body of one of his workers to hungry lions.
[22] Muzrai, 2003.
[23] C. L. Morna, "Frontline States Prepare for Competition with South Africa," *African Business*, October 1990.
[24] E. Leistner, Ibid, I992.
[25] J. Daniel, V. Naidoo and S. Naidu, *"South Africa Have Arrived: Post-Apartheid Corporate Expansion into Africa,"* In: Daniel John, Habib Adam and Southall Roger (eds.), State of the Nation: South Africa, Cape Town: HSRC Press, 2003, 368 -369.
[26] K. Booth and Peter Vale, "Security in Southern Africa: After Apartheid, Beyond Realism," *International Affairs*, London, Volume 71, No. 2, 1995: 287.
[27] Ibid, 288.
[28] C. Alden and M. Soko, "South Africa's Economic Relations with Africa: Hegemony and Its Discontents," *Journal of Modern Africa*, 43, 3, 2005: 368.
[29] Peter Meyns, "From Co-ordination to Inegration: Institutional Aspects of the Development of the SADC," In: H. Dieter (ed.), *The Regionalism of the World Economy and Consequences for Southern Africa*, Marburg: Metropolis-Verlag, 1997, 167.
[30] Alden and Soto, Ibid, 2005: 368.
[31] D. Flames, "Conceptualising Regional Power in International Relations: Lessons from the South Africa Case," *GIGA Research Programme: Power, Violence and Security, No. 53*, 2007: 22. Access at www.giga. Com.
[32] Ibid, 27.
[33] D. McKinley, "South African Foreign Policy towards Zimbabwe under Mbeki," *Review of African Political Economy*, Volume 31, No. 100, 2003.
[34] Taylor, 2004.
[35] Daniel et al. Ibid 368–90.
[36] F. Ahwireng-Obeng and P. J. McGowan, "Partner or Hegemony? South Africa in Africa," In: J. Broderick, G. Burford and G. Freer (eds.), *South Africa's Foreign Policy: Dilemmas of A New Democracy*, New York: Palgrave Macmillan, 2001, 74.
[37] Nelson Mandela, "South Africa's Future Foreign Policy," *Foreign Affairs*, 72, 5, 1993: 89.

[38] N. Grobbelaar, "Can South African Business Drive Regional Integration?," *South African Journal of International Affairs*, 2, 91-106, 2004.

[39] N. Dlamini-Zuma, "South Africa's Foreign Minister's Address," *South African Journal of International Affairs*, 8, 2, 2001: 21–6.

[40] B. Vickers, *Investment Policy in South Africa: Performance and Perceptions,* Johannesburg: Institute for Global Dialogue, 2003: 29.

[41] Akor, 2011.

[42] Ibid.

[43] John J. Mearsheimer, *The Tragedy of Great Power Politics*, New York: W. W. Norton and Company, 2001: 56.

[44] R. Chase et al., "Pivotal States and US Strategy," *Foreign Affairs*, 1996.

[45] John M. Mbaku, "NEPAD and Prospects for Development in Africa," *International Studies*, Volume 41, no. 4, 2004, pp. 390-393.

[46] Olayiwola Abegunrin, *Nigerian Foreign Policy under Military Rule,* 1966-1999, Westport, CT: Praeger Publisher, 2003, p. 151.

In: Africa
Editor: Olayiwola Abegunrin
ISBN: 978-1-62948-561-4

Chapter 7

SUDAN: PEACE, DEVELOPMENT AND THE U.S. CONSTITUENCY FOR AFRICA

Mae C. King
Department of Political Science,
Howard University, Washington, D. C. US

INTRODUCTION

Sudan is an ancient, complex country strategically located in the Horn of Africa. Prior to the secession of South Sudan on July 9, 2011, Sudan had the largest territory of any country in Africa, and a population of about 40 million. Nine countries share borders with Sudan. These include Ethiopia, Democratic Republic of the Congo, Uganda, Chad, and Egypt. Such extensive borders still make Sudan vulnerable to interference by external governments and non-state actors. The country was divided into twenty-five states, each with an elected governor. The government of the Republic of Sudan is headed by President Omar al-Bashir, who has been targeted by "regime change" policies of the United States and Britain.

The focus of this chapter is on Sudan and the US constituency for Africa prior to the secession of the South. Essentially, this is a manipulated constituency camouflaged in "democracy", and "human rights" garb. It is dedicated to the division of the country in a manner that will effectively subjugate the bulk of its oil, agriculture, and water wealth to the control of western commercial and "humanitarian" interests that dominate South Sudan.

The secession of South Sudan was the realization and triumph of the long-standing imperial British "southern" policy of separating north and south Sudan and thwarting the development of a strong Sudanese nation [1]. The separation has created a new weak oil rich dependent state in Africa. South Sudan is a land locked country with a population of about 8 million. Despite her oil wealth and fertile agricultural land, South Sudan owes her "independent" existence ultimately to the political and military support provided by the US government, other NATO countries, and western based "humanitarian" advocacy groups. Consequently, the wealth of this new state will most likely be dominated by these interests. The needs and wishes of this external constituency will be given priority over those of the domestic population. Indeed, the majority of the population of South Sudan is likely to remain impoverished and insecure, as their internal differences are further exploited by external interests and the conflict persists. The continued militarization of the country will divert critical resources from human development to armaments, readily supplied by western powers and arms dealers to Sudanese to continue killing each other.

THE POLITICAL DYNAMICS OF CONFLICT IN SUDAN

Sudan is challenged by conflict internally and externally generated. Conflict in the north and various rebel groups in the south have been prevalent off and on since independence [2]. In January 2005 a Comprehensive Peace Agreement (CPA) was signed that purported to end the Civil War between the Government of Sudan and the People's Liberation Army/Movement (SPLA/ SPLM) that was fought from the 1980's to 2005. Historically, the domestic politics of Sudan has been characterized by sectarian, ethnic, sectional, communal and nationalist rivalry that often manifest itself in open conflict with or rebellion against the ruling authorities. The politics associated with the Mahdist Movement (the Mahdiyya), the Khatmiyya, the Ana Nya as well as the Sudan People's Liberation Movement and the Southern Sudan Independence Army exemplify the high degree of heterogeneity that mark the Republic of Sudan [3]. However, the Mahdist Movement was also an integrative force that united people across ethnic and regional boundaries to oppose British imperialism. In 1881, the founder of the Movement, Mohammed Ahmad Ibn Abdullah proclaimed himself the *Mah*di, "one sent by God to rectify injustices and unrighteousness …" [4] His victory against the

British imperial army at Khartoum in 1885 immortalized him as a national hero of Sudan.

The complexity of Sudan's politics is intensified by the penetration of the politics of imperial and regional powers into the domestic arena. The legacy of British imperialism and its racialization of ethnic or tribal identities to form more narrow political identities, continue to impact the domestic politics of Sudan [5]. Meanwhile, the "missionary factor" exemplified by advocacy groups in the US has influenced US foreign policy toward Sudan. The latter has nurtured a southern separatism and secessionism consistent with the old British "southern" policy in the country. The latter policy gave Christian missionaries "exclusive charge of educational and social policy, discouraged collaboration between pastoralists and agricultural groups, criminalized movement between south and north and was overall designed to create two different countries" and prohibit the development of the Sudanese nation [6]. The US government and the dominant elements of the US constituency for Africa supported a divided Sudan. Christian religious and advocacy groups are key elements of this constituency. Their support for a divided Sudan was usually rationalized on the basis of the false propagandistic "genocide" and "slavery" labels applied to the conflict between the government of Sudan and the western and southern regions of the country [7].

The US government and some religious advocacy groups tend to support divisive secessionist movements in resource rich African countries. The attempted secession of Biafra in Nigeria [8] and Katanga in the Congo are examples of this behavior [9].

Respect for territorial integrity and sovereignty of African countries is abandoned for access to and control of natural resources. Indeed, the civil wars in Africa since independence have been manipulated and driven largely by greed and a desire to control resources such as oil, diamonds, cobalt, uranium, coltan, copper and others. Countries that possess such resources are more likely to experience civil wars [10]. The oil in Sudan is a major factor that explains the United States extensive involvement in this conflict despite contrary "humanitarian" claims.

The US policy toward Africa is shaped by a US constituency for Africa that is dominated by corporate and non-governmental "humanitarian" interests. The historic African Diaspora in the US has little influence within this constituency. Although historically African Americans advocated progressive policies toward Africa, the current constituency tends to support policies that maintain the essence of a colonialism or imperialism that subjugates, divides and perpetuates dependency.

Historic progressive policies, for example, opposed the global trade in African slaves; European colonialism, and the partitioning of Africa; supported African independence and liberation movements; and encouraged independent economic development in Liberia and elsewhere in Africa [11]. The current constituency tends to support neo-liberal policies of "free trade", "privatization", "human rights", and "democracy". The African American members of Congress (AAMC) are an element of this constituency for Africa. The current US policy toward Sudan reflects the inimical impact of such policies on the unity and development of African countries. First, priority is given to corporate interests that seek to promote US commercial interests often to the detriment of the general welfare of African citizens. Second, the "humanitarian" NGOs seek to protect western defined "human rights" and "democracy," even through foreign military intervention and secession. The cumulative consequence is an Africa policy that is hostile in camouflaged ways to the development of an integrative, unified African nation-state with institutions, authority and power to provide for the general welfare and to establish and protect the rights, privileges and obligations of its citizens. A look at US policy toward Sudan, as expressed in some key selected congressional action, and the voting behavior of African American members in this regard, will help illuminate the nature of the constituency that most command the attention of Congress in shaping policy toward Sudan.

Congress and US Policy toward Sudan

Since 1990 to 2010 about 532 bills or resolutions from multiple congresses have addressed the Sudan issue. Some of these focused specifically on the Sudan. Others considered the issue, for example, within a larger context of economic growth and development, terrorism, conflict in Africa, or appropriations legislation. Congressional action on Sudan echoed the dominant corporate mainstream media on the issue. Essentially, the media was critical of the government of Sudan and virtually aligned itself with southern Sudan and Darfur in western Sudan in their opposition to Sudan's national government. Sudan's oil is located largely in these areas of the country.

In echoing the media, Congress was sometimes acting on flawed information disseminated by advocacy and non-governmental groups, such as, Save Darfur Coalition, Enough, Christian Solidarity International, the American Jewish Committee, Southern Baptist Convention, Christian Aid and Others [12].

One of the most egregious allegations made was one regarding "slavery" and "slave redemption". The idea was advanced that there was government sponsored "slavery" and "slave redemption" in Sudan. The 'slaves' were allegedly captured in southern Sudan by "Arab" militias. This fraud was eventually exposed. However, many Americans, including members of Congress, embraced this fallacy. The Washington Post, February 26, 2002, and CBS 60 minutes May 16, 2002 exposed this slave narrative as a fraud and scam. The "slaves" were some villagers who had been recruited and trained to act the part. They were "redeemed" by rather gullible westerners for a fee, for example of $500 or more, paid to the "slave-holders" who turned out to be rebel soldiers or simply hustlers.

This false "slave" narrative helped mobilize support for the southern Sudan rebels among NGOs in the US including civil rights groups. Congress echoed the "slave" narrative, for example, in House Resolution (H. R.) 3766, July 9, 1996. A bill was introduced "to prohibit economic assistance, military assistance or arms transfers to the government of Sudan until appropriate actions is taken to eliminate chattel slavery in Sudan". (H. R. 3766). The bill also committed the US government to opposing any financial assistance to Sudan from any of the international financial institutions to which the US is a member (H. R. 3766, sec. 5) [13]. These included the World Bank, the International Development Association, the African Development Bank, the African Development Fund and the International Monetary Fund (IMF). The bill called for a "Slavery Monitor" to be based in the US Mission in Khartoum when reestablished. The US President was to prepare and transmit to Congress every six months "a report that describes all forms of covert and overt forms of slavery in Sudan". [14] Several African Americans members of Congress were among the chief sponsors of this bill. The government of Sudan vigorously protested these false allegations of slavery. However, the advocacy groups, especially under the umbrella of the Save Darfur Coalition (SDC), penetrated the churches, universities, and even high schools in America with this false "slave" narrative. Indeed, it was referenced in much legislation dealing with the Sudan issue (e.g., H. R. 82, H.R. 112).

The US Congress also played a key role in promoting the "genocide" narrative. Again, Congress was influenced by corporate and NGO advocacy interest groups. The government of Sudan was alleged to be carrying out a genocidal war in Darfur in the western region of Sudan. This region possesses notable oil and water resources.

Significantly, if the wealth producing regions of the south and west could be detached from the Sudanese state and constituted as "independent states" with "client regimes", supported and maintained by the United States and Britain; the generality of the Sudanese people in these regions and elsewhere in the country will be victims of "imperial" or "clientele democracy". Such regimes will give priority to the economic and security interests of their external clients rather than to the general welfare of the Sudanese people. The Sudan nation-state would be denuded. The fifty years of independence of the Democratic Republic of the Congo illustrate the bitter fruits of western clientele regimes in Africa.

Horrific violations of human rights were undoubtedly committed by all parties involved in the conflict in Darfur. The U. N. International Commission of Inquiry on Darfur reported in January 2005 that there was no evidence of genocide [15]. The Darfur conflict is rooted in historic ethnic or tribal struggles for scarce resources, with farming communities pitted against pastoral. Climate change, the availability and prevalence of weapons, the subsequent rebellion against the state itself in 2003, and international and regional interference in this conflict all helped to escalate and prolong it [16].

The Sudan Peace Act [17] was passed by Congress in 2002. The Act exemplifies international interference in the conflict and the internationalizing of Sudan's civil war. It also illustrates the embrace by Congress of the mindset of the US constituency for Africa, especially as represented by Save Darfur Coalition. This Coalition has more than "180 faith-based advocacy and humanitarian organizations." [18] Among other things, the Act declares the war in Darfur to be an act of genocide, asserts the existence of government sponsored slavery in the Sudan, commits the US to take "multilateral efforts to deny the Government of Sudan access to oil revenues to ensure that the Government of Sudan neither directly or indirectly utilizes any oil revenues to purchase or acquire military equipment or to finance military activities". At the same time, $100,000,000 was authorized for assistance to areas of the Sudan that "are not controlled by the Government of Sudan (H. R. 5531, Sec. 5a, and b)."

An in depth analysis of the Sudan Peace Act reveals a legislative action that fundamentally establishes a framework for guaranteeing the secession of southern Sudan and the dismantling of any unified Sudanese state. The Act, for instance, provided assistance (including military) to southern Sudan to develop independent political and economic structures. At the same time, it instituted economic sanctions on the national government of Sudan, and called on the U. N. Security Council to impose an arms embargo on the Government of Sudan. It also called for the settlement of the conflict in Sudan according to the Machakos Protocol of July 2002 (Sec. 6a, b).

This Protocol was negotiated in consultation ("guidance") with the then US Special Envoy to Sudan, Senator Danforth. The Protocol was inserted into the Comprehensive Peace Agreement (CPA) between the Government of Sudan and the SPLM/A. It called for an internationally monitored referendum for the people of southern Sudan "to confirm the unity of Sudan by voting to adopt the system of government established under the peace agreement; or to vote for secession". [19] A fair vote would have required the people of the entire country to vote on the issue of unity. No secessionist movement can be expected to vote to remain in a national entity it has rebelled against. The people of the southern United States would never have voted to remain in the Union of the United States of America if given this option (by Britain, e.g., who was sympathetic to the South).

The CPA is an externally driven agreement imposed on the Government of Sudan by the US and its allies, including those in the Horn of Africa region. The United States and the United Kingdom, with supporting roles of Italy, Norway, Ethiopia, Eritrea, Uganda, Djibouti and Kenya were the key forces behind the CPA. Significantly, the US had already provided at least $20 million dollars to Sudan's neighbors, Ethiopia, Eritrea and Uganda to support rebel forces in the Sudan [20]. Meanwhile, these are the countries represented in the Independent Assessment and Evaluation Commission (AEC) responsible for overseeing the implementation of the CPA along with equal representation from the Government of Sudan and the SPLM/A. Neither the Sudan Peace Act, nor the CPA that emanated from it will end the conflict in Sudan. Instead, a new context for violence is established as neocolonial and imperial forces [21] will continue to express themselves through a client regime in South Sudan.

Congressional legislative action consistently encouraged the indictment and arrest of President Omar al-Bashir for alleged crimes against humanity. The National Islamic Front (NIF) government was accused of genocidal war in southern Sudan, support of terrorism and gross human rights violations [22]. Although, the Sudan Peace Act authorized the US Secretary of State to collect information about genocide, war crimes and other violations of "international humanitarian law" by all parties to the conflict, senior officials of the government of Sudan were referenced. Congress urged the US to utilize the U. N. Security Council to help implement its Sudan policy. The US was instrumental in getting the U. N. Security Council to refer the situation in Darfur to the International Criminal Court (ICC) for investigation. The ICC later issued an indictment and warrant for the arrest of President al-Bashir for war crimes, but not genocide.

The latter charge, however, was reinstated by appeal judges of the ICC in February 2010. A top U. N. investigator of the Darfur conflict, Andrew Cayley has stated that there is no basis for genocide charges against President al-Bashir. "It is difficult to cry government led genocide in one breath and then explain in the next why 2 million Darfuris have sought refuge around the principal army garrisons of their province". [23]

The indictment issued by the ICC for the arrest of President Omar al-Bashir is a political not legal action. It reflects the double standards that still prevail in an international system dominated by Europeans and their descendants in America. Sudan, like the US, has not ratified the Rome Treaty that established the ICC, and does not recognize its jurisdiction over its sovereignty or nationals. Articles 13b and 16 of this Treaty contain structural flaws that subject the question of justice to international power politics. These articles tie the Court to the U. N. Security Council, the most undemocratic organ of the United Nations. They allow the Council to refer "situations" to the ICC for investigation. In this arena, only the weak will be referred, punished or persecuted, while the powerful go free. The Security Council has never, and never will as currently constituted, referred the situations in Iraq, Palestine/Israel, or Afghanistan to the ICC for investigation, even though crimes against humanity have been committed in these areas.

African American Members of Congress and US Sudan Policy

The African American members of Congress (AAMC) hardly reflected any critical thinking or historical knowledge or understanding of the Sudan issue. There appeared to be no awareness of the historical context and the global economic forces that were fuelling the conflict in Sudan [24]. The AAMC engaged in and supported a discourse that construed the political violence in Sudan to be primarily internally generated. The allegations of slavery and genocide, implicitly racially based, probably were key factors that account for their voting behavior.

The Sudan issue, of course, had been inserted into the US "war on terror". The "Janjaweed", for example, was referred to as government sponsored "Arab" militias attacking "black Africans". However, in the US "Janjaweed" was a term used more for propaganda than clarity since the "Arabs" referenced were usually black.

The people of Darfur who have been victims of violence tend to refer to anybody on horseback or camelback who attack them a "Janjaweed. These may be militias or rebels. Nevertheless, the AAMC, like the corporate and advocacy interests, blamed primarily the government of Sudan for the horrific violence in the country. The role of imperialism, the Cold War, and international interventions of various sorts in creating the environment that sustain political violence in Sudan was not acknowledged.

The AAMC echoed the narrative of the advocacy and corporate interests in their discourse and vote on the Sudan issue. They were often at the forefront in sponsoring punitive legislation dealing with Sudan. In the House of Representatives, for example, Democrat Donald Payne of New Jersey sponsored or co-sponsored, often with Republican Frank Wolf of Virginia, several of the major resolutions or bills dealing with Sudan. He introduced H. R. 3766, on July 9, 1996 that called for the prohibition of economic, military and arms transfers to the Government of Sudan until appropriate action was taken to "eliminate chattel slavery". Rep. Payne was joined by at least five other members of the AAMC as co-sponsors of the resolution.

When US Special Envoy to Sudan, Maj. General J. Scott Gration, attempted to work with officials of the Sudanese Government in resolving the conflict, he faced severe criticism from advocacy groups that dominate the U. S. constituency for Africa. The AAMC did not voice any significant support for Gration's approach to the issue. Rep. Frank Wolf, who often worked with Rep. Payne on this issue, strongly criticized Gration saying he failed to recognize the true nature of the Government of Sudan under President al-Bashir. Wolf called on President Obama to give the Sudan issue back to Ambassador Susan Rice and Secretary of State Hillary Clinton [25]. A coalition of 25 advocacy groups endorsed Wolf's appeal. Enough advocacy groups had been very critical of Maj. General Gration and unrelenting in its call for a referendum on secession of southern Sudan. It targeted key members of the National Security Council "deputies committee" with a message to this effect with an announcement in *The Washington Post* of January 22, 2010. [26] Some members of the AAMC were co-sponsors of the Sudan Peace Act, probably the most comprehensive congressional action dealing with the Sudan issue. Representatives Donald Payne and Barbara Lee were among the co-sponsors. In supporting the Act, Rep. Payne called for a "movement in this country to focus on Sudan. We must make this a number one priority". [27] However, this Act focuses more on selective punishment than peace. It laid the foundation for the CPA agreement that provided for the division of Sudan into two countries.

The agreement is a catalyst for disunity on the entire African continent. In Africa "infant" nation-states are still trying to achieve national integration within the boundaries of the territorial states bequeathed by colonial powers at independence. Altogether, the 43 African American members of Congress have not articulated a progressive perspective, informed by history and legacy, on the Sudan issue. They followed the "human rights" and "democracy" advocacy groups and the corporate interests that dominate the US constituency for Africa. These groups often shape the foreign policy of the US government toward Africa. This policy may be detrimental to the security and general welfare of African people [28].

CONCLUSION

Sudan and the Sudanese people continue to be imperiled as the US constituency for Africa becomes more and more advocates of the expansion of imperial privileges and powers disguised in the narratives of "humanitarian intervention", "human rights", and "democracy". The US led NATO savage bombing and destruction of Libya; the slaughter and torture of tens of thousands of Libyan civilians; the brutal assassination of the Libyan Head of State, Colonel Muammar Qaddafi, and the barbaric desecration of his body; is a recent example and consequence of western "humanitarian intervention" in Africa [29] Libya, like South Sudan, is resource rich in oil. Hence, despite the secession of South Sudan and its declaration of "independence" violence still plagues the new state. In January 2012, fighting between two South Sudanese ethnic groups might have left thousands dead and about 50,000 people in need of assistance [30]. The government of South Sudan also seized Sudan's share of the oil produced in the south and confirmed that South Sudan would build a pipeline that would not cross Sudanese territory [31]. This provocative action reflects more of an external agenda of "regime change" in Sudan and perpetual instability, rather than peace, in resource rich African countries. Division of the oil was to be negotiated not usurped. Meanwhile, the Obama administration is providing South Sudan with more military weapons and defense assistance [32].

The division of Sudan is a triumph for the policy of "divide and rule". It represents the resurgence of colonialism with its foreign domination in disguises of "human rights", "democracy" and "humanitarianism". South Sudan is a weak, dependent state that would not exist except for western political and military support.

Its creation may deprive the masses of the Sudanese people of sharing in the oil wealth of the Sudanese nation. The secession also encourages the further balkanization of Sudan and of Africa and the establishment of client regimes. These regimes are compelled to give priority to serving and protecting external interests rather than promoting the peace and welfare of the domestic population. They are an impediment to development. The US constituency for Africa, as currently constituted, lends its support to this wily imperial project. Thus, the US constituency for Africa as constituted and dominated by the American corporate interest is promoting instability and militarization of not only South Sudan but the entire African continent.

References

[1] See Mahmood Mamdani, *Saviors and Survivors: Darfur, Politics and the War on Terror,* New York: Patheon Books, 2009, pp. 174-177.

[2] Ali Mazuri, *Africa's International Relations: The Diplomacy of Independence and Change*, Boulder: Westview Press, 1979, pp. 187-188. Also see Peter Woodard, *The Horn of Africa: Politics and International Relations*, London: I. B. Tauris Publishers, 1996, p. 40.

[3] Woodard, Ibid. pp. 36-60.

[4] William Polk, *The Arab World Today*, Cambridge: Harvard University Press, 1991, p. 154.

[5] Mamdani, Op. cit. pp. 146-176.

[6] Ibid. 175-176.

[7] David Hoile, *Images of Sudan: Case Studies in Propaganda and Misrepresentation*, London: European Sudanese Public Affairs Council, 2003, pp. 46-56.

[8] See General Olusegun Obasanjo, *My Command*: *An Account of the Nigerian Civil War1967-1970*, London: Heinemann, 1980, pp. 146-158. Also see John de St. Jorre, *The Nigerian Civil War*, London: Hodder and Stoughton, 1972, pp. 272-273.

[9] Mazrui, op. Cit., pp. 149-150.

[10] Paul Collier, "Natural Resources, Development and Conflict: Channels of Causation and Policy Interventions", World Bank, Washington, D. C., 2003.

[11] See Elliot Skinner, *African Americans and US Policy Toward Africa, 1850-1924*, Washington, D. C.: Howard University Press, 1992.

[12] Hoile, Op. Cit., pp. 46-65; Mamdani, Op. Cit. pp. 25-38.

[13] 104th Congress, 2nd Session, H.R. 3766, July 9, 1996, Sec. 5.
[14] Ibid. Sec. 3, 4.
[15] Mamdani, Op. Cit., p. 42.
[16] David Hoile, *Darfur: The Road to Peace*, London: European-Sudanese Public Affairs Council, 2008, pp. 141-171.
[17] "Sudan Peace Act", 107th Congress, 2nd Session, H.R. 5531 (Began January 23, 2002).
[18] Mamdani, Op. Cit., p. 23.
[19] Comprehensive Peace Agreement Between the Government of the Republic of Sudan and the Sudan People's Liberation Movement/Sudan People's Liberation Army, http://Sudan Comprehensive Peace Agreement 2005, Part B, Sections 2, 5.
[20] *The Washington Post*, November 10, 1996.
[21] Allison J. Ayers, "Sudan's Uncivil War: the global-historical constitution of political violence", *Review of African Political Economy*, vol. 37, no. 124, June 2010.
[22] H. R. 75, 106th Congress; H. R. 402, 108th Congress; H. R. 159, 111th Congress, 2009.
[23] Cited by Colum Lynch, "Genocide Case Against President of Sudan to be Reconsidered", *The Washington Post*, February 4, 2010, p. A8.
[24] Ayers, Op. Cit.
[25] "Congress Reviews US Policy toward Sudan", http://www.voanerus.com/english/news/USA.
[26] *The Washington Post*, January 22, 2010.
[27] *Congressional Record*, June 13, 2001, p. 10529.
[28] See, for example, Julie Hearn, "The 'Uses and Abuses' of Civil Society in Africa", *Review of African Political Economy*, March 2001, no. 87, vol. 28. Also Greg Cameron, *"Taking Stock of Pastoralist NGOs in Tanzania,"* Ibid.
[29] *The Washington Post*, June 20, 2011, pp. Ai, A9; October 22, 2011, pp. A1, A8.
[30] *The Washington Post*, January 7, 2012, p. A8.
[31] Ibid. November 23, 2011, p. A8.
[32] Ibid, January 7, 2012, p. A8.

In: Africa
Editor: Olayiwola Abegunrin
ISBN: 978-1-62948-561-4

Chapter 8

African and African American Perspectives on Race and Human Rights Discourse

James Pope
Adjunct Professor, Department of African American Studies,
Virginia Commonwealth University,
Richmond, VA, US

Introduction

From 1940 to 1950, not discounting the totality in impact of global political and economic restructuring after the Second War World and the rise of African and Diasporic anticolonialism, there are two events that are considered to have shaped the human rights universe. It is from this period we saw the development and ratification of the United Nations Charter (1945) and the Universal Declaration of Human Rights (UDHR—1948). From this point, these tools have been used as a platform from which governments, international non-governmental organizations (INGOs), activists, and advocates have sought to deal with injustices. There is a consensus among states, academics, and human rights advocates that the UDHR is the most significant embodiment of human rights standards.[1] Some describe it as showing signs of having achieved the status of holy writ within the human rights movement. [2] Others describe it as the 'spiritual parent' of all other human rights documents. [3] In short, it is considered to be the *parent document*, the primary spark of idealism on human rights. In some sense, it is considered to be the '*constitution*' of the entire human rights movement…the single most invoked human rights instrument. [4] Subsequent to this, a series of tools and standards have been developed to serve as the framework through which the complexities of issues related to human rights are addressed. These tools and standards are commonly referred to as the human rights corpus. Human rights are a consistent part of contemporary international affairs. [5] Subjects in the global stage not only center on issues such as war and trade, but pivot on vital issues concerning human rights. [6] Since the adoption of the UDHR, human rights have been institutionalized and internationalized. [7] The discourse that has since developed has become the primary platform used by world leaders, human rights professionals, advocates, lawyers, and activists to address issues germane to human rights in international affairs. [8] In fact, with the adoption of these instruments, many scholars and advocates suggest that it was at this moment, the movement for human rights was born. [9]

Given these facts, one could safely assume that the issues the corpus claims to protect would be sufficiently addressed. However, despite the acceptance of a *universal* conceptual framework of human rights, coupled with the explosion of INGOs and governments claiming to uphold the explicit and implicit principles within the human rights corpus, Africans and people of African descent (the Africana or African world proper. These concepts will be used interchangeably thorughout) are consistently faced with dire daily choices. According to any report one chooses to examine, people of the African world are consistently located on the dismal end of the analytical spectrum on most issues germane to human rights: education, mortality, wealth disparities, health—HIV/AIDS, poverty, hunger, the list goes on.

This leaves one to wonder, what is wrong? Why is the Africana world negatively and disproportionately affected by issues germane to the full range of human rights? Why are the gaps in human development indicators such as, but not limited to, education, wealth, health, growing instead of shrinking? Why, with the proliferation of systems and institutions that have been created to monitor, protect, and champion human rights for *all*, Africans and people of African descent are continually faced with the reality of passing on the generational task of enduring a myriad of obstacles that drastically restrict life choices that engender overall success?

The answers may be found in the following interconnected strains of thought: (1) the human rights discourse in its current praxis—specifically, its development and interaction with the cultural-ideological class character of race—present real limitations in addressing the issues relevant to majority of the Africana world; and (2) the historical transference and continuity of a critical human rights consciousness has been fractured in the Africana world. No longer mass in character in its opposition to the global implications of race and capitalism, the range of thought and activity in relation to addressing social and economic inequities, globally and locally, are limited.

The absence of an identifiable movement highlights this notion. In essence, what we must ask in this present moment is captured in one over-arching question: are human rights in its current praxis adequate in addressing the issues faced by the African world? In order to begin to address this question, it would serve us well to understand the role of race in the theory and practice of human rights by exploring its origins and evolution.

How Is Race Situated in Human Rights Discourse?

Race is a cultural-ideological class construct. It has played and is playing a deleterious role in human rights discourse, which systematically prevents it from adequately and substantively addressing issues that are faced by Africans and people of African descent. This is mainly due to two identifiable and interconnected realities: (1) the complexities found in experiences with racism, imperialism, colonialism, and the proliferation of capitalism; and (2) how the various forms of resistance to this experience produced a more nuanced and deeper understanding of human rights that actually calls into question its praxis. Today, more than ever it is vital to expand, explore, and understand how race—stripped of its now debunked pseudo-science of biological inferiority—as a culturally engrained ideologically-driven tool of the elite class has permeated social structures and forms of consciousness. Central to their maintence of positions of authority are modes and methods that are used to create contradictory states of lived experiences.

Accordingly, it becomes important to restate the previously mentioned interconnected strains of thought as being captured in the following question: What has been the impact on the critical human rights consciousness of the African world as result of the impact of the cultural-ideological class character of race on human rights? Exploring this will not only lead to our understanding of why there is a fracture in African world resistance centered on an advanced conceptualization of human rights? But, why is there a lack of international mass organizing and mobilization between Africa and her Diaspora? This is despite the fact that there is an identifiable historical legacy and non-linear continuity of African and Diasporic resistance being firmly placed within the context of a deeper understanding of the ideas and practice of human rights. It cannot be lost that at the center of this resistance was the common understanding of the interconnectedness of African and people of African descent experiences with racism, colonialism, and imperialism. However, with the drive to universalize a specific Europeanized human rights project, the successes and failures of these important contribtuions are silenced or studied as being separate from the dominant narrative.

The conceptualization of race and its integration into the structures, systems, and institutions that order thoughts and guide behaviors of one group of people towards another group of people has evolved over time and space. Based on class rationalizations and racial assumptions of differences that are natural within the human family, race as a cultural-ideological class construct has been a fluid structuring and ordering mechanism used to divide the world into hierarchical, fragmented categories. Its use as a tool of mental, spiritual, and physical oppression has had disastrous effects upon those who employ its oppressive power as well as those who are the target of this power. This dialectic has permeated the conscious and unconscious behaviors and ideas which guide human interaction. Exploring race in this form and its implications on human rights is of vital interest to addressing the inadequacies of the current discourse as well as the global problems it is intent to deal with. Once framed in this way, it becomes clear that there is a sub-text within the human rights corpus that gives primacy to Europe, which drives it praxis. [10]

Being so, what role does this sub-text play in the theory and practice of human rights? Here it is argued that one of the more subtle impacts is on the critical human rights consciousness of the African world. However, this sub-text alone is not enough to understand the fracture. The external influences of racism and colonialism placed concerted pressure on Africans and people of African descent working for social justice within an advanced understanding of human rights locally and globally. This pressure resulted in the stifling or dismantling of the Africana *avant garde* international left. [11] Because of direct attempts to hide or dismiss their contributions of revolt against imperialism, racism, and capitalism, racial and class-based distinctions have been allowed to flourish and fragment the continuity in their thought and action as it relates to informing a legacy of critical human rights consciousness. Historically, the discourse on race in its *pseudo*-scientific form rested primarily on the biological arguments of superiority. These arguments have since been dismissed. In fact, there is a dominant narrative that refers to the current period as being *post-racial*. Depsite this proclaimation, the implications of race are real and still identifiable. To understand the breadth and depth of its impact on a global scale, a more evolved understanding of race and its relationship to the interdependent, intersecting African and Diasporic discourses on human rights must be forged.

ORIGINS AND INVENTION OF RACE AS A WORLDVIEW

Before moving further, it will be vital to the purpose of this inquiry to frame race within its cultural-ideological class character. It has been suggested that few topics in Western intellectual and social history have been subject to as much investigation, speculation, analysis, and theoretical scrutiny as race has been over the past 450 years. [12] Despite whatever overtures of race-neutrality are championed, it does not matter whether we accept race as a God-given denouement of the complexity of an imperfect world or as a misguided conception of group relationships, race is a pervasive element in the cognitive patterning of Western thought and experience. [13] According to Charles W. Mills, in the *Racial Contract* (1997), the ideas the make up race are considered so fundamental and intrinsic to our construction of perceptual and explanatory frames of reference; its meaning or its reality is generally not questioned. It is accepted as being part of the natural order of things—a universal truth.

Still, research on race shows that there is enormous ambiguity, much confusion, and little to no agreement on its meaning. In fact, the concept of race and its historical implications are systematically being eliminated from educational textbooks. In one study, it is suggested that has been a progressive project that has an identifiable origin. The decline occurred precipitously during the late 1970s, when either the term was no longer mentioned in texts or the authors argued that races do not exist or is not scientifically real. [14] This lack of support for the retention of the concept of race as a scientific concept was seen as a shift to a no-race position in the science of humankind. [15] When examined more closely, this becomes far more 'revolutionary', especially when it is considered that race as primary tool of classification emerged from the rise of scientific racism. In fact, when we explore the origins of our current conceptualizations of race we find that its evolution from a scientifically applied concept to a culturally ingrained worldview was linked with European contact with other peoples of the world. This contact was guided by the ideological interests of elite classes. Beginning in the 15th century, Europeans began to venture out from geographical, cultural, and social isolation to *explore* the rest of the world to aquire material wealth.

Within the next 500 plus years, European exploration, expansion, colonial settlement, and exploitation changed the course of human history as well as constructed peculiar conceptualizations of the value of human groups. In the process of this exploration and exploitation, they encountered awesome and complex political, economic, cultural, and social ways of life which proved to be alien and unexpected. [16] More often than not, these encounters seem to have strained and challenged the European imagination, prompting a wide-range of speculations and pseudo-interpretations of their so-called new discoveries. [17] As a consequence, in order to grapple intellectually and practically with these *alien* societies, meanings and identities were imposed upon them that fit within their own cultural understandings, historical experience, and preconceptions of what the world was all about. [18] Somewhere in this process, the use of race to characterize differences among people was employed. However, in the English language, the concept has had a dozen distinct meanings dating from medieval times. [19] In its semantic form referring to particular groups of human beings, English ideas of race have a particular historical trajectory. Examining its etymology, race appears to be obscure, although most dictionary descriptions assert that it most likely has its origins from Italy, thus assuming a Latin origin. [20]

Over the centuries there has been debate on this view. In 1926, it was argued that there is not a Latin term from which it is known to have evolved. [21] In 1951, a zoologist argued that it derived from the Arabic term *ras*, meaning chief head, origin, or beginning. [22] From here it was speculated that it was diffused into Spanish to form *raza*, which means a kinship group or follower of a headman. [23] There is another argument that suggests that race was derived from the Latin word *ratio* in an accusative form that had similar meaning to other classificatory terms such as species, kind, and nature, coming to Italian as *razza* and from there to other related languages. [24] To add legitimacy to this latter argument, it was noted that the earliest usage of *race* in the English language occurs in a 16th century poem entitled, "*The dance of the seven deadly synnis*" or "*backbyttaris of sindry racis,*" written by William Dunbar. [25] The transformation of *ratio* to Italian *razza* and subsequently into modern languages as being the true direction of linguistic development was agreed upon by etymologists. [26] Other usages of race, albeit rare can be found in the late 16th century in two ways: (1) as a group of persons, animals, or plants, connected by common descent or origin; and (2) a group or class of persons animals, or things, having some common feature or features. [27]

During the latter part of the 16th century, only occasionally do we find race as being used to refer to humans; although some contemporaries of Edmund

Champion author of *The History of Ireland* used it to refer to the 'Irish race'. [28]

Nevertheless, as the historical evidence suggest, race did not appear in the English language with direct reference to humans until the 17th century. Here, we can identify that it was used in several ways: "First, it was used to refer to the characteristics or common qualities of certain types of people. For example, John Bunyan references a 'race of saints' in his *Pilgrim's Progress*. While William Shakespeare, along with others, associated race with the idea of the inherited disposition or temperament of individuals. In this frame of reference, other writers seemed to convey a sense that it referred to a class or type of person, i.e. race of bishops or the race of womankind. Secondly, was a more incipient technical usage employed by *'learned men'* when attempting to describe and classify different human groups, occasionally using interchangeably with species as a general mode of categorizing peoples." [29]

In the earliest Spanish dictionary, the 1611 Tesoro de la Lengua Castellana o Espanola of Covarrubias Horozco, it specifically identifies *raza* as referring to the caste or quality of authentic horses which are branded for recognition. [30] In addition to this, two other meanings are given, with one of them referring to humankind.

As global interactions began to evolve within European historicity, *raza* begins to take on a negative connotation to identify the existence of Moorish or Jewish ancestry. [31] During the Spanish Inquisition race was applied to differentiate religious affiliations particularly Jewish and Christians. Thus, by 1737, the Diccionario de la Lengua Castellana gives the first and primary meaning to race when it suggests that it means "a ***caste or quality*** of origin or lineage." This gives creditability to the idea that race could have been a folk concept in the Romantic languages (such as Spanish, Italian, French, and Portuguese), which evidently comes from breeding domestic animals. [32] In addition to this, race has a long history in the folk cultures of the Latin world, which dates far back into ancient agrarian communities to refer to a ***persons' ability*** to breed animals. Consequently, it is not a far intellectual stretch to suggest that Spanish writers, explorers, and thinkers used the term in several ways when referring to new people encountered in their travels.

As a result of 15th and 16th century Spanish hegemony in Europe and of the seas, contact with other Europeans increased dramatically. It cannot be lost that during these periods contact based primarily on economic interests increased at a very rapid rate, especially on the part of merchants, adventurers, and their representatives in London. Notwithstanding, various intermarriages between English and Spanish royalty which led to instances such as the

Spanish King, Philip, ruling England for several years in conjunction with his wife, Mary, daughter of Henry VIII. Together, giving the first glimpse into the identifiable moments of historical transference of race being utiltized to understand and deal with global economic, cultural, social, and political changes.

With this, it is most assuredly possible that with this increase in contact and intermingling, the English adopted the term race from the Spanish, applying it to the indigenous peoples of their conquered terriorties, which included the so-called New World (North America). Therefore it is logical that during this time, the pronunciation of *razza* could have easily been transformed into English *race* in the same manner consistent with other known linguistic transformations. So, history teaches that from the 16th to 18th centuries, race developed as a classificatory term in the English worldview similar to and interchangeable with people, nation, kind, type, variety, or stock. [33]

To solidify this evolution, in the latter part of the 18th century, scholars actively engaged in projects that investigated, classified, defined, and elevated the notion of race to being the major symbol and mode through which human group differentiation was interpreted. A cultural-ideological prism, if you will. This project of differentiation was aggressively and extensively applied to non-European peoples and in some cases to groups within Europe that varied in some way from what was considered the subjective norm. [34]

Therefore, the historical record shows that race became the most useful tool that conveyed qualities and degrees of human differences that had become increasingly consonant with the English worldview of the worlds' people of color. [35] This proved to be an easy analogy of inheritable and unchangeable features from breeding animals to human beings. Thus, providing early evidence that race was not arbitrarily applied. In fact, it can be suggested that there were useful and substantive aspects of its referential meaning that were utilized as the primary mechanism to convey value on individual and group differences. As a consequence, it was eminent that race evolved to inform, structure, and guide the European world view of other societies and people.

It then becomes important to note that, in North America, the English developed and expanded the implications of race as a social, economic, political, and cultural tool of exclusion and categorization that informs our current global conceptualizations and practices of race.

In fact, race as developed by Europeans in North America and exported around the world are based on several distinct points of evolution: "First, the dichotomous race categories of black and white are set and inflexible. The assumptions and rationalizations are locked in step with these categories. Therefore, these sets of assumptions and rationalizations follow the group or individual no matter how high up the social, political, or economic ladder one climbs. Caste then becomes the major point of reference. [36] Secondly, the category *black* or *African American* is defined by any known descent from a Black ancestor (African). This conflates and socially homogenizes individuals with a wide range of phenotypes into one racial category. Third, one cannot transcend or transform one's race status, no legal or a social mechanism exists for changing one's race. Accordingly, not only is race is highly institutionalized in the collective consciousness of Americans and Europeans; it is institutionalized in the sub-systems and sub-structures of society such as schools, employment, churches, etc. Boundaries are rigidly drawn." [37]

Therefore, analysis on any phenomenon related to race must account for this period in the evolutionary cycle of race from a unconscious external descriptor to a cultural-ideological class construct that has permeated every social institution linked with human interaction. This includes the way human rights norms and standards are conceptualized and implemented.

This is because humans cannot operate outside of the knowledge systems of their cultures and the assumptions that are found within them. Indeed the state of this knowledge, both technological and social, as well as perceived cultural values and standards all determine the directions along which that system and sub-systems will develop. [38] In essence, if we operate through systems of knowledge that are born out of contradictory and self-centered perceptions and perspectives, then the institutions and structures that order and guide the thought and actions of those within it will mirror contradictory and self-centered patterns. Myths, specialized language, complex systems of knowledge which only serve the rationale and interests of an elite class are interdependent and have direct influence on conscious and unconscious thoughts and behaviors no matter how far from reality they are created. The primary example of this is found in the blind adherence to capitalism, despite its innate exploitative character.

Today, the biological idea of race as a useful tool is more often than not rejected. It is argued that it is a myth or an abstraction that does not correspond with reality and complexities of humanity. Nevertheless, all of this has been quite confusing to those who grapple with the political, cultural, social, and economic realities of race and its accompanying marginalization. The major reason for this confusion is that the cultural-idoelogical class character of race prohibits many from being able to make the necessary distinction between natural biological variations and the social meanings that were constructed and imposed on those varying features. [39] This dialectic creates an environment, which suggests that race is not real, yet deadly relevant. Nevertheless, race does exist as it is infused with idoleogical and cultural interests of the dominant class. However, it should not be viewed as something that is biologically tangible and existing in the outside world that has to be discovered, described, and defined but as a creation with direct and concentrated consequences. [40] It is a product of the human mind a human invention.

From the beginning, it reflected a particular way of looking at and interpreting human differences—physical, mental, and spiritual. It is inextricably linked with certain presumptions and beliefs developed by European thinkers and English colonists from the 16th to the 18th centuries. As it was during this period the concept was transformed from a mere tool of classification to a sort of practice as developed from the cultural worldview of a particular class that expressed certain attitudes and informed prejudgments toward non-European people that fit idoleogical purposes, especially towards the peoples of the African World. Captured in these attitudes and prejudgments was the drive to exert power. As a way of imposing order and understanding on the complex realities where one group asserts dominance over others, an equally complex conceptualization of race was developed to rationalize their exploitation. [41] Accordingly, the Europeans who came to dominate during the 17th and 18th century laid the framework for a world where whiteness achieved a level of supremacy, while non-European peoples could not escape the status of inferior or lower-status peoples.

Race was use to convey a model of the world as being divided into exclusive groups of people that were naturally ranked vis-à-vis one another. [42] What this suggests, is that dominance is a key component to the use of race. As a consequence, its political dimensions are then unmasked. It is further suggested that forceful subjugation of other groups is a characteristic of those that are most exclusive in their conception of the kinship bond. [43] People who have the strongest and most narrowly defined conception of kinship have a tendency to be more warlike to protect these bonds. This is done so that the history of successful social interaction not only breeds what can be called the '*dominant race*', but this so-called dominant race also becomes the political race over other races. Being such, this politically powerful people create systems and institutions of social, economic, cultural, etc. interaction within a particular worldview. Essential to this worldview is the responibility to secure the consent of the dominated to maintain their positions of moral, political, and economic authority. Therefore, the processes of *mystification,* where the construction of social, political, and economic relations based on the interest of the elite class mask, conceal, and obscure the systems, process, and institutions of domination, subordination, and exploitation, becomes vital to maintaining this hegemony. These processes are constructed and vigorously protected in order to guide and structure the marginalized range and scope of thought and behavior to be always linked to the interest of the elite class (the colonial master). [44] Those who are considered to be lacking in this sense will not only be lacking in the capacities for this kind of racial or political dominance, but will come under more forceful control of the political or dominant group(s).

What this then suggests is that people who have not been successful in acquiring dominance, the people who have not been able to force their group identity upon another people will be called the inferior people." [45] They will be called the backward people, even though it is a historical fact that they have contributed more to the civilization than those who have been able to secure political conquest and hold political power. [46] History teaches a wake of horrendous human misery and intractable social, economic, political, and moral problems were given to the world from these processes.

Although the patterns and practices of a racial worldview have evolved relative to the social, political, cultural, and economic contexts of a particular society, the ideological components are essentially the same. [47] This rests on the following points of similarity: "each society have race classifications identified in law; all have structured and institutionalized racial classifications based on a hierarchy; each have associate stereotypical behavior with each racial category; and all hold, at least abstractly, that racial characteristics physical and behavioral are innate and unalterable." [48]

As we can now see with race and its evolution as an cultural-ideological engineered conditioner of human interaction based on class rationalizations, the practice or implications of a racial worldview that produce instances of conscious and unconscious behaviors is a more salient project with global implications. A project that has severe implications on human interactions, that has permeated even the most *sacred* of discourses including the human rights discourse. As a consequence, race requires a different conceptual framework; its socio-cultural history must be holistically examined. The intellectual scope has to shift from units of analysis, to exploring how ideas, their relationships, and the cultural matrix within ideological features emerge, function, and evolve. [49]

Instead of looking outwardly for some esoteric genesis, it is essential we peel away the intricate layers of Western cultural and intellectual history and look at the material conditions, forms of knowledge, motivations and objectives, and levels of consciousness of those who imposed the ideas of race on human interactions. [50] This becomes essential to contemporary understanding of those who continue to accept it as a useful component of human interaction. In human rights, this requires a more vigorous and substantive project to explore the deep interconnected layers of contradictory and unacceptable notions of justice, peace, and equality embedded within the dominant discourse. Race as a cultural-ideological class construct requires a concerted effort to address its evolutionary nature not only as an idea, but also how its practice order, structure, and influences systems of thought and behaviors.

Race/Racism and Its Global Vitality

We are currently living in an age where poverty and disease are big business. In a world where race and class produces and reproduces ways of interacting. Its has attached itself to our very construction of individual and group realities, therefore guiding and informing conscious and unconscious acts of overt and covert racism as being natural and universal occurrences. Assessing the implications of race upon human rights discourse and critical consciousness is vital in order to engage in a substantive restructuring of world order. The interrogation of a racial paradigm is critical because it can be exported to the rest of world. [51] The current human rights discourse is dominated by concepts and ideas that were formed in European historicity; therefore it must not be lost that it also contains its negativities.

In the 21st century, with the rapid development of new technologies and global connectivity, race, gender, and class issues constantly intersect and remold each other. [52]

With this, a paradigm shift in understanding race has also occurred. In the U.S., race has been reconfigured and restructured. With the elimination of state-sanctioned racial segregation in the latter part of the 20th century, an ideology of color blindness which is an underlining central theme to the myth of a racial democracy has been promoted around the globe. [53] However, it has been suggested that the ideology of color blindness is a smoke screen for a more dangerous and disturbing mission; more than to simply make race neutral. [54] Within this frame of reference, all colors of value become white, with *neutral* within this frame of reference functioning as a euphemism for White. [55] Hidden under the progressive idea that race is a social construct is an insistence that race will not matter even in circumstances where racial inequities prevail, here color blindness becomes racial blindness. [56] This has been the situation in South Africa since the end of apartheid. Those who consider themselves liberals and, in many ways some, progressives defend this ideology of color blindness, while selectively blinding themselves to real implications of a highly racialized and class-oriented society.

This same ideology or worldview can be extracted from and identified within the human rights discourse. Human rights are touted as being universal thereby apolitical. However, the seemingly apolitical character of the human rights discourse obscures its true character and the cultural identity of the norms it seeks to universalize. [57] In fact, those who attempt to critique the current human rights discourse are greeted with a litany of criticisms that attempt to discredit them as being undemocratic, apologetists, and delusional. The central function of the current human rights discourse purports itself as being universal, neutral, and apolitical in character, a discourse that comes from and can be used by all people. However, when closely assessed with conceptual and practical clarity, this simply is not the case. There is something seriously wrong with the foundations upon which the universal discourse is built. The deep-rooted implications of this argument cannot simply be dismissed, as the evolution and interaction of race and class has put serious limitations on the effectiveness of the human rights discourse. Not exploring the interaction of race in human rights conceptualization and practice is counter-productive. This negation, allows for the negation of individual and collective responsibilities and duties of those who purport the sanctity of human rights. But, more importantly, it promotes an implicit dismissal of the roots of many of the problems faced by Africans and African descendant peoples all over the world who have been historically and are still being marginalized.

To abandon using race as an explicit physical category of differentiation does not mean that its cultural-ideological character is not available. By this it is meant to suggest that using a categorical term such as race, with all its intended processes to capture the totality of a people or a person in one universal frame of reference has serious implications. We can see this in the interdependent processes of the Trans-Atlantic Slave trade, the imperial and colonial projects in Africa and Latin America (this includes the Carribean), and their subsequent instances, which have observable impact today. The cultural-ideological shift to dehumanize a people brought with it a legacy of inequities that permeate every aspect human interaction.

In the 21st century, the entrenchment of the cultural-ideological class character of race is pervasive and must be interrogated with the upmost sense of urgency. This urgency sits squarely upon the understanding of the increasing importance of utilizing a more holisitic and deeper understanding of human rights in order to effectively and substantively address issues of Africans and people of African descent. This is not to say the idea of a universal human rights discourse is unattainable, rather its philosophical and conceptual foundations must with deliberate speed be restructured or evolved. Although we can identify issues that historically, systematically, and disproportionately affect the African world, such as poverty, HIV/AIDS, etc. These in reality cut across the socially constructed boundaries between those who have and those who do not have. In essence, with the saliency and aggressive proliferation of systemic exclusion and continued marginalization of the contributions African world to human rights understanding and practice, the implications have with great speed become global problems. The issues that the human discourse and its proponents claim they are addressing in the *Developing World* are beginning to affect the so-called First and Second Worlds. [58] Opposed to the theory outlined by Samuel Huntington in *Clash of Civilizations*, the clash is actually between those who propagate a culture of oppression and those who seek a culture of freedom for all. [59]

Racialized Discourse as Human Rights Practice

Peculiarly, even today, Africans and people of African descent are not considered to be actors, creators, nor implementers of the human rights corpus. Despite having an identifiable legacy and continuity of thought and action that is undeniably linked to the ideas and purpose of a human rights tradition, the Africana world are not actors, but essentially acted upon. They are the objects in human rights discourse. This objectification automatically removes agency from the oppressed and places them within the perpetual state of being victims. This project essentially requires the oppressed to consciously and unconsciously accept a position of inferiority, waiting for the saviors to rescue them from their state of pre-modernity.

Most scholars of human rights, citizenship, and democracy simply ignore the centrality of race in the formulation of the ideas, systems, and institutions that are lauded as the universal standard to which all others must adhere. This particularistic worldview serves as being natural and complete; the foundation upon which all human interaction must be launched. This frame of logic is taken for granted and is not seen as being political or as a form of domination. [60] Accordingly, Enlightenment philosophers such as Voltaire, Rousseau, Kant and Condorcet are universalized. [61] The idea of democracy, the gift of the Greeks and their contributions to civilization are invoked with passion and vigor when human rights are discussed. However, it is a *lost* fact that democratic citizenship, as expounded by Athens—was quick to exclude others. The inclusion of '*Others*' was seen as the negation of order and the rule of law. [62] In fact, it is *missed* that it was Aristotle who created the notion of *ius sanguinis* (meaning '*right of blood*', '*by blood*') to be an exclusionary tool serving the interest of the dominant class. [63] An evolution of this worldview is later found in the words of David Hume (1753) in *Of National Character*, where he asserts that:

> I am apt to suspect the negroes…to be naturally inferior to white…not to mention our colonies, there Negro slaves dispersed all over Europe, of which non ever discovered any symptoms of ingenuity;…In Jamaica…they talk of one negro as a man of arts and learning; but it is likely he is admired for very slender accomplishments, like a parrot who speaks a few words plainly. [64]

The father of modern moral theory, Immanuel Kant adds to this, writing in *Observations on the Feeling of the Beautiful and Sublime* that; "so fundamental is the difference between races of man…it appears to as great in regard to mental capacities as in color so that a clear proof that what a Negro said was stupid was that this fellow was black from head to toe." [65]

It must not be overlooked that during this period the discourse on rights, liberty, justice, equality were being developed and elaborated upon. In 1646 Richard Overton, a Leveler philosopher summarized the emerging and soon to be dominant strain of Western thought on rights when he asserts that:

> to every individual in nature is given an individual property by nature to not be invaded or usurped by any. For every one…has a self- property, else could he not be himself, and this no second may presume to deprive any without manifest violation and affront the very principles of nature and of the rules of equality and justice between man and man. [66]

In essence, as John Locke would later write, "every man has a property in his own person." [67] This idea of self-propriety which evolved into demands for a list of natural or human rights can be categorized into civil and political rights, which is the form of rights advanced by English liberals such as Locke and Overton. This frame of reference was often narrowly applied to individuals and often linked to a defense of existing and increasing inequality in private property. [68] Nevertheless, along with this English liberal strain of thought concerning (human) rights, a more group-oriented way of looking at rights began to take shape with the Diggers. [69]

One of the leading Digger philosophers, Gerrard Winstanley, preceding Karl Marx by two centuries, asserted that genuine freedom is possible only with the existence of common ownership of property, and offered a powerful critique of the effects of rising agrarian capitalism on poor and middling farmers. [70] Writing in 1649, Winstanley argues that; "buying and selling is the great cheat that robs and steals the Earth from one another. It is that which makes some lords, and others beggars, some rulers, others to be ruled, and makes great murderers and thieves to be imprisoners and hangers of little ones." [71]

These events were further developed with the onset of the French and American revolutions. The outcome of both events proved to provide an even sharper contrast between the growing views on human rights, which placed emphasis upon the individual and their civil and political rights. [72]

Further adding to the development from this period, Thomas Jefferson, Benjamin Franklin, John Hancock, James Madison, George Washington to name a few, contradictorily participated and profited from the global impact of the enslavement of Africans, all while being revolutionary proponents of liberty, justice, and equality. [73] With this abbreviated outline of the historical development of the dominant worldview on human rights, race as a cultural-ideological class tool of dominance was prevalent and merged into the formulation and structuring of human interactions. During these instances of human development, Africans and people of African descent were objects (property), therefore considered to be non-human in human rights discourse. How has this changed, today?

A further exploration of race, class, ideology, and human rights can be found in Rousseau's logic when he asserted the following: "after years of Europeans swarming all over the world…I'm convinced that we have known no other men than Europeans." [74]

Notwithstanding the obvious, malicious, and ill-informed strain of thought in the above quote, history teaches that there is an abundance of evidence that contradicts this claim of European superiority. The multiple incursions into continental Africa and the conquest of the Americas changed any Western claim to moral and ethical superiority maintained vis-à-vis the old worlds. No matter how awful the Mayan and Aztec civilizations are portrayed, history teaches that this time the Europeans were greater in their slaughter, than those with whom they compared themselves. [75]

Fredrick Douglass, a person of African descent adds legitimacy to this fact in a speech he delivered on July 5, 1852. Fredrick Douglass asks:

> ...Fellow-citizens, pardon me, allow me to ask, why am I called upon to speak here to-day? What, to the American slave, is your 4th of July? I answer; a day that reveals to him, more than all other days in the year, the gross injustice and cruelty to which he is the constant victim...There is not a nation on the earth guilty of practices more shocking and bloody than are the people of the United States, at this very hour... Go where you may, search where you will, roam through all the monarchies and despotisms of the Old World, travel through South America, search out every abuse, and when you have found the last, lay your facts by the side of the everyday practices of this nation and you will say with me that, for revolting barbarity and shameless hypocrisy, America reigns without a rival.... [76]

The lands upon which Europeans and Americans colonized experienced a warrior-citizen, a genocidal destroyer of culture and tradition. [77] To undertake such a critical view on human rights leaves one to wonder: Is this simply a reaction to nonrelavant historical instances? The answer is emphatic no! It is, however, a call for a serious and substantive interrogation into the *universal* ideas of a democratic society that informs the human rights discourse. There are other worldviews that focus on finding a path toward freedom, justice, and equality. Are these worldviews so incompatible with the dominant European worldview, that they should be ignored? Can we or should we abolish the conception of racial equality? Can there ever be equality?

If human rights are the rights that one has simply because they are born in the human family, then only human beings have human rights. If one is not a human being, then by definition one cannot have human rights. Because only people are human beings, it would seem obvious that only individuals can have human rights. [78] Herein lies the major problem, Africans and people of African descent were not seen as humans. Accordingly, in the origins of modern Europe and the subsequent historicity, the now dominant liberal view of human rights being essentially relegated only to civil and political rights did not apply to *non-humans* or *property,* of which Africans and people of African were defined. [79] The existence of targeted and persistent inequality despite identifiable universal human rights standards is a direct contradiction of their universality. Accordingly, the current conceptualization and practice of human rights is proving to be inadequate in addressing historical and contemporary problems produced from the entrenchment of and application of race as a cultural-ideological class construct in the African world.

Impact of Race on Human Rights Discourse

With this, there are a few points of limitation that are important to explore and expand upon. [80] First, the human rights discourse is stuck within a bourgeois liberal individualism ethos. [81] The epistemology of this ethos is built upon systems of exclusion and perceived notions of supremacy and inferiority in humanity that are nothing more than class rationalizations of natural occurring phenomena. Accordingly, those scholars, activists, and policymakers who subscribe to this dominant frame of reference fully reject group-based claims or expressions unless they are regulated to the private sphere. [82] The human rights discourse focuses on the idea of the autonomous individual who is located within a universe of abstract rights, devoid of racially constraining social structures. [83] Important to note is that this race neutral or color-blind position uses the same global neoconservative rhetoric that has dominated global racial justice debates since the dismantling of Jim Crow in the United States as well as Apartheid in South Africa. [84]

The commitment to equality is loosely structured within manipulable civil and political compromises and is the primary mechanism of addressing issues plaguing the non-White world. The central problem with this frame of reference is that it is narrowly focused and interprets the goal of human rights in a way that precludes concern for historical and contemporary implications resulting from race and class inequalities. It is the premise of color-blindness that inequality will be solved with individual advancement. Thus, collective actions are not encouraged nor endorsed by the dominant theory and practice of human rights. This form of logic presents an interesting point of contention, as agitation within the African world was collective and mass in character. Resistance started with mass mobilization and the organized actions of the people. Moreover, it is this very collective action that has enhanced the boundaries of democracy, justice, rights, equality, peace, etc. The real problem is that it not only challenges the credibility of human rights as currently practiced, but calls into question its foundational principles and ideological positioning. As a consequence, it concurrently serves as a critique of the thoughts and actions of its adherents. Nevertheless, universal claims of human rights that continue to implicitly (or explicitly) ignore the implications of race and class in its theory and practice will continually and systemically impede the trajectory of creating global democracitc societies. [85]

The second point of limitation is found in the assertion that nation-states are *not* deeply racialized. [86] The dominant historical narrative and leading rationale in the formation of nation-states is given as being constructed on the basis of general will and for the protection of the citizen. A construct that is void of race, class, and culture, as it was born out of the collective need for order under the *rule of law*. If this is true, then it begs to be asked: if nation-states are indeed not racialized, then why must they provide for and guarantee full citizenship to non-whites—the *Others*? [87]

It must not be lost that the formation of nation-states and its political reigns precipitate the development of founding myths, such as myths of origins. [88] This practice is a gift with particular roots. Scholars argue that the origins and development of the nation-state is found in the historical continuum of Europe. [89] The "bourgeoisie use of print and press, their appeals to and seduction of the classes they intended to dominate facilitated the fabrication of these national myths. The sole purpose of these myths were to be recognized in the official instruments of class hegemony: national creeds, social ideologies, philosophical tenets, constitutions, etc. They functioned to legitimate the social orders that they create. As they begin to inform the social consciousness of everyone forced and who choose to freely be a part of the social order, these myths are substituted for real history. They provide the appearance of being a factual-based historical narrative when they are actually nothing more than class-serving rationales for exploitation." [90]

In fact, when properly contextualized, the documents that are said to encapsulate the ideals of the nation are nothing less than the expressions of the interests and creed of an elite class. [91]

An ascriptive racial status is the main organizing principle of Western social, economic, and political institutions, the ways and means of interacting, that produce real-life differences that cannot be understood purely in representational terms. [92] Access to social, political, and economic capital and the various arrangements and rearrangements that are produced vary greatly depending on what resources are obtained, who is excluded from them, and what is demanded in exchange to obtain them. [93] This produces or perpetuates conditions where exclusivity and identity determines whether or not one is allowed to freely function in society. [94] In such an environment one must find ways to live, either by accepting ones place in it, even if that means one has to accept a dehumanized existence or unrelentingly resist it *by any means necessary*. With this resistance, a critical human rights consciousness becomes an essential building block to situate a counter response to redress injustices.

Third, the human rights discourse ignores the role of different power relations among individuals as well as members of social groups or nation-states. [95] As currently practiced, human rights discourse does not fully grapple with the presence of inequitable power relations as a product of the development, implementation, and maintenance of race and class. There are two integral and interdependent aspects inherent in citizenship—membership and equality. The idea of membership invokes the notion that one is recognized as a person with the full capability to exercise their humanity in a democratic society such as participating in the development of that society's productive forces. Therefore, it is a logical and fundamentally safe assumption that those who are considered to be members are equal with respect to the rights and duties associated with that membership. [96] Furthermore, individual, and in large respect group, autonomy provides the platform for being able to participate in the governing of the nation-state, in an ongoing dialogue, or both. [97]

The uneven distribution and access to the various forms of capital consistently masks the unequal power relations that are systemically and historically beneficial to the interests of the dominant class. Moreover, it has increasingly becoming less helpful to stigmatized groups, who have demanded policies that combat racism and discrimination. [98] Despite having fought and died in efforts to expand the ideas of justice, freedom, and equality, data shows that review of any human development index, Africans and people of African descent consistently rank among the lower end. [99] Couple this with the idea that Africans and people of African have not been granted full membership into the global human family, the fact remains that without citizenship in either the human family or a nation-state, full participation is not a realizable goal no matter how far one can stretch their imaginations. It is without doubt and requires little analysis to assert that citizenship and human rights can work to create equality and justice only when differences natural within the human family are no longer the basis of exclusion, oppression, and fear. The only question that arises is whether a just and equal society is materially profitable to power elite.

Finally, the dominant narrative of human rights portrays an ahistorical understanding of the development of its discourse. [100] Specifically, it ignores the fact that the African world grappled with the expansion and application of justice, peace, and equality through its protracted interaction with the forces of slavery, racism, imperialism, and colonialism longer than the corpus has been enshrined in international law, treaties, standards, and norms.

Moreover, the liberal tradition, which informs human rights conceptualization and practice, purposefully does not say anything about the fact that exclusion of some groups from democratic processes has from the beginning been integral to the entitlement of other groups. [101] In the U.S., no matter how hard the power elite attempt offer their rationale of some mythological "super individualism", no one can refute nor ignore the fact that the nation was built upon the backs of people of color and their forced and coerced labor. In the case of Europe's level of civilization, their democratic societies are a product of their economic (substantially aided by the bible and the gun) successes found in the natural and human resources that were (are) stripped from their colonies in Africa, Latin America, and Caribbean. [102] After the fight for independence begin to settle, the people, the subjects of these colonial empires did not enter global politics as full-fledged participants, but as a people that were ruled—alien *Others* in their own ancestral lands. [103] The various processes that were used to dehumanize African peoples to justify their domination, was easily translated to them being defined as incompetent and undeserving of the ability to govern themselves. Afterall, they are deemed to be a backward people.

Accordingly, U.S. and European intermediaries were formed to *speak for* and *on behalf* of the subjected peoples who were judged to be backward. [104] This way of interacting is found in the dominant human rights praxis. The historical consequences and contemporary implications of direct imperialism and (neo)colonialism are overlooked, and in most cases eagerly defined as being irrelevant. [105] This is especially the case since we are now largely considered to be in the era of post-colonial, post-race, post-everything that links inequities to the cultural-ideological worldview and interests of the dominant class. The ideas of justice, equality, and freedom are severely degenerate when transformed into a means for establishing and maintaining authority for an elite class. [106]

REFERENCES

[1] Makau Mutua, "Standard Setting in Human Rights: Critique and Prognosis," *Human Rights Quarterly*, 29(3), (2007): 547-630; Jack Donnelly, *Universal Human Rights in Theory and Practice*, Ithaca, New York: Cornell University Press, 2003; Johannes Morsink, *The Universal*

Declaration of Human Rights: Origins, Drafting and Intent, Pennsylvania: University of Pennsylvania Press, 2000; David Forsythe, *Human Rights in International Relations*, 2nd edition, New York: Cambridge University Press, 2006; Thomas Buergenthal, *Human Rights in a Nutshell*, 3rd edition, St. Paul Minnesota: West Publishing Company, 2002.

[2] Mary Glendon, "Knowing the Universal Declaration of Human Rights," *Notre Dame Law Review*, 73(5), (1998): 1153-1190.

[3] Henry Steiner, "Political Participation as a Human Right," *Harvard Human Rights Yearbook*, 1 Spring, (1988): 77-134; Makau Mutua, "Standard Setting in Human Rights: Critique and Prognosis," *Human Rights Quarterly*, 29, (2007), 547-630.

[4] Philip Alston and Henry Steiner, *International Human Rights in Context: Law, Politics, Morals, 2nd edition*, Oxford: Oxford University Press, 2000.

[5] Office of United Nations High Commissioner for Human Rights (OHCHR), "Human Rights Corpus," retrieved April 20, 2011, from: http://www2.ohchr.org/english/law/

[6] Forsythe, *Human Rights in International Relations*; Donnelly, *Universal Human Rights in Theory and Practice.*

[7] Sarah Mendelson, "Dusk or Dawn for the Human Rights Movement?," *Washington Quarterly*, 32(2), (2009): 103-120.

[8] Office of the United Nations High Commissioner for Human Rights, "Core International Human Rights Instruments," retrieved April 22, 2011, from: http://www2.ohchr.org_/english/law/

[9] Steiner, Henry J., Ryan Goodman & Philip Alston, *International Human Rights in Context: Law, Politics, Morals* Oxford: Oxford University Press, 2008.

[10] The grand narrative of the human rights discourse contains a subtext which depicts an epochal contest pitting savages on one side and victims and saviors on the other. This narrative was constructed by thinkers, scholars, and jurists in the 16th, 17th, and 18th century. It is now being refined, implemented, and expanded by the 'modern authors' of the human rights discourse which includes the United Nations, Western states, international NGOs, senior Western academics, practitioners, advocates, and some activist. This idea is explored in more detail by Makau Mutua, see: Makau Mutua, "Savages, Victims, and Saviors: the Metaphor of Human Rights," *Harvard International Law Journal*, 42(1), (2001): 201-245.

[11] The period between the 1940s and 1950s witnessed crisis and opportunity not only in global political and economic relationships, but also in struggles for freedom in the African world. With the end of WWII, African and Diasporic (Africana) resistance rested on the praxis of individuals and institutions that were forged in an anti-colonial, anti-imperialist, and anti-racist ideology. They represent the 'avant garde international left' (See Penny Von Eschen, *Race Against Empire: Black Americans and Anti-Colonialism, 1937-1957,* Ithaca, New York: Cornell University Press, 1997). This group of activist/scholars sought to find ideological symmetry and behavioral expression with radical elements all over the Africana world. They consisted of individuals and organizations such as W.E. B. Du Bois, Paul Robeson, C. L. R. James, Claudia Jones, William Patterson, Council on African Affairs, National Negro Congress (Civil Rights Congress), Southern Negro Youth Congress to name a few. To be more clear, this concept is expanded and defined because within their praxis we find several important and interdependent points of continuity: there was a clear presence of internationalism; clear efforts in creating a counter discourse—verbal and/or written; a deep understanding of human rights; a clear revolutionary—based ideological frame of reference that guides liberation efforts; and clear adherence to the importance of creating institutions which embodied these components in a concerted and sustained effort for a (re)ordering of fundamental social, economic, political, cultural structures. The motivating impetus of their efforts was an understanding that race and racism was rooted in capitalism and imperialism. It was argued that the bonds in which black Americans shared with colonized people were rooted not only in common culture but a shared history of the racism spawned by slavery, colonialism, and imperialism (Jack O'Dell, *Climbin Jacobs Ladder: The Black Freedom Movement Writings of Jack O'Dell* , Nikhil Singh (editor), California: University of California Press, 2010).

[12] Audrey Smedley, *Race in North America: Origin and Evolution of a Worldview*, Colorado: Westview Press, 1999, 1.

[13] Ibid.

[14] Alice Littlefield, "Redefining Race: The Potential Demise of a Concept in Physical Anthropology," *Current Anthropology*, 23(6), (1982): 641-656; Smedley, *Race in North America: Origin and Evolution of a Worldview,* 2.

[15] ibid; ibid.

[16] Smedley, *Race in North America: Origin and Evolution of a Worldview.*
[17] Ibid.
[18] Smedley, *Race in North America: Origin and Evolution of a Worldview,* 37.
[19] Ibid.
[20] Ibid.
[21] H. W. Fowler, *A Dictionary of Modern English Usage*, New York: Oxford University Press, 2009 [1926]; 1962; Smedley, *Race in North America: Origin and Evolution of a Worldview.*
[22] Cedric Dover, "Letter to the Editor," *Man*, April, number 9, 1951.
[23] Ibid.
[24] J. C. Tevor, "Letter to the Editor," *Man*, April, number 96, 1951, This was in response to the Letter to the Editor that was written by Dover in number 95; Smedley, *Race in North America: Origin and Evolution of a Worldview,*38.
[25] Ibid.
[26] Leo Spitzer, *Essays in Historical Semantics*, New York: S. F. Vanni, 1948.
[27] The Oxford English Dictionary of Historical Principles, Oxford: Oxford University Press, 2007 [1933].
[28] James Myers, *Elizabethan Ireland*, Hamden, Connecticut: Archon Books, 1983; Smedley, *Race in North America: Origin and Evolution of a Worldview.*
[29] Smedley, *Race in North America: Origin and Evolution of a Worldview,* 38-39.
[30] Ibid.
[31] George Frederickson, (2002) *Racism: A Short History*, Princeton, New Jersey: Princeton University Press.
[32] Smedley, *Race in North America: Origin and Evolution of a Worldview, 39.*
[33] Ibid.
[34] Ibid.
[35] ibid, 40.
[36] Oliver Cox, *Caste, Class and Race: A Study in Social Dynamics*, New York: Monthly Review Press, 1948.
[37] For a discussion on hegemony and consent see: Antonio Gramsci, *The Antonio Gramsci Reader: Selected Writings, 1916-1935*, David Forgacs (editor) New York: New York University Press, 2000 Smedley, *Race in North America: Origin and Evolution of a Worldview,*8-9.

[38] ibid, 3.
[39] ibid, 5.
[40] Ibid.
[41] ibid, 7.
[42] Ibid.
[43] Alain Locke, *Race Contacts and Interracial Relations*, Washington, D.C.: Howard University Press, 1992.
[44] See Karl Marx, (1845-46) *German Ideology.*
[45] Locke, *Race Contacts and Interracial Relations,* 22.
[46] ibid, 23.
[47] Smedley, *Race in North America: Origin and Evolution of a Worldview.*
[48] ibid, 8.
[49] Ibid.
[50] ibid, 14.
[51] Clarence Lusane, *Race in the Global Era: African Americans at the Millennium*, Boston: South End Press, 1997, xvi.
[52] Ibid.
[53] ibid, xv.
[54] ibid, 137.
[55] Kimberlé Williams Crenshaw, "Color-Blind Dreams and Racial Nightmares: Reconfiguring Racism in the Post-Civil Rights Era," in Toni Morrison and Claudia Lacour, (eds.), *Birth of a Nation 'hood*, (New York: Pantheon, 1997).
[56] Lusane, *Race in the Global Era: African Americans at the Millennium,* 137-138.
[57] Makau Mutua, *Human Rights: A Political and Cultural Critique*, Philadelphia: University of Pennsylvania Press, 2004.
[58] The use of first, second, third; developed, developing, underdeveloped, etcetera as a descriptive of other regions of the world is a glaring indicator of the reality in promoting and propagating counter-productive ideologies that function and flourish in the ideas and behaviors of the dominant culture guiding, ordering, structuring human interactions. The use of language is an important tool in promoting peace and cooperation or oppression and violence.
[59] Samuel Huntington, *Clash Of Civilizations: The Remaking of World Order*, New York: Simon & Schuster, 1998.
[60] Charles Mills, *The Racial Contract*, Ithaca: Cornell University Press, 1997.

[61] Eduardo Bonilla-Silva, "Look, A Negro": Reflections on the Human Rights Approach to Racial Inequality," in Angela Hattery, David Embrick, and Earl Smith (eds.), *Globalization and America*, (New York: Rowman & LittleField Publishers, 2008), 9-21.

[62] Stephen Castles and Alastair Davidson, *Citizenship and Migration: Globalization and the Politics of Belonging*, New York: Routledge, 2000; Cheikh Anta Diop, *Pre-colonial Black Africa*, New York: Lawrence Hill Books, 1987.

[63] Castles and Davidson, *Citizenship and Migration: Globalization and the Politics of Belonging*; Bonilla-Silva, "*Look, A Negro:" Reflections on the Human Rights Approach to Racial Inequality,"*10.

[64] Eric Morton, Race and Racism in the Works of David Hume, *Journal on African Philosophy,* 1(1), (2002)1-27; David Hume, Of National Character, in *The Philosophical Works of David Hume*, Volume III, Bristol: Thoemmes Press, 1996: 1753, 228; David Goldberg, *Racist Culture*, London: Blackwell, 1993.

[65] Emmanuel Eze, "The Color of Reason: The Idea of Race in Kant's Anthropology," in Katherine Faull (ed.), *Anthropology and the German Enlightenment*, (Pennsylvania: Bucknell University Press, 1995), 196-237; Mills, 1997: 70; Immanuel Kant, *Observations on the Feeling of the Beautiful and Sublime*, translated by John T. Goldthwait, Berkeley: University of California Press, 1960, 111-113.

[66] Curtis Stokes, "Introduction," in Curtis Stokes (ed.), *Race and Human Rights,* (Michigan: Michigan State University Press, 2005), xiv; Richard Overton, "An Arrow Against All Tyrants," in Andrew Sharp (ed.), *The English Levelers: Cambridge Texts in the History of Political Thought*, (Cambridge: Cambridge University Press, 1646; 1998), 54.

[67] John Locke, *Two Treaties of Government.*

[68] Stokes, *Race and Human Rights,* xiv.

[69] Ibid.

[70] Ibid.

[71] Christopher Hill, *Winstanley: The Law of Freedom and Other Writings*, Cambridge: Cambridge University Press, 2006; Stokes, *Race and Human Rights,* xiv; Gerrard Winstanley, "*A Declaration From the Poor People of England, 1649,"* available at http://www.bilderberg.org/land /poor.htm; David Petegorsky, *Left-Wing Democracy in the English Civil War*, London: Alan Sutton Publishing, 1997.

[72] Lynn Hunt, *Inventing Human Rights*, New York: W. W. Norton and Company, 2008; The *French Revolution and Human Rights: A Brief Documented History*, New York: Bedford/St Martin's, 1996.

[73] Joe Feagin, *Racist America: Roots, Current Realities, and Future Reparations*, New York: Routledge, 2000; Ronald Walters, *The Price of Reconciliation*, Michigan: University of Michigan Press, 2008; Randall Robinson, *The Debt: What America Owns Black America*, New York: Plume, 2001; Ambrose Lane, *For Whites Only? How and Why America Became a Racist Nation*, 2nd edition, Indiana: Author house, 2008.

[74] Castles & Davidson, *Citizenship and Migration: Globalization and the Politics of Belonging,* 48; Bonilla-Silva, *"Look, A Negro:" Reflections on the Human Rights Approach to Racial Inequality,"* 10.

[75] Castles and Davidson, *Citizenship and Migration: Globalization and the Politics of Belonging,*50; Bonilla-Silva, "*Look, A Negro;" Reflections on the Human Rights Approach to Racial Inequality,*"11.

[76] Delivered on July 5, 1852, Fredrick Douglas was asked to give a speech at an event commemorating the signing of the Declaration of Independence, held at Rochester's Corinthian Hall.

[77] Castles and Davidson, *Citizenship and Migration: Globalization and the Politics of Belonging*; Also see, Ayi Kwei Armah, *Two Thousand Seasons*, Chicago: Third World Press, 1980.

[78] Donnelly, *Universal Human Rights in Theory and Practice.*

[79] Stokes, *Race and Human Rights,* xix.

[80] These limitations were illuminated by Eduardo Bonilla-Silva and are presented and elaborated upon here.

[81] Bonilla-Silva, *"Look, A Negro:" Reflections on the Human Rights Approach to Racial Inequality,"*11.

[82] For more see: Angela Hattery, David Hambrick, and Earl Smith, *Globalization and America*, Lanham Maryland: Rowman & Littlefield, 2008.

[83] Lani Guinier and Gerald Torres, *The Miner's Canary: Enlisting Race, Resisting Power, Transforming Democracy*, Cambridge, Mass: Harvard University Press, 2002; Bonilla-Silva, "*Look, A Negro;" Reflections on the Human Rights Approach to Racial Inequality,*" 11.

[84] Bonilla-Silva, *"Look, A Negro:" Reflections on the Human Rights Approach to Racial Inequality".*

[85] Guinier and Torres, *The Miner's Canary: Enlisting Race, Resisting Power, Transforming Democracy.*

[86] Bonilla-Silva, *"Look, A Negro:" Reflections on the Human Rights Approach to Racial Inequality".*

[87] David Goldberg, *The Racial State*, London: Blackwell, 2001; Bonilla-Silva, *"Look, A Negro:" Reflections on the Human Rights Approach to Racial Inequality,"* 12.

[88] Ernst Cassirer, *The Myth of the State*, Connecticut: Yale University Press, 1961; Robert Dahl, *Pluralist Democracy in the United States: Conflict and Consent*, Chicago: Rand McNally, 1968; Cedric Robinson, *Black Marxism: The Making of the Black Radical Tradition*, Chapel Hill, North Carolina: University of North Carolina Press, 1983, 186; Karl Marx & Friedrich Engels, *Collected Works of Karl Marx and Friedrich Engels, 1845-1847, vol. 5*, New York: International Publishers, 1976

[89] Eric Hobsbawm, *Nations and Nationalism since 1780: Programme, Myth, Reality, 2nd ed.* Massachusetts: Cambridge University Press, 1992; Benedict Anderson, *Imagined Communities: Reflections on the Origin and Spread of Nationalism*, New York: Verso, 1991; Basil Davidson, *The Black Man's Burden: Africa and the Curse of the Nation-State*, New York: Three Rivers Press, 1992.

[90] Robinson, *Black Marxism: The Making of the Black Radical Tradition,*186.

[91] Ferdinand Lundberg and Carol Bram, *Cracks in the Constitution*, New York: Lyle Stuart, Inc., 1982; Robinson, *Black Marxism: The Making of the Black Radical Tradition*, 186.

[92] Evelyn Glenn, *Unequal Freedom: How Race and Gender Shaped American Citizenship and Labor*, Cambridge, Mass.: Harvard University Press, 2002, 14-15; Bonilla-Silva, *"Look, A Negro:" Reflections on the Human Rights Approach to Racial Inequality,"* 12.

[93] Alejandro Portes and Patricia Landolt, The Downside of Social Capital, *The American Prospect*, 26,(1996):18-25.

[94] Ibid.

[95] Neil Stammers, *Human Rights and Social Movements*, London: Pluto Press, 2009; Howard, *Human Rights and the Search for Community,* 46.

[96] Timothy Gaffaney, *Freedom for the Poor: Welfare and the Foundations of Democratic Citizenship*, Boulder, Colorado: Westview Press, 2000.

[97] Timothy Gaffaney, *Freedom for the Poor: Welfare and the Foundations of Democratic Citizenship*; Cairns, "Empire, Globalization, and the Fall and Rise of Diversity."; Edward Said, *Culture and Imperialism*, New York: Vintage Books, 1993; Castles and Davidson, *Citizenship and Migration: Globalization and the Politics of Belonging;* Daniele

Archibugi, David Held, and Martin Kohler, *Re-Imaging Political Community: Studies in Cosmopolitan Democracy*, California: Stanford University Press, 1998..

[98] Sophie Body-Gendrot and Marilyn Gittel, Empowering Citizens: From Social Citizenship to Social Capital in Sophie Body-Gendrot and Marilyn Gittel (eds.), *Social Capital and Social Citizenship,* (Lanham, Maryland: Lexington Books, 2003).

[99] The Human Development Index (HDI) is a composite statistic used to rank countries by level of "human development" and separate developed (high development), developing (middle development), and underdeveloped (low development) countries. The statistic is composed from data on life expectancy, education and per-capita GDP (as an indicator of standard of living) collected at the national level. They are found in the United Nations Development Program's (UNDP) Human Development Reports (HDRs). For more information see: http://hdr.undp.org/en/. In addition to these reports, other statistics collected by international NGOs, IGOs, activist and advocacy groups (such as Human Rights Watch, Doctors Without Borders, and Oxfam), and think tanks, such as Institute for Policy Studies in Washington, DC).

[100] Bonilla-Silva, *"Look, A Negro:" Reflections on the Human Rights Approach to Racial Inequality".*

[101] This fact has been thoroughly developed in the work of scholars in the Dependency school. Individuals found within this tradition are Andre Gunder Frank, Samir Amin, and Immanuel Wallerstein; Walter Rodney, *How Europe Underdeveloped Africa*, Washington, DC: Howard University Press, 1981; Manning Marable, *How Capitalism Underdeveloped Black America*, Cambridge, Mass.: Southend Press, 1999.

[102] Beetham, *Democracy and Human Rights*; Bonilla-Silva, *Look, A Negro:" Reflections on the Human Rights Approach to Racial Inequality,"* 13.

[103] Robinson, *Black Marxism: The Making of the Black Radical Tradition*; Alan Cairns, Empire, Globalization, and the Fall and Rise of Diversity in Alan Carins, John Courtney, Peter MacKinnon, Hans Michelmann, and David Smith (eds.), *Citizenship, Diversity, and Pluralism: Canadian and Comparative Perspectives*, (Montreal: McGill-Queen's University Press, 1999); Edward Said, .

[104] Edward Said, *Culture and Imperialism*, New York: Vintage Books, 1993; Cairns, "*Empire, Globalization, and the Fall and Rise of Diversity*".

[105] Cairns, "*Empire, Globalization, and the Fall and Rise of Diversity*";Kwame Nkrumah, *Neo-colonialism: The Last Stage of Imperialism*, New Jersey: Humanities Press International, 1965.

[106] Douglas Lummis, *Radical Democracy*, Ithaca, New York: Cornell University Press, 1996: 20

In: Africa
Editor: Olayiwola Abegunrin
ISBN: 978-1-62948-561-4

Chapter 9

The Historical and Strategic Significance of Africa in World Affairs

Olayiwola Abegunrin
Professor of International Relations and African Studies,
Department of Political Science, Howard University,
Washington, D.C., US

> "It is impossible to separate the affairs of Africa from the affairs of the world as a whole. Not only has the history of Africa been too closely involved with Europe and the Western hemisphere, but that very involvement has been the driving force in bringing about major wars and international conflicts for which Africans have not been responsible. Africa has too long been the victim of disruptive aggression, which still attempts to make a hunting ground of our continent." [1]

Africa: The Cradle of Mankind

Geography is the mother of history. Nowhere in the world is this more powerfully illustrated than in Africa. The most potent force in Africa's experience is Africa's environment, the combined elements of geo-physical features, location and climate. Together they have given rise to three momentous paradoxes of the African history. First, Africa has been a continent of abundant natural resources but the poorest continent. Second, partly because of this paradox, Africa has been the first habitat of Man but the last to become habitable. And thirdly, linked to these two ironies is the contradiction of Africa as a cradle of civilization but most of its first fifty years of independence is pre-occupied of instability and civil wars. [2]

The British naturalist/Scientist Charles Darwin first proposed his theory of evolution in 1859 in his book (*The Origin of Species*). [3] When he finally applied this theory to the origins of human beings in 1871 (*The descent of Man*), [4] he suggested that the birthplace of humankind was probably Africa. At that time in the middle and late nineteen century, Darwin's theory of evolution provoked serious controversy all over Europe. First, for religious reasons; because Darwin's theory challenged the Biblical belief that God created humankind and all other living creatures in a single, spontaneous seven days of creation. [5] Second, Darwin's theory of evolution publications came at the peak of European colonialism and imperial expansion around the world and particularly in Africa. Consequently, Darwin's theory challenged the European notions of racial superiority. With Darwin's theory the Europeans found it very difficult to accept that their own ancient ancestors had originally descended from Africa, a place the Europeans called the *Dark Continent.* However, since the 1930s scientific research in the savannah grasslands and woodlands of eastern, southern, and northern Africa have provided sufficient evidence to confirm the truth of Darwin's theory; that Africa is indeed the cradle of humankind. [6]

In 1931 Louis Leakey from Kenya discovered on Rusinga Island in Lake Victoria a creature in the ape line, called *proconsul,* with a larger brain than any preceding primate and eyes more clearly focused in stereoscopic vision. This *proconsul* was found in a geological stratum dated to about twenty-five million years ago. Again in 1959 Leakey and his wife Mary Leakey found in the Olduvai Gorge in Tanzania the skull of a more advanced creature they called *Zinjanthropus*, man of *Zinj* (the early Arab name for East Africa). *Zinjanthropus* was found with chipped pebble tools. Potassium argon dating carried out by scientists from the University of California at Berkeley conclusively established that Zinjathropus lived between one and a half, one and three-quarter million years ago. According to Ali Mazrui:

> Further evidence to suggest that Africa is probably Man's first home came in 1984, when two Kenyans Kamoya Kimeu and Richard Leakey, son of Louis Leakey, discovered much of a skeleton of a twelve-year-old boy in a swamp on the western shore of Lake Turkana. The boy seems to have been

> an example of Homo erectus, one step along in the evolutionary scale between Homo habilis and Homo sapiens, *the thinking man or modern man*. All these archaeological discoveries increase the possibility that human genesis occurred in Africa; that if there is a Garden of Eden where the first man and woman lived, that garden was in Africa. [7]

Thus, Africa is not merely the probable cradle of Man and its initial culture; the continent is also the genesis of civilization. [8]

Africa is a paradox which illustrates and highlights neo-colonialism. Her earth is rich, yet the products that come from above and below her soil continue to enrich, not Africans predominantly but groups and individuals who operate to Africa's impoverishment. With an estimated population of one billion, about twelve percent of the world's population, Africa accounts for only two percent of the world's total production. Yet survey of Africa's natural resources show the continent to have immense, untapped wealth. Africa's iron reserves are put at twice the size of United States' and two-thirds those of the former Soviet Union's on the basis of an estimated two billion metric tons. Africa's calculated coal reserves are considered to be enough to last for three hundred years. [9] Today, new petroleum fields are being discovered and brought into production all over the continent. Africa has more than forty percent of the world's potential water power, a greater share than any other continent. However, production of primary ores and minerals, considerable as it appears, has touched only the fringes of the African population.

Africa is the second largest continent in size in the world next to Asia. [10] While it is the most central of all the continents in geographical location, politically, economically and militarily, it is the most marginal continent. [11] Physically, it is divided almost in half by the equator and the only continent traversed by the tropics of Cancer and Capricorn. Economically, it is very strategically placed in relations to the oil routes and some critical as well as essential minerals of the world. [12] Paradoxically, its political leverage in world affairs is insignificant or at best, modest. What then are implications of Africa being historically important, physically central and strategically located, but politically peripheral to the world affairs? Physically on the map of the world, as noted above, Africa is not only firmly central and strategically located. It is also the only continent that is cut almost into two halves by the equator and is traversed by the Tropics of Cancer and Capricorn. Africa is bounded by the two busiest Oceans in maritime and trade activities, the Atlantic Ocean to the South and West, and the Indian Ocean to the East. [13]

To the North-East is the Red Sea, and to the North of Africa lays the biggest and busiest land-bound waterway in the World, the Mediterranean Sea.

In addition, Africa's centrality has other dimensions. Africa has one of the oldest commercial routes to the Far East, dating back to the 15th century when Vasco da Gama, the Portuguese's explorer, landed in Mozambique in 1482 in his efforts to find a sea route to India and the Far East. [14] Circumventing the African continent by way of the Cape Sea route in the south was part of this process of facilitating Europe's maritime trade and communication with the countries in Asia, South-East Asia and the Pacific Islands.

Second, the Ocean route around the African continent remains very important and essential for Euro-Asian communications and commerce from the days of the spice trade in the fifteenth Century to the period of Industrial Revolution in the ninetieth century, and to date. The Cape route along the South African Coast has served the cause of rubber trade from Malaya, Jute from India, wood and meat from Australia and New Zealand, and precious metals and spices from the Asian continent. These same routes have served textiles and industrial equipment trade from Europe to the Asian and Pacific countries.

Third, strategically Africa is the gateway to Eastern and Western Europe. Africa's sea route is the lifeline for the oil trade with Europe and North America. The sea-lanes around the Northeast Coast of Africa (especially the Red Sea and the Mediterranean Sea) made it economically cheaper to transport petroleum and other products from the Middle East and the Gulf States Region to Europe and North America. Two million barrels of oil/petroleum are shipped through the Suez Canal every day. Starting from the 1970s, the Indian Ocean carried 40 percent of British's trade and about 25 percent of Japanese's trade. Since the 1960s and the beginning of the twenty-first century, virtually most of the exported petroleum products (oil) from the Middle-East to Europe and to North America needed the two basic and vital African routes either passing through the Suez Canal in the Northern-Eastern Africa or the Cape Sea route in the Southern Africa. [15]

Strategic Importance of Africa's Mineral Resources in the Global Economy

Economically and strategically, Africa is very important in terms of supply of many strategic minerals to the global economy (see table 9.1), particularly Europe, North America and China. [16] While Africa produces and has ten of the most highly sought after minerals and agricultural products including gold, diamond, uranium, oil, cobalt, zinc, copper, chrome, platinum, coltan, exotic woods, cocoa, rubber, and coffee. South Africa is the world's largest producer of gold. Globally, South Africa is one of the world's leading mining countries with many quantities and a broad range of mineral reserves. It has the world's largest reserves of platinum, manganese, chrome and gold. [17] In addition, Africa has the best diamond and the largest reserves of this strategic mineral in the world. [18]

Table 9.1. Africa's Strategic Minerals

Oil
Uranium
Diamond
Gold
Natural Gas
Coltan
Copper
Cobalt
Platinum
Chrome
Manganese
Iron ore
Bauxite
Phosphates
Potassium
Coal
Vanadium
Zinc

Sources: compiled by the Author, Olayiwola Abegunrin.

To demonstrate the strategic importance of Africa's natural resources to the global community it should be noted that the uranium used for the "Atomic Bomb developed by the United States, under the Manhattan Project, and deployed in Hiroshima and Nagasaki, Japan to end the Second World War in 1945, was obtained from Africa, specifically, from (former Belgian Congo) the Democratic Republic of Congo (DRC)." [19]

This evidence was confirmed in Albert Einstein's letter of August 2, 1939, to President Franklin Roosevelt in which he states that: "The United States has only very poor ores of uranium in moderate quantities. There is some good ore in Canada and Czechoslovakia, while the most important source of uranium is the Belgium Congo" [20] In addition, the Democratic Republic of Congo is the world's largest producer of cobalt. Cobalt is a very essential and important mineral which is used chiefly for magnetic alloys. Another very important mineral produce in Africa is coltan.

Eighty percent of world production of Coltan which is a very essential mineral for the production of cell phone is produce in the Democratic Republic of Congo. [21] Of all of Africa's strategic minerals, the most exploited by Europe and North America is uranium, which has acquired prominence in the global community, particularly in this age of nuclear proliferation. Uranium has been mostly exploited in Namibia, South Africa, Congo, Niger Republic, and Republic of Chad. Republic of Mali is now producing uranium, gold and oil. [22]

For a long time, uranium in South Africa was extracted mostly as a byproduct from the country's gold mines, with the bulk of production mined by Anglo-American Corporation, Gold Fields, and General Mining Corporation.

The first ore company to concentrate production on uranium, Beisa Mine in the Central Free State Province in South Africa was commissioned in 1981. With uranium output of 1,093 tons in 1999, [23] South Africa is the third largest uranium producer in Africa, and one of the world's leading producers. Namibia is Africa's largest uranium producer with 6,689 tons in 1999, and the world's fourth largest producer. Rossing Uranium, a Namibia based subsidiary of the Rio Tinto Group, which has its headquarters in London and Melbourne, Australia, noted that, "Namibia will be able to supply a growing global demand for nuclear fuel as well as potential nuclear plants in Namibia." [24] Republic of Niger is Africa's second producer of uranium, and is one of the world's leading producers. [25]

The major customers for the Namibian, Nigerien, and South African uranium are the European countries, and the United States. Africa's iron ore reserves are twice those of the United States, and its reserves of chrome are the most important and the largest outside Russia. United States imports 98 percent of its manganese needs with Africa accounting for 50 percent. [26]

Table 9.2. The Ten Top Diamond Producing Countries in the World

Rank	Country	% of World-wide Production	Rank	Country	Value in U.S. Dollars
1	Russia	22.40%	1	Botswana	$2,940
2	Botswana	19.90%	2	Russia	$1,989
3	Democratic Republic of Congo	18.60%	3	Canada	$1,646
4	Australia	13.20%	4	South Africa	$1,458
5	South Africa	9.10%	5	Angola	$1,300
6	Canada	8.10%	6	Democratic Republic of Congo	$790
7	Angola	4.80%	7	Namibia	$698
8	Namibia	1.30%	8	Australia	$343
9	Ghana	0.60%	9	Other	$132
10	Brazil	0.40%	10	Brazil	$35
	Other	1.50%			
		100.00%			

Sources: www.cheap-diamond.com/countries.

Nearly half of the world's diamonds come from Africa, especially West, Central and Southern Africa. And since 2005, Zimbabwe [27] has become one of the leading diamond producing countries in Africa. In Southern Africa, investors from Britain, the United States, and especially De Beers Corporation, plays a dominant role in Africa's diamond industry. Botswana is the world's leading producer of gem quality diamonds producing 28.4 million carats in 2002, and 30.4 million carats in 2003 with the diamond industry accounting for 83 per cent of Botswana's export earnings. Indeed, six of the ten largest diamond producing countries in the world (Russia, Botswana, Democratic Republic of Congo, Australia, South Africa, Canada, Angola, Namibia, Ghana, and Brazil), are in Africa (see table 9.2). [28]

Historically, Cecil Rhodes set up the mining company De Beers in South Africa in 1888. De Beers was the name of the Boer/white farm where the first diamond was found in 1867 in South Africa. [29] It should be noted that the farmer De Beers, illegally occupied African land (Griqualand) where the first diamond was found in South Africa. By 1893, Cecil Rhodes (a white settler) began excluding everybody else from the diamond selling business. However, he gave the contract to 10 Jewish firms in London, to sell African gems (diamond). With this contract, Rhodes gave them a boost and an advantage which they maintain up to the present day. In 1947, the World Diamond Congress was formed by these same firms, but has no single African representative on its governing body. [30] Cecil Rhodes, a British colonizer/setter, and imperialist made fortune from gold and diamond in Southern Africa in the nineteenth century with his British South African Chartered Company (BSAC). With the wealth he acquired from diamond, and gold in Southern Africa, he endowed Annual Rhodes scholarships in 1902 for Commonwealth and United States students to study at Oxford University. Ironically, Africans were excluded out of the Rhodes' Will Statement. [31] Initially, Africans were not supposed to go to Oxford University as Rhodes' Scholars, although the endowment came from the African resources of diamonds and gold.

AFRICA'S GROWING IMPORTANCE IN THE GLOBAL ECONOMY

The U.S. House of Representatives Subcommittee on Africa barely a month after September 11 observed that the policy of putting Africa on the back burner could no longer continue. Thus, later in 2002 policymakers at a Conference at the Center for Strategic and International Studies in Washington, D.C. confirmed that the African continent must be seen as strategically important to the United States interests, largely because of terrorism and oil. [32] It should be remembered that the formulation of the U.S. policy towards Africa, since the 1950s under President Eisenhower, has always been based on the strategic importance of mineral resources of the continent for the national interest of the United States. [33] The United States' interest in Africa's oil continues to increase significantly, and it will continue for a long time.

The U.S. Navy has installed a radar system in Sao Tome and Principe to guarantee maritime security in the Gulf of Guinea, a Key West African supplier to the U.S. oil market. [34] "It has been estimated that imports of African oil reached 921 million barrels or 18.7 percent of the U.S. total in 2005, surpassing imports from the Middle East, which were 839 million barrels, or 17 percent. Imports from Africa have increased by 51 percent since

2000 at the same time supplies from the Middle East fell from more than 900 million barrels to 839 million or from 22 percent to 17 percent of total U.S. imports." [35] A former Assistant Secretary of State for African Affairs, Charles Snyder once said that:

> It used to be kind of a cruel joke twenty years ago when some of us tried to pretend Africa might rise to the level of a strategic interest, but thanks to the oil deposits that we are finding every day in Africa. I can say with a straight face 30 percent of our oil will come from there, and I promise you it is a strategic interest. [36]

Adding to the supply uncertainties, the United States faces new competition for oil from an energy-hungry China. In January 2006, China's state-run oil corporation -China National Oil Corporation (CNOOC) paid $2.3 billion for 45 percent stake in Nigeria's offshore oil. [37] In addition to investments in oil, agriculture, and infrastructure, China secured a $311 million contract with the Nigerian Government in 2004 to build and launch a communications satellite known as NIGCOMSAT-1. When this satellite is completed it will provide communications services over Africa and parts of the Middle East and Southern Europe. A Chinese state-owned Aerospace Company, Great Wall Industry Corporation, will monitor the satellite from a ground station in northwestern China. It will also train Nigerian engineers to operate a tracking station, and manage the satellite from a control station in Nigeria. [38] A new 150-bed hospital was commissioned in January 2013 in Abuja, capital of Nigeria, in partnership with China. Known as the China-Nigeria Friendship Hospital, marks the 42nd anniversary of the establishment of diplomatic relations between China and Nigeria. [39]

The Forum on Sino-China-African Cooperation held in Beijing in November 2006 was attended by 48 African Heads of State and Government. [40] The forum was given wide global prominence as a pointer to several of the Sino-African dynamic. The Summit approved a three year action plan to create a "new strategic partnership" between China and Africa based on equality and mutual benefit. The Plan included a doubling of aid to Africa from 2006 levels by 2009, a $5 billion China-Africa Development Fund, and as of 2012 this fund has been increased to $10 billion, [41] debt cancellations, and a further opening of the Chinese markets to exports from Africa by increasing from 190 to 400 products.

The *new strategic partnership* between Africa and China also intends to increase the number of products receiving zero-tariff treatment, and pledged to build 30 hospitals, 30 malaria treatment centers, and 100 rural schools in African countries. [42] China is also helping in agriculture and food security, in its attempts to improve food production in African countries in areas such as irrigation, fertilizer, storage and research into variety of seeds.

UNITED STATES POLICY TOWARD AFRICA SINCE SEPTEMBER 11, 2001

According to current estimate, by 2015 Africa will be supplying the United States 25 percent of its oil needs. Many African countries are now oil producers (see table 9.3 for details). Africa has the best light crude Petroleum, especially, Nigeria with Bonny light crude and sulfur free which is highly prized in the Global oil market because it is easily refined into gasoline. [43] The Gulf of Guinea, starting from Angola all the way to Senegal is very strategic in energy supply to the United States and the global economy. "More than one hundred thousand jobs in the United States, notably, in Texas, Louisiana and California are linked to African oil investments, and this is increasing annually." [44]

One of the hottest foreign policy issues since 2000 in the United States is energy independence, largely because the United States has been unable to find alternative sources of energy. The world is reaching oil peak as the situation concerning its price has shown since October 2007, when the price first reached $90 per barrel, and is destined to skyrocket as the supplies fail to meet increase demand. [45] In addition, the revolt in North Africa, starting in January 2011 in Tunisia and Egypt, sent fresh fears of supply crunch to the international oil market. [46]

Thus, as of July 2011, crude oil prices shot up to $108 per barrel according to the OPEC daily basket price. [47] The spring revolution in North Africa (in Tunisia, Egypt and Libya) has contributed to the rise in oil price. As far as crude oil is concerned, there is a possibility that the price may continue to rise because of the unstable global economy since 2008, and the price will continue to fluctuate. [48] Thus, anxiety of political violence and tension around the world, especially in North Africa and the Middle East had once again driven up the political premium for oil. [49]

Table 9.3. African Oil Production by Country, 1993-2003 (Thousand Barrels Per Day)

Year	1993	1994	1995	1996	1997	1998	1999	2000	2001	2002	2003
Algeria	1329	1324	1327	1386	1421	1461	1515	1576	1562	1681	1857
Angola	504	557	633	716	741	731	745	746	742	905	885
Benin	3	2	2	2	1	1	1	1	1	N/A	N/A
Cameroon	130	115	106	110	124	105	95	88	80	72	68
Chad	N/A	N/A	N/A	N/A	^	^	^	^	^	^	40
Congo Brazzaville	185	185	180	200	225	264	293	275	271	259	243
Congo (DRC)	25	25	28	30	28	26	24	25	24	23	22
Egypt	941	921	924	894	873	857	827	781	758	753	750
Equatorial Guinea	5	5	7	17	60	83	100	113	181	237	249
Gabon	305	337	356	365	364	337	340	327	301	295	240
Ghana	N/A	6	6	7	5	5	6	6	6	6	6
Ivory Coast	N/A	N/A	6	16	14	10	10	5	7	10	20
Libya	1402	1413	1439	1452	1489	1480	1425	1475	1425	1376	1488
Morocco	^	^	^	^	^	^	3	^	^	^	^
Nigeria	1985	1988	1998	2138	2302	2163	2128	2104	2199	2013	2185
Senegal	^	^	^	^	^	^	^	^	N/A	N/A	N/A
South Africa	8	9	9	8	15	15	32	32	23	20	16
Sudan	2	2	2	5	9	12	63	174	211	233	255
Tunisia	99	93	90	89	81	83	84	78	71	73	66
Uganda	N/A	N/A	N/A	N/A	^	^	^	^	5	5	10

N/A - Not Available.

^ - Less than 0.5.

Sources: BP Annual Statistical Review, and Oil and Gas Journal, 1993-2003.

After the September 11, 2001 attacks, the United States has pursued a more aggressive foreign policy towards Africa under the pretext that Africa now posse some national security threat to the United States. Intending to stabilize the continent in order to have access to Africa's natural resources to the benefit of United States interests, however, this policy is characterized by increased military cooperation between the Pentagon, State Department, and host African governments, as well as a more robust NATO/United States military presence throughout the continent. A good example is the 2011 NATO-U.S. war on Libya that led to the assassination of Muammar Ghaddafi on October 10, 2011. [50] The fact on the ground demonstrates that "United States policy goals are more focused on securing access to African resources, especially oil, through the militarization of individual African states' armed forces. These concrete transactions which make up the militarization efforts are providing intelligence, logistics, equipment, and counter terrorism training to host governments." [51]

In 2007, the George W. Bush administration created a separate Africa Command AFRICOM [52] to oversee military activity on the continent, fueling fears among Africans that the United States was militarizing its foreign policy toward Africa and looking to construct new military bases in the continent. Since 2007 U.S. has spent $1 billion in Trans-Saharan Africa in what is known as *Sahara Counter-terrorism strategy.* [53] In return the United States interests are favored above more domestically based economic, political, and social priorities. African leaders and above all, the African peoples should know their socio-economic and socio-political interests rather than just following the imperialists' national interest at their own expense. The results are African leaders with a well-armed military able to dominate their political rivals with the blessing of the United States under the disguise of War on Terror. [54] For instance, the 2006 Ethiopian invasion of Somalia on the ground that Somalia is a terrorist haven because is sympathetic to the terrorist cause that is spearheaded by AL Qaeda against the United States.

United States has raised its Africa priority after September 11, 2001, and shifted its policy focus by use of military and international institutions such as NATO and U.N. towards Africa. [55] Thus, what we have been witnessing appears to be the same policies of militarization and exploitation long familiar to the continent, especially since the Berlin Conference of the partition of Africa of 1884-1885, by the European leaders. [56]

THE BRICS AND THE SCRAMBLE FOR AFRICAN RESOURCES

The new entry of Brazil, Russia, India and China (BRICS) [57] that have literally invaded the continent of Africa and not with arms has demonstrated the strategic importance of Africa in the global economy. Instead, they have invaded Africa with money, goods, ideas, and drilling and mining equipment. The countries that were largely absent just a few years ago, the BRICS are now gradually but surely edging out Western countries in Africa in the areas of trade and investment, and to some degree development aid. Especially, India and China and to a certain degree Brazil have increased their engagement in Africa in dramatic ways. The BRICS countries are becoming major players in the continent, which has not only changed Africa's traditional trade and investment relations but also created significant opportunities and challenges for Africa's economies. There is no doubt that Africa's growth in the twenty-first century will be influenced by its relationship with the BRICS. [58]

One of the most important dimensions of this burgeoning relationship is foreign direct investment (FDI). Although most FDI to Africa still comes from the United States, Western Europe and Japan, the largest increases in FDI to Africa in recent years has come from the BRICS. Since 2001, FDI flows from the BRICS to Africa have increased consistently, only falling slightly in 2009 due to the global economic crisis. While the bulk (most) of the BRICS' FDI to Africa has been concentrated in Angola, South Africa, Nigeria, Sudan, Ghana, Libya and Morocco, the BRICS have recently taken a greater interest in investing in other countries across Africa. While this positive outlook for Africa since foreign direct investment can be a strong catalyst for economic growth and development, there are serious concerns over the BRIC countries' appetite for the African continent's natural resources. Some analysts have characterized the BRICS as leading a modern day scramble for Africa. However, the BRICS are already major players in the exploitation of key natural resources in Nigeria, Sudan, the Democratic Republic of Congo and Angola. For instance since 2008, Brazil and China have expanded their investments in oil in Angola, Nigeria and Sudan, in mining in Liberia and Mozambique, and in gas in Nigeria.

However, the BRICS are beginning to invest in other sectors of African economy as well. For example, India is diversifying its investment portfolio in Africa to include textiles, small and medium-sized enterprises, social services such as health and education, information, communication technology and automobiles. BRIC countries are also now heavily involved in massive construction projects all over Africa. [59] They are also involved in building of roads, dams, hydroelectric power stations, railways and buildings. In addition, trade between the BRICS and Africa has expanded greatly and in some cases the BRICS have replaced Africa's traditional trading partners, even though exports to the BRICS from Africa are still mainly dominated in natural resources. BRIC countries are also becoming important actors in development aid to Africa. In addition to concessionary and soft loans, lines of credits and grants, the BRICS and especially China, are providing project aid to expand and improve Africa's infrastructure. [60]

BRICS and Africa's Development

While the BRICS are opening up opportunities for Africa to diversify its trading partners in the new global markets and to forge new mutually beneficial partnerships, these opportunities come with major challenges. The new and recent attention on Africa by the BRICS is not solely based on an altruistic goal to improve the economic well-being of Africans. Rather, BRIC countries are trying to maximize their own strategic economic and political interests by engaging with African countries. Therefore, African policy makers and their leaders must also be strategic in thinking and in dealing with BRIC countries just as they should be with other foreign partners.

One issue that requires careful attention and management from African policy makers is natural resources exploitation contracts. There are growing concerns over the lack of transparency in the signing of these contracts with the BRICS. In some cases, BRIC countries seem unconcerned with corruption and may even be contributing to the survival unaccountable regimes. In addition, there are increasing concerns over BRIC projects in Africa that fail to maintain internationally accepted environmental standards. Therefore, African nations must invest in the contracting process and African policy makers must push for more transparency in the contracting process. The international community must also subject the BRICS to accepted accountability restraints with regard to the exploitation of natural resources.

The issue of growing project aid from the BRICS also requires some careful consideration by African leaders and policy makers. While such aid is helping Africa narrow the infrastructure gap, it is important that this aid not be used as a way to endow monopoly rights for the BRICS in the exploitations of

Africa's natural resources or to hold African countries hostage to future contracts related to new projects and maintenance. "Africa's relationship with emerging partners (BRICS) is more complex and will boost the continent if states negotiate wisely." [61]

Ultimately, African leaders and their policy makers must work to shift Africa's relationship with the BRIC s from the position based primarily on natural resources to one that advances the continent's long term economic growth and development trajectories. The prospects for long-term growth in African economies will depend on the transformation of their current production structures. Thus, African leaders and their policy makers must identify and demand that the BRICS focus on those investments that best contribute in the transformation and economic development of African continent.

CONCLUSION

African countries have all the weapons they could use to benefit from their economic resources, provided they could get all their forces together in a united front. "United we stand, divided we fall." African countries should come up with a new strategy on how they can benefit from their natural resources of the minerals, the black gold-oil, and blue gold-gas for the good and development of the continent of Africa for the African peoples.

The African countries/leaders should and need to unite and speak with one voice and use their God given rights-their natural resources which are highly in demand in the global markets as economic weapon of diplomacy-*soft power*, in negotiating with the Western, and BRICS Countries to win and gain their economic benefits and rights they deserve. It is not going to be easy for the African countries to get recognition from the West and gain economic benefits they deserve for their natural resources they produce and consume by the World powers. We have to sacrifice certain things and our leaders must behave them-selves, get their acts together as responsible leaders to be trusted and serve the interests of the African peoples, and not sold out to the (imperialists) outside powers, be it the Western powers or BRICS powers.

The psychological dependency on Western World orientation is a great weakness to African political leaders and above all to the new generation of African youths that are negatively affecting the socio-economic and socio-political development of the continent of Africa. This is very important and critical issue, and a potential crisis that the African leaders must face and address it seriously and find effective solutions before it is too late, because Africans are not only weak economically and unstable politically; but most important and very frightening is that Africans are losing their culture, values and ways of lives and even sense of African historical tradition of who we are and where are we going.

The history of Africa's political and military weaknesses, insecurity, dependency, economic underdevelopment and political instability has continued to haunt African leaders and thinkers. It was a small wonder that former President Ahmed Sekou Toure of Guinea once queried whether it was because of the "inferiority of Africa's means of self-defense that it was subjected to foreign domination." [62] Whereas Africa's political and military weaknesses served as a prelude to colonization, peace, security, and survival of the continent are very vital in the new scheme of international order. The scramble for African natural resources, and wealth, *the black gold-oil and the blue gold-gas* should not and must not be the priority or the yard stick for the Western and other Great Powers in their treatment of the Africans. Therefore, because of its strategic importance, economic potential and political relevance in the world affairs, Africa should not be ignored in the new global affairs (economy) of the twenty-first century.

REFERENCES

[1] Kwame Nkrumah, *Africa Must Unite*, London: Panaf Books, 1963, p. 194.

[2] See Kevin Shillington, *History of Africa, 2nd edition*. New York: Palgrave Macmillan, 2005; and Sanford Ungar, *Africa: The People and Politics of An Emerging Continent*. New York: Simon & Schuster Inc., 1986.

[3] Charles Darwin, *The Origin of Species*, London: John Murray, 1860.

[4] Ibid, *The descent of Man*, London: John Murray, 1871.

[5] *The Holy Bible*, Genesis chapter 1, verses 1-31.

[6] Kevin Shillington, Ibid, see chapters 1 & 2.

[7] Ali A. Mazrui, *The Africans: A Triple Heritage*. Boston, MA: Little, Brown and Company Inc., 1986, pp. 41-42.

[8] See the following, Chancellor Williams, *The Destruction of Black Civilization: Great Issues of A Race from 4500 B.C. to 2000 A.D.* Chicago, IL: Third World Press, 1987, George James, *The Stolen Legacy*, San Francisco, CA: Julian Richardson Associates Publishers,

1954. Reprinted in 2001, and Matthew Ashimolowo, *What is Wrong with Being Black*, Shippensburg, PA: Destiny Image Publishers, Inc., 2007.

[9] Kwame Nkrumah, *Neo-Colonialism: The Last Stage of Imperialism*, London: Panaf Books, 1965, p. 1.

[10] Sanford J. Ungar, *Africa: The People and Politics of An Emerging Continent*. New York: Simon Schuster, 1985, pp. 10-20.

[11] Sanford Ungar, p. 10.

[12] Oye Ogunbadejo, *The International Politics of Africa's Strategic Minerals*, Westport, CT: Greenwood Press, 1986, pp. 36-62.

[13] James Duffy, *Portuguese Africa*. Cambridge, MA: Harvard University Press, 1961, pp. 25-27.

[14] Ibid, pp. 36-62.

[15] Olayiwola Abegunrin, *Africa in Global Politics in the Twenty-First Century: A Pan-African Perspective*, New York: Palgrave Macmillan, 2009, p. 114.

[16] Martin Jacques, *When China Rules the World: The End of the Western World and the Birth of A New Global Order*, New York: Penguin Books, 2012.

[17] Putsch Commey, "Mining: Dethroning King Monopoly," *New African*. London, September 2002, pp. 50-51.

[18] Martin Bailey, "Rossing Helps Profits but Fuel Protests," *African Business*, London, July 1982, pp. 32-33. Also see Luyton Driman, "BBC Viewpoint: Is Africa Open for Business?" www.bbcnews.com Accessed June 5, 2006.

[19] Olayiwola Abegunrin, op. cit, p. 115.

[20] For full details of how the uranium was obtained by the United States from the Democratic Republic Congo (the former Belgian Congo) during the Second World War through the Belgian government, which was the former colonial power. See Donna Uthus Gregory, editor, *The Nuclear Predicament: A Sourcebook*. New York: St. Martin's Press, 1986, pp. 39-40.

[21] *The Express Tribune*, 2010, "Is Your Cell Phone Soaked in Congolese Blood?" Http://www.tribune.com.pk. Also see T-Mobile, "Coltan, Gorillas and Cell Phone," 2011, Retrieved April 6, 2011 from www.cellular-news.com/coltan

[22] Sudarsan Raghavan, "Foreigners in a Leading Role: Mali's Local Uprising Increasingly Taken Over by Outside Islamist Fighters" *The Washington Post,* January 29, 2013.

[23] World Energy Council Member Committees 2000/2001; *Uranium 1999*: Resources, Production and Demand, 2000, OECD Nuclear Energy Agency and International Atomic Energy Agency Reports, 2001, pp. 10, 18 and 20.

[24] Special Reports, "Namibia Set To Be Global Uranium Supplier," *United Press International*, March 26, 2007.

[25] Ibid. Also see U.S. House of Representatives, Subcommittee on Africa, Committee on International Relations, "Africa and the War on Global Terrorism," November 15, 2001.

[26] Olayiwola Abegunrin, Africa in Global Politics in the Twenty-First Century p. 116.

[27] Tafadzwa Chiremba, "Zimbabwe Gems Deemed Fit for Export," *The Sunday Mail*, Harare, Zimbabwe, June 26-July 2, 2011, p. 7.

[28] Diamonds Mining, *Mining Weekly*, Johannesburg, May 10, 2006. Also available on www.miningweekly.co.za/min/sector/diamonds. Accessed on May 24, 2006.

[29] African Diamond, "Patterns of Inequality," Jewish/European Business. http://www.nefertamu.tripod.com

[30] Ibid.

[31] "Death of Mr. Rhodes," *The Times*, London: March 27, 1902, p. 7. Also see Anthony Thomas, *Rhodes: The Race for Africa*, London, Bridge, 1997.

[32] Olayiwola Abegunrin, *Nigerian Foreign Policy under Military Rule, 1966-1999.* Westport, CT: Praeger Publishers, 2003, p. 179. Also see Shai Oster, "Oil Fuels Unrest in Nigeria," *The Wall Street Journal*, March 21, 2005, p. A15.

[33] For details on the foundation of the U.S. Foreign policy toward Africa see, Andrew DeRoche, *Black, White, and Chrome,* Trenton, NJ: Africa World Press, 2001.

[34] "U.S. Navy to Set up Sao Tome Radar for Gulf of Guinea Security," *REUTERS*, December 7, 2006.

[35] "Blood and Oil," *New York Times Editorial*, April 16, 2006. Also see Rob Crilly, "Oil from Africa Comes with Political Instability," *USA TODAY,* May 1, 2006. Also available @ www.USATODAY.com. Accessed on May 24, 2006.

[36] Charles Snyder, Speech at the American Enterprise Institute, Washington, D.C. April 13, 2004.

[37] *Nigeria Today Online,* "China Seals $2.3 billion Nigerian Oil Deal," January 10, 2006.

[38] Emeka Anuforo, "Nigeria Launches Satellite," *The Guardian,* Lagos, May 13, 2007.

[39] *Nigerian Daily Trust*, Abuja, January 28, 2013. Also see *The Weekly China Briefing*, Center for Chinese Studies, Stellenbosch University, South Africa, February 1, 2013.

[40] Edwin Madunagu, "China's Return to Africa," *The Guardian*, Lagos, December 14, 2006.

[41] "China-Africa Development Fund," *The Weekly Briefing,* Center for Chinese Studies, Stellenbosch University, South Africa, December 2012.

[42] "China-Africa Relations: A win Strategy," *African Business*, London, March 2007, p. 4.

[43] David Goldwyn and J. Stephen Morrison, "Promoting Transparency in the African Oil Sector: Report of the Center for Strategic and International Studies Task Force on Rising U.S. Energy Stake in Africa, CSIS, Washington, D.C., March 2004. Also available at www.csis.org/files/media Accessed on April 13, 2011.

[44] David Yergin, *The Prize: The Epic Quest for Oil, Money and Power*. New York: Simon and Schuster, 1991, pp. 567-572.

[45] Paul Blustein and Craig Timberg, "High Oil Prices Met with Anger Worldwide: Both Rich and Poor Countries Make Moves to Appease Citizens," *The Washington Post*, October 3, 2005. Also see Mike Oduniyi, "Niger Delta Threat Raises Oil Prices to $70 per barrel," Available on www.allafrica.com. Accessed on April 13, 2006.

[46] "Crude Oil Futures Climb Above $71 per Barrel," Available on www.allafrica.com. Accessed on April 19, 2006.

[47] *OPEC Daily Basket Price*, July 27, 2011, retrieved from http://www.opec.org/ opec_web/en/923.htm. Also see Simone Baribeau, "Stocks Nosedive As Oil Hits Record," *The Washington Post*, June 27, 2008. And see Peter Fritsch and Kelly Evans, "How Economy Could Survive Oil at $100 A Barrel." *The Wall Street Journal*, September 29-30, 2007, P. A1. Also see Matt Chambers, "Crude Oil Reaches Fresh High as Futures Rise 11% in a Week," *The Wall Street Journal*, October 17, 2007, P. C11. Steven Mufson, "Strike on Iran Would Roil Oil Markets, Experts Say," *The Washington Post*, October 26, 2007.

[48] "Unrest in North Africa and the Middle East," *The Washington Post*, February 8, 2011.

[49] Steve Hendrix and Anthony Fayola, "Gaddafi Forces, Rebels Continue to Fight for Control of Oil Depot," *The Washington, Post*, March 8,

2011. See also Marc Fisher and Liz Sly, "Protest Fervor in Arab World Grows," *The Washington Post*, February 28, 2011, pp. 1 & 9.

[50] Joby Warrick and Liz Sly, "Impasse in Libya Growing More Likely," *The Washington Post,* April 2, 2011.

[51] Olayiwola Abegunrin, "Africa Command Center (AFRICOM) and U.S. Foreign Policy of Militarization of Africa under the Obama Administration," in Adebayo Oyebade (editor), *United States' Foreign Policy in Africa in the Twenty-First Century: Issues and Perspectives*, Durham, NC: Carolina Academic Press, 2013.

[52] Ibid.

[53] Craig Whitlock, "In North Africa, A Decade of Anti-Terror Errors," *The Washington Post*, February 5, 2013.

[54] Robert J. Samuelson, "A New Era for Oil," *The Washington Post*, March 30, 2005.

[55] See Thomas Pakenham, *The Scramble for Africa: White Man's Conquest of the Dark Continent from 1876-1912*, New York: Avon Books, 1992, pp. 239-256.

[56] See Olayiwola Abegunrin, op. cit. p. 124.

[57] Michael T. Klare, *Resource Wars: The New Landscape of Global Conflict*, New York: Henry Holt and Company, 2002. Also see Martin Jacques, *When China Rules the World: The End of the Western World and the Birth of A New Global Order*, New York: Penguin Books, 2012.

[58] Nicholas Norbrook and Marshall Van Valen, "Friend or Foe?: For Better or For Worse China, Brazil and India Shake up Africa." *The Africa Report,* London, No. 31, June 2011, pp. 22-27.

[59] Stephen S. Cohen d J. Bradford DeLong, *The End of Influence: What Happens When Other Countries Have the Money,* New York: Basic Books, 2010.

[60] Valerie Noury, "What BRICS Membership Means to Africa," *African Business,* London, June 2011, pp. 37-39.

[61] Nicholas Norbrook and Marshall Van Valen, "Africa's Emerging Partners: For Better or for Worse," *The Africa Report,* London, June 2011, pp. 22-27.

[62] Conakry: Guinea National Broadcasting Service, quoted in Ali A. Mazrui, *The African Condition*, London: Cambridge University Press, 1980, p. 122.

SELECTED BIBLIOGRAPHY

Abegunrin, Olayiwola, Africa in Global Politics in the Twenty-First Century: A Pan- African Perspective, New York: Palgrave Macmillan, 2009.

__________________, "The Genesis of the Crisis in the Niger Delta," Being a paper delivered at the Public Workshop on Nigeria U.S. Institute of Peace, Washington DC March 22, 2006.

__________________, Nigerian Foreign Policy under Military Rule, 1966-1999 Westport, CT: Praeger Publishers, 2003.

__________________, Nigeria and the Struggle for the Liberation of Zimbabwe: A Study of Foreign Policy Decision Making of An Emerging Nation. Stockholm, Sweden: Bethany Books, 1992.

__________________, Economic dependence and regional Cooperation in Southern Africa: SADCC and South Africa in Confrontation. Lewiston, NY: The Edwin Mellen Press, 1990.

__________________, "The Military, and Nigerian Political Economy in the Global System," In Kwadwo Konadu-Agyemang (editor), Africa's Development in the 21st Century: Some Pertinent Issues, Opportunities and Challenges. New York: Ashgate International, 2006.

__________________, "The Soviet/Russian Involvement in Southern African Liberation Struggle, 1960-1990," in Maxim Matusevich (editor), Africa in Russia, Russia in Africa: Three Centuries of Encounters. Trenton, NJ: Africa World Press, 2006.

__________________, "Chief M.K.O. Abiola's Presidential Ambitions and Yoruba Democratic Rights," in Toyin Falola (editor), Yoruba Identity and Power Politics Rochester, New York: University of Rochester Press, 2006.

__________________, "Restructuring Nigerian Federalism: The Imperative of A Sovereign National Conference," in Segun Gbadegesin, editor, The

Imperative of Cultural Democracy in Nigeria: Reflections From the Yoruba Diaspora, Mitchellville, MD: Pinnacle Publications, 2006.

________________, "Zimbabwe-U.S. Relations," Encyclopedia of Global Perspectives on the United States, Great Barrington, MA: Berkshire Publishing Company, 2006.

________________, "The South African Truth and Reconciliation Commission: Review Essays", African Studies Review, Vol. 45, no. 3 (December 2002), 31-34.

________________, "Nigeria: Federalism, Resource Control and Restructuring", Journal of Nigerian Affairs, Vol. 10, no. 1 (March 2002), 11-21.

________________, "Nigeria's Foreign Policy: A Democratic Kickstart, 1998-1999." Government and Politics Journal, 11, no. 6 (March 2002).

________________, "Federalism, Political Instability and Struggle for Democracy in Nigeria," in Bamidele Ojo (editor), Problems and Prospects of Sustaining Democracy in Nigeria: Voices of A Generation, Huntington, New York: Nova Science Publishers, 2001.

________________, "Post Apartheid South Africa: An Analysis on Regional Perspectives," Journal of the Third World Spectrum, 6, no. 2 (Fall 1999), 19-41

________________, "African Regional Organizations," in Joel Krieger (editor), The Oxford Companion to Politics of the World, New York: Oxford University Press, 1993.

________________, "Prospects and Possibilities of SADCC as A Regional Organization," The Quarterly Journal of Administration (OAU: Ile-Ife), Vols. 1-2 (October 1989-January 1990), 25-30.

________________"Zimbabwe's Foreign Relations Since Its Independence," Scandinavian Journal of Development Alternatives, Stockholm, Sweden: vol. 6, December 1987, 93-107.

________________, "Angola and the Soviet Union Since 1975," Journal of African Studies (UCLA), Vol. 14, no. 1 (Spring 1987), 25-30.

________________, "Southern Development Coordination Conference: Politics of Dependence," in Ralph Onwuka and Amadu Sesay (eds.), The Future of Regionalism in Africa. New York: Macmillan Press, 1985.

________________, SADCC: Towards Integration of Southern Africa for Liberation," A Current Bibliography on African Affairs, Vol. 17, no. 4 (1984-1985), 93-107.

________________, "Liberation Struggle in South Africa," Renaissance Universal Journal, 4, 1-2 (1984).

__________________, “The West and South Africa,” Renaissance Universal Journal, 4, 1 (1984).

__________________, “The Arabs and the Southern African Problems,” International Affairs, Volume 60, no. 1(Winter, 1983-1984), 97-105.

__________________, “Soviet and Chinese Military Involvement in Southern Africa,” A Current Bibliography on African Affairs, 6, 3(1983-1984), 52-83.

__________________, “The U.S. Policy of Containment: A Case Study of Cuban Missile Crisis,” The Quarterly Journal of Administration (QJA), Vol.6, nos. 1-2(January 1982), 103-116.

__________________, “Western Options vis-à-vis South Africa,” The Western Journal of Black Studies, Vol. 6, no. 4 (Winter 1982), 231-240.

__________________, “The Southern Nine,” A Current Bibliography on African Affairs, 14, 4, 1981-1982, 331-334.

__________________, “Nigeria and the Politics of the U.S. on the Liberation of Zimbabwe,” Journal of African Studies of China, Taiwan, Republic of China, No. 8 (January 1981), 166-231.

__________________, and Olusoji Akomolafe (editors), Nigeria in Global Politics: Twentieth Century and Beyond, Essays in Honor of Professor Olajide Aluko. New York: Nova Science Publishers, 2006.

__________________, and Franklin Vivekananda (editors), The Political Economy of South-South Cooperation: Towards A New International Economic Order. Stockholm< Sweden: Bethany Books, 1998.

__________________, and H.E. Newsum, United States Foreign Towards Southern Africa: Andrew Young and Beyond. London and New York: Macmillan and St. Martin’s Press, 1987.

__________________, and Ralph Onwuka and Dhajoo N. Ghista (editors), Africa Development: The OAU/ECA Lagos Plan of Action and Beyond. Lawrenceville, VA: Brunswick Publishing Company, 1985.

Aborisade, Oladimeji and Robert J. Mundt, Politics in Nigeria, 2nd edition, New York: Longman, 2002.

Achebe, Chinua, Things Fall Apart, Ibadan: Heinemann Educational Books, 1959.

Adebajo, Adekeye, Building Peace in West Africa: Liberia, Sierra Leone, and Guinea-Bissau Boulder, CO: Lynne Rienner Publishers, 2002.

Adedeji, Adebayo (editor), Africa within the World: Beyond Dispossession and Dependence. London: Zed Books, 1993.

Adekunle, Abiodun A. (editor), The Nigeria – Biafra War Letters: A Soldier’s Story, Volume I. Atlanta, GA: Phoenix Publishing Group, 2004.

Adeniji, Oluyemi, Essays On Nigerian Foreign Policy, Governance, and International Security. Ibadan, Nigeria: Dokun Publishing House, 2000.

Akadiri, Oladele, Diplomacy, World Peace and Security. Akure, Nigeria: Ondo State Government Printing Press, 2003.

Ake, Claude, Democracy and Development in Africa. Washington, D.C.: The Brookings Institution, 2001.

Akiba, Okon, Nigerian Foreign Policy towards Africa: Continuity and Change. New York: Peter Lang, 1998.

Akindele, Rafiu and Bassey E. Ate (editors), Selected Readings on Nigeria's Foreign Policy and International Relations. Ibadan: Vantage Publishers, 2000.

____________ (editor), The Organization of African Unity, 1963-1988. Ibadan: Vantage Publishers, 1988.

Akinrinade, Sola and Amadu Sesay (editors), Africa in the Post Cold War International System. Washington, D.C: Pinter, 1998.

Akinsanya, Adeoye A., "Multinational Corporations in South Africa, Armed Conflict and Majority Rule in South Africa," International Review of Politics and Development, 3, June 2005, 14-51.

__________________,"Foreign Economic Control and Non-Alignment in Global Affairs, Pakistan Horizon, 45, April 1992, 69-93.

__________________, Multinationals in A Changing Environment: A Study of Government-Business Relations in the Third World. New York: Praeger Publishers, 1984.

Akinsanya, Adeoye A. and John A. Ayoade (eds.), Readings in Nigeria Government and Politics, Ijebu-Ode: Gratia Association International, 2005.

Akinsanya, Adeoye, A, and Gordon J. Idang (eds), Nigerian Government and Politics, 1979-1983, Calabar, Cross River State: Wusen Publishers, 2002.

Akinyemi, A. Bolaji, "Mohammed/Obasanjo Foreign Policy." In Oyeleye Oyediran (editor), Nigerian Government and Politics under Military Rule, 1966-1979, Lagos: Macmillan Press, 1979.

_______________, Foreign Policy and Federalism: The Nigerian Experience (Ibadan: Ibadan University Press, 1974.

Alao, Abiodun, The Burden of Collective Goodwill: The International Involvement in Liberian Civil War. Aldershot: Ashgate Publishers, 1996.

___________, Zimbabwe's Foreign Policy. Master's Thesis, Department of International Relations, Obafemi Awolowo University, Ile-Ife, Nigeria, 1985.

Aluko, Olajide, Africa and the Great Powers in the 1980s. Lanham, MD: University Press of America, 1987.

____________, Essays on Nigerian Foreign Policy. London: Allen and Unwin, 1982.

___________, (ed.), Foreign Policies of African States. London: Hodder and Stoughton, 1977.

___________, Ghana and Nigeria, 1957-1970: A Study in Inter-Africa Discord. New York: Barnes and Noble, 1976.

___________, "Nigeria, the United States and Southern Africa," African Affairs, 78, no. 310, January 1979.

Anglin, Douglas, Zambian Crisis Behavior: Confronting Rhodesia's Unilateral Declaration of Independence. Montreal: McGill University Press, 1996.

Asante, S.K.B., Pan-African Protes: West Africa and Italo-Ethiopian Crisis, 1934-1941. London: Longman, 1977.

Assensoh, A.B. and Yvette M. Alex-Assensoh, African Military History and Politics: Coups and Ideological Incursions, 1900-Present. New York: Palgrave, 2001.

Ayittey, George, B.N., Africa Unchained: The Blue Print for Africa's Future. New York: Palgrave-Macmillan, 2005.

________________, Africa in Chaos, New York: Palgrave-Macmillan Press, 1998.

________________, Africa Betrayed, New York: Palgrave-Macmillan Press, 1992.

Balewa, Abubakar Tafawa, Mr. Prime Minister: A Selection of Speeches made by the Right Honorable, Sir Abubakar Tafawa Balewa. Lagos: National Press Limited, 164.

Barber, James and John Barratt, South Africa's Foreign Policy: The Search for Status and Security 1945-1988. New York: Cambridge University Press, 1990

Baregu, Mwesiga and Christopher Landsberg (editors), From Cape to Congo: Southern Africa's Evolving Security Challenges. Boulder, CO: Lynne Rienner Publishers, 2003

Basedau, Matthias and Andreas Mwhler (eds.), Resource Politics in Sub-Saharan Africa. Hamburg: Institute of African Affairs, 2005.

Birmingham, David, Kwame Nkrumah Father of African Nationalism. Athen, OH: Ohio University Press, 1998.

Briand, Michael (Editor), Dialogue in Williamsburg: The Turning Point for South Africa? San Francisco, CA: Institute for Contemporary Studies, 1989.

Broderick, Jim, Gary Burford and Gordon Freer (Editors), South Africa's Foreign Policy: Dilemmas of A New Democracy. New York: St. Martin's Press, 2001.

Burstein, Stanley, Ancient African Civilizations: Kush and Axum. Princeton, NJ: Markus Wiener Publishers, 1998.

Calderisi, Robert, The Trouble With Africa: Why Foreign Aid Isn't Working. New York: Palgrave Macmillan, 2006.

Carter, G.M. and P. O'Meara (editors), Southern Africa: The Continuing Crisis. Bloomington, IN: Indiana University Press, 1979.

Cervenka, Zdenek, The Unfinished Quest for Unity in Africa and the OAU. London: Julian Friedmann, 1984.

Chazan, Naomi, and Robert Mortimer, et al, Politics and Society in Contemporary Africa, 3rd edition. Boulder, CO; Lynne Rienner Publishers, 1999.

Cheru, Fantu, African Renaissance: RoadMaps To the Challenge of Globalization. New York: Zed Books, 2002.

Chiedu, Kingsley, "Fighting Africa's Killer Diseases," West Africa. London, June 2003.

Christie, Kenneth, The South African Truth Commission. New York: St. Martin's Press, 2000.

Clapham, Christopher, Africa and the International System: The Politics of State Survival. New York: Cambridge University Press, 1996.

Collins, O. Robert (editor), Documents From the African Past. Princeton, NJ: Markus Wiener Publishers, 2001.

Commission for Africa, Our Common Interest: Report of the Commission for Africa. London: British Press, 2005.

Comprehensive Peace Agreement Between the Government of the Republic of Sudan and the Sudan People's Liberation Movement/Sudan People's Liberation Army, http://Sudan Comprehensive Peace Agreement 2005.

Damachi, Ukandi C. Leadership Ideology in Africa: Attitudes toward Socioeconomic Development. New York: Praeger Publishers, 1976.

Decalo, Samuel, Coups and Army Rule in Africa: Studies in Military Style, New Haven, CT: Yale University Press, 1977.

Deegan, Heather, The Politics of New South Africa: Apartheid and After. New York: Longman, 2001.

______________, South Africa Reborn: Building A New Democracy. London: UCL Press Limited, 1999.

DeRoche, Andrew, Black, White and Chrome: The United States and Zimbabwe, 1953-1998. Trenton, NJ: Africa World Press, 2001.

Diop, Cheika Anta, Black Africa: The Economic and Cultural Basis for A Federated State. Trenton, NJ: Africa World Press, 1987.

Dompere, Kofi Kissi, African Union: Pan-African Analytical Foundations. London: Adonis & Abbey Publishers Ltd, 2006.

Eades, Lindsay Michie, The End of Apartheid In South Africa. Westport, CT: Greenwood Press, 1999.

Easterly, William, The White Man's Burden: Why The West's Efforts To Aid The Rest Have Done So Much Ill And So Little Good. New York: The Penguin Press, 2006.

Edgar, Robert E. (editor), Sanctioning Apartheid. Trenton, NJ: Africa World Press, 1990.

Edie, Carlene J., Politics in Africa. Belmont CA: Thomson Wadsworth, 2003.

El-Ayouty Yassin and William Zartman (eds.), The OAU after Twenty Years. New York: Praeger Publishers, 1985.

Ellis, Stephen, "Liberia 1989-1994: A Study of Ethnic and Spiritual Violence," African Affairs, 94, no. 375, April 1995.

Esedebe, Olisanwuche, Pan-Africanism: The Idea and Movement, 1776-1991. Washington, D.C: Howard University Press, 1994.

Etuk, Emma S., Listen Africans: Freedom is under Fire. Washington, D.C.: Emida International Publishers, 2002.

Evans, Graham, "South Africa's Foreign Policy after Mandela: Mbeki and His Concept of an African Renaissance," The Round Table, 352, 1999.

Francis, David J., Uniting Africa: Building Regional Peace and Security Systems. Burlington, VT: Ashgate Publishing Company, 2006.

Fawole, Alade W., Nigeria's External Relations and Foreign Policy under Military Rule (1996-1999). Ile-Ife: Obafemi Awolowo University Press, 2003.

Forest, Joshua Bernard, "Ethnic-State Political Relations in Post-apartheid Namibia." Journal of Commonwealth and Comparative Politics, 32, no. 3, 1994.

Gambari, Ibrahim A. Theory and Reality in Foreign Policy Making: Nigeria After the Second Republic. Atlantic Highlands, NJ: Humanities Press International, 1989.

Gault, Hunter Charlayne, New News Out of Africa: Uncovering Africa's Renaissance, New York: Oxford University Press, 2006.

Gibson, Richard, African Liberation Movement: Contemporary Struggle Against White Minority Rule. New York: Oxford University Press, 1972.

Grundy, Kenneth, W. Confrontation and Accommodation in Southern Africa: The Limit of Independence. Berkeley, CA: University California Press, 1963.

Gumede, William Mervin, Thabo Mbeki and the Battle for the Soul of the ANC. Cape Town: Zebra Press, 2005.

Guyer, I. Jane, African Studies in the United States: A Perspective. Brunswick, NJ: African Studies Association Press, 1996.

Haarlov, Jens, CDR Research Report No. 14, Regional Cooperation in Southern Africa: Central Elements of the SADCC Venture, Copenhagen: Centre for Development Research, 1988.

Hanlon, Joseph, "African Debt Hoax." Review of African Political Economy, 25, no. 77, September 1977.

Harbeson, W. John, and Donald Rothchild (editors), Africa in World Politics: Post Cold War Challenges, 3rd edition. Boulder, CO: Westview Press, 2000.

Harvey, Robert, The Fall of Apartheid: The Inside Story From Smut to Mbeki. New York: Palgrave and Macmillan, 2001.

Hill, Robert A., Pan-African Biography. Los Angeles, CA: Crossroads Press, 1987.

Hirsch, L. John, Sierra Leone: Diamonds and the Struggle for Democracy. Boulder, CO: Lynne Rienner Publishers, 2001.

Hoile, David, Images of Sudan: Case Studies in Propaganda and Misrepresentation, London: European Sudanese Public Affairs Council, 2003.

Hunter, Susan, Black Death: AIDS in Africa. New York: Palgrave Macmillan, 2003.

Ihonvbere, Julius, O. and Timothy Shaw, Illusion of Power: Nigeria in Transition. Trenton, NJ: Africa World Press, 1998.

Isbister, John, Promises Not Kept: The Betrayal of Social Change in the Third World, West Hartford, CT: Kumarian Press, 1998.

Johnson, Phyllis and David Martin, Destructive Engagement: Southern Africa at War. Harare: Zimbabwe Publishing House, 1986.

Jorre, John de St., The Brothers War: Biafra and Nigeria. Boston, MA: Houghton Mufflin Company, 1972.

Kaplan, Robert D., The End of the Earth: A Journey to the Frontiers of Anarchy. New York: Vintage Books, 1996.

Keller, J. Edmond, and Donald Rothchild (eds.), Africa In The New International Order: Rethinking State Sovereignty and Regional Security. Boulder, CO: Lynne Rienner Publishers, 1996.

______________, and Louis A. Picard (editors), South Africa in Southern Africa: Domestic Change and International Conflicts. Boulder, CO: Lynne Rienner Publishers, 1989.

Khadiagala, M. Gilbert, Allies in Adversity: The Frontline States in Southern Africa Security. Athens, OH: Ohio State University Press, 1994.

__________________, and Terrence Lyons (editors), African Foreign Policies: Power and Process. Boulder, CO; Lynne Rienner Publishers, 2001.

Khapoya, Vincent B., The African Experience: An Introduction, 2nd edition. Upper Saddle River, NJ: Prentice Hall, 1998.

King James, The Holy Bible, St. Matthew, Chapter 13, Verse 12.

King, Mae, C. Basic Currents of Nigerian Foreign Policy. Washington, D.C: Howard University Press, 1996.

Knott, David, "Interest Grows in Africa Oil and Gas Opportunities," Oil and Gas Journal no. 41, May 1997.

Kodjo, Edem, Africa Tomorrow, New York: Continuum Publishing Company, 1987.

Konadu-Agyemang, Kwadwo and Kwamina Panford, editors, Africa's Development in the Twenty-First Century: Pertinent Socio-Economic and Development Issues, New York: Ashgate Publishing Company, 2006.

Krafona, Kwesi, The Pan-African Movement: Ghana's Contribution, London: Afroworld Publishing CO. 1986.

Lake, David, A. and Donald Rothchild (editors), The International Spread of Ethnic Conflict. Princeton, NJ: Princeton University Press, 1998.

Landsberg, Christ, "Promoting Diplomacy: The Mandela-Mbeki Doctrine," Journal of Democracy, Volume 11, No. 3, 2000.

Langley, J. Ayodele, Pan-Africanism and Nationalism in West Africa, 1900-1945: A Study in Ideology and Social Classes. London: Oxford University Press, 1973.

_______________, Ideologies and Liberation in Black Africa, 1856-1970. London: Rex Collings, 1979.

Lapping, Brian, Apartheid: A History. New York: George Braziller, 1989.

Legum, Colin, Africa Since Independence. Bloomington and Indianapolis, IN: Indiana University Press, 1999.

__________, Pan-Africanism. London: Pall Mall Press, 1962.

Lemarchand, Rene, "Burundi in Comparative Perspective: Dimensions of Ethnic Strift." In John McGarry and O'Leary (editors), The Politics of Ethnic Conflict Regulation, London: Routledge, 1993.

Lezhnev, Sasha, Crafting Peace: Strategies To Deal With Warlords In Collapsing States. Lanham, MD: Lexington Books, 2005.

Love, Janice, Southern Africa in World Politics: Local Aspirations and Global Entanglements. Boulder, CO: West-view Press, 2005.

Low, Eric P.' The Rise, Fall, and Legacy of Apartheid. Westport, CT: Praeger Publishers, 2004.

Mahmood Mamdani, Saviors and Survivors: Darfur, Politics and the War on Terror, New York: Patheon Books, 2009.

_____________, Citizen and Subject: Contemporary Africa and The Legacy of Late Colonialism. Princeton, NJ: Princeton University Press, 2002.

Mandela, Nelson, Long Walk to Freedom: The Autobiography of Nelson Mandela. Boston, MA: Little, Brown and Company, 1994.

____________, "South Africa's Future Foreign Policy." Foreign Affairs, 72, no. 5, 1993.

____________, Intensify the Struggle to Abolish Apartheid: Nelson Mandela Speeches. New York: Pathfinder, 1990).

____________, Nelson Mandela: I am Prepared to Die. London: International Defence and Aid Fund for Southern Africa, 1984.

Mandivamba, Rukuni, "Challenges of the Agriculture sector from 2000" Harare, University of Zimbabwe Publications, 2006.

Manyeruke Charity, "The Spaces of Women in Zimbabwe" SALARN Newsletter, Volume 1 Issue 4, Harare.

Martin, Guy, Africa in World Politics: A Pan-African Perspective. Trenton, NJ: Africa World Press, 2002.

Mathurin, Owen Charles, Henry Sylvester Williams and the Origins of the Pan-African Movement, 1869-1911. Westport, CT: Greenwood Press, 1976.

Matusevich, Maxim, No Easy Row for A Russian Hoe: Ideology and Pragmatism in Nigerian-Soviet Relations, 1960-1991. Trenton, NJ: Africa World Press, 2003.

Mazrui A. Ali, A Tale of Two Africas: Nigeria and South Africa as Contrasting Visions, London: Adonis and Abbey Publishers Limited, 2006.

__________, Towards A Pan-Africana: A Study of Ideology and Ambition. Chicago, IL; The University of Chicago Press, 1971.

___________, Africa's International Relations: The Diplomacy of Dependency and Change. Boulder, CO: Westview Press, 1979.

____________, and Michael Tidy, Nationalism and New States in Africa. Portsmouth, NH: Heinemann Educational Books, 1984.

Mbeki, Thabo, "Speech Delivered at the Launching of the African Renaissance Institute." October 11, 1999, Pretoria, 1999.

Meredith, Martin, Diamonds, Gold and War: The British, The Boers and The Making of South Africa. New York: Public Affairs, 2007.

Mohamoud, Abdullah A. (ed.), Shaping A New Africa. Amsterdam: KIT Publishers, 2007.

Morgan, Dan, et al, "Farm Program Pays $1.3 million Billion to People Who Do not Farm: Reaping Money for Nothing," The Washington Post, July 2, 2006.

Moyo, Sam, The Land Question in Zimbabwe, Harare: SAPES, 1995.

Mshomba, Richard E., Africa in the Global Economy Boulder, CO: Lynne Rienner Publishers, 2000.

Nkrumah, Kwame, I Speak of Freedom: A Statement of African Ideology. London: William Heinemann Limited, 1961.

_______________, Towards Colonial Freedom: African in the Struggle Against World Imperialism. London: Heinemann, 1962.

_______________, Africa Must Unite. London: Heinemann, 1964.

_______________, Neo-Colonialism: The Last Stage of Imperialism. New York: International Publishers, 1965.

Nnoli, Okwudiba, Ethnicity and Development in Nigeria. Brookfield, VT: Ashgate Publishing Company, 1995.

Nsekela, Amon, J. (editor), Southern Africa: Towards Economic Liberation, London: Rex Collings, 1981.

Ntalaja-Nzongola, Georges, The Congo, From Leopold to Kabila: A People's History, New York: ZED Books, 2005.

Nyang, S. Sulayman, Islam, Christianity and African Identity. Brattleboro, VT: Amana Books, 1984.

Nyerere, K. Julius, Man and Development, New York: Oxford University Press, 1974.

_______________Uhuru Na Ujamaa: Freedom and Socialism. New York: Oxford University Press, 1968.

Obasanjo, Olusegun, Africa Embattled, Ibadan: Fountain Publications, 1988.

___________________, My Command: An Account of the Nigerian Civil War 1967-1970, London: Heinemann, 1980.

O'Connell, James, "Political Integration: The Nigerian Case," in Arthur Hazlewood, African Integration and Disintegration. London: Oxford University Press, 1967.

Ogunbadejo, Oye, International Politics of Africa's Strategic Minerals. Westport, CT: Greenwood Press, 1985.

______________, "Soviet Policy in Africa." African Affairs, 79, no. 316, July 1980.

Ogwu, Joy, "South Africa and Nigeria's Relations with the World." Paper Presented at the Nigeria-South Africa Dialogue, Johannesburg, South Africa, August, 1999.

_________, Nigerian Foreign Policy: Alternative Future. Lagos: Nigerian Institute of International Affairs, 1986.

Olorunyomi, Sola, AFROBEAT: Fela and the Imagined Continent. Trenton, NJ: Africa World, 1998.

Oluleye, James E., Military Leadership in Nigeria 1966-1979, Ibadan: University Press, 1985.

Onwuka, Ralph, I. and Olajide Aluko (editors), The Future of Africa and The New International Economic Order. New York: St. Martin's Press, 1986.

______________, and Amadu Sesay (editors), The Future of African Regionalism. New York: St. Martin's Press, 1985.

Osaghae, Eghosa E., Nigeria since Independence: Crippled Giant, Bloomington, IN: Indiana University Press, 1998.

Osia, Kunirum, Israel, South Africa and Black Africa, Lanham, MD: University Press of America, 1982.

Our Common Interest, Report of the Commission for Africa, Chaired by Tony Blair, the British Prime Minister, London, British Information Service, 2005.

Oyebade, Adebayo and Abiodun Alao (editors), Africa After the Cold War: The Changing Perspectives on Security. Trenton, NJ: Africa World Press, 1998.

Oyugi, Awlter, O, et al, Democratic Theory and Practice in Africa. Nairobi: Heinemann, 1988.

Paton, Alan, Cry, The Beloved Country, New York: Scribner, 1987.

Payne J. Richard and Jamal R. Nassar, Politics and Culture in the Developing World: The Impact of Globalization. New York: Longman, 2003.

Perkins, John, Confessions of an Economic Hit Man. San Francisco, CA: Berrett-Koehler Publishers, Inc., 2004.

Peterson, Lennart, Post Apartheid Southern Africa: Economic Challenges and Policies for the Future. New York: Routledge, 1998.

Pobi-Asamani, Kwadwo, O. W.E.B. Dubois: His Contributions to Pan-Africanism. San Bernardino, CA: The Borgo Press, 1994.

Prendergast, John, "Our Future failure in Somalia: U.S. Counterterrorism Policy is Empowering Islamist Militias," The Washington Post, June 7, 2006.

Reno, William, Warlord Politics and African States. Boulder, CO: Lynne Rienner Publishers, 1999.

Report of an Independent Task Force, More than Humanitarianism: A Strategic U.S. Approach toward Africa, New York: Council on Foreign Relations, 2006.

Reynolds, Andrew (editor), Election '94 South Africa: The Campaign, Results and Future Prospects. New York: St. Martin's Press, 1995.

Robinson, Simon, and James Nachtwey, "The Tragedy of Sudan," Time Magazine. October 4, 2004.

Rodney, Walter, How Europe Under Developed Africa. Washington, D.C: Howard University Press, 1994.

Rotberg, Robert and Greg Mills (editors), War and Peace in South Africa: Crime, Drugs, Armies and Trade. Washington, D.C: Brookings Institution Press, 1998.

Rotimi, Kemi and Ogen, Olukoya. "Jaja and Nana in the Niger Delta region of Nigeria: proto-nationalists or emergent capitalists. Journal of Pan African Studies. December 2008.

Schraeder, Peter J., African Politics and Society: A Mosaic in Transformation,2nd edition. Belmont, CA: Thomson Wadsworth, 2004.

Schrire, Robert, Adapt or Die: The End of White Politics in South Africa. New York: The Ford Foundation, 1991.

Seidman, Ann, The Roots of Crisis in Southern Africa, Trenton, NJ: Africa World Press, 1985.

Spence, Jack, E., After Mandela: The 1999 South African Elections. London: Royal Institute of International Affairs, 1999.

Shaw, Timothy, M. and Olajide Aluko (editors), Africa Projected: From Recession to Renaissance by the Year 2000? New York: St. Martin's Press, 1985

______________________________ (editors), The Political Economy of African Foreign Policy: A Comparative Analysis. New York: St. Martin's Press, 1984.

______________________________ (editors), Nigerian Foreign Policy: Alternative Perceptions and Projections, New York: St. Martin's Press, 1983.

Shepard, B. Robert, Nigeria, Africa and the United States: From Kennedy to Reagan. Bloomington, IN: Indiana University Press, 1991.

Singh, Jerome, A. "Why AIDS in South Africa Threatens Stability and Economic Growth in other Parts of Africa," The Lancet, Volume 364, No. 9449, 2004.

Skinner, Elliot, African Americans and U. S. Policy toward Africa, 1850-1924, Washington, D C: Howard University Press, 1992.

Snow Donald M. National Security For A New Era: Globalization and Geopolitics. New York: Longman, 2004.

Soremekun, Fola, Angola: The Road to Independence. Ile-Ife: Obafemi Awolowo University Press, 1983.

Soyinka, Wole, You Must Set Forth At Dawn: A Memoir. New York: The Random House Publishing Group, 2006.

____________, The Open Sore of A Continent: A Personal Narrative of the Nigerian Crisis. New York: Oxford University Press, 1996.

____________, The Economist, September 1995.

Sparks, Allister, Beyond The Miracle: Inside The New South Africa. Chicago: The University of Chicago Press, 2003.

____________, Tomorrow Is Another Country: The Inside Story of South Africa's Road to Change. Chicago: The University of Chicago Press, 1995.

____________, The Mind of South Africa. Chicago: The University of Chicago Press, 1989.

Stockwell, John, In Search of Enemies: A CIA Story. New York: W.W. Norton and Company, 1978.

Stremlau, J. John, A House No Longer Divided: Progress and Prospects for Democratic Peace in South Africa. New York: Carnegie Commission on Preventing Deadly Conflict, 1997.

______________, The International Politics of the Nigerian Civil War, 1967-1970. Princeton, NJ: Princeton University Press, 1977.

Sullivan, Kevin, "In War-Torn Congo, Going Wireless to Reach Home: For Poor, Cell-phones Bridge Digital Divide," The Washington Post Foreign Service, July 9, 2006.

Swarns, Rachel L. "Awe and Unease as South Africa Stretches Out," The New York Times, February 17, 2002.

Taras, Raymond C. and Rajat Ganguly, Understanding Ethnic Conflict: The International Dimension, Second Edition. New York: Longman, 2002.

Taylor, Ian, NEPAD: Toward Africa's Development or Another False Start? Boulder, CO: Lynne Rienner Publishers, 2005.

Thomas, Caroline, and Peter Wilkin (editors), Globalization, Human Security and The African Experience. Boulder, CO: Lynne Rienner Publishers, 1999.

Thompson, Leonard, A History of South Africa. New Haven, CT: Yale University Press, 1990.

Thompson B. Vincent, Africa and Unity: The Evolution of Pan-Africanism, London: Longman, 1969.

Thomson, Alex, An Introduction to African Politics, New York: Routledge, Taylor and Francis Group, 2000.

Tieku, Thomas Kwasi, "Explaining the Clash, and Accommodation of Interests of Major Actors in the Creation of African Union," African Affairs, April 2004, Vol., 103, No. 411.

Timberg, Graig, "How AIDS in Africa Was Overstated: Reliance on Data From Urban Prenatal Clinics Skewed Early Projections," The Washington Post Foreign Service, April 6, 2006.

Todd J. Moss, African Development: Making Sense of the Issues and Actors. Boulder, CO: Lynne Rienner, 2007.

Tutu, Desmond, The Rainbow People of God: The Making of A Peaceful Revolution. New York: Double Day, 1994.

Ungar, Sanford J., AFRICA: The People and Politics of An Emerging Continent. New York: Simon & Schuster Inc., 1986.

UNAIDS, AIDS Epidemic Update, December 2002, Geneva, Switzerland: UNAIDS and WHO, 2002.

United Nations Development Program, Human Development Report, 2002, New York: Oxford University Press, 2002.

United Nations Development Program, Human Development Report, 2003. New York: Oxford University Press, 2003.

United Nations Development Program, Human Development Report, 2004, New York: Oxford University Press, 2004.

Van Der Veen, Roel, What Went Wrong with Africa, New York: Amsterdam: KIT Publishers, 2004.

Venter, Denis, "South African Foreign Policy Decision-making in the African Context," In Gilbert M. Khadiagala and Terrence Lyons (editors), African Foreign Policies: Power and Process, Boulder, CO: Lynne Rienner Publishers, 2001.

__________, "Wind of War Set to Blow Across Angola." Jane's Intelligence Review, 10, no. 10, October 1998.

Villa-Valencia, Charles and Wilhelm Verwoerd (editors), Looking Back Reaching Forward: Reflections on the Truth and Reconciliation Commission of South Africa, Cape Town: University of Cape Town Press, 2000.

Vogt, Margaret A. (editor), Liberian Crisis and ECOMOG: A Bold Attempt at Regional Peace Keeping. Lagos: Gambumo Publishers, 1992.

Watts, Michael, "Resource Curse? Governmentality, oil and power in the Niger Delta, Nigeria." Geopolitics, Volume 9, Number 1, 2004.

Watts, Michael (2006). "Empire of Oil: Capitalist Dispossession and the Scramble for Africa." Monthly Review, Volume 58, Number 4.

Watts, Michael (2007). "Petro-Insurgency or Criminal Syndicate? Conflict & Violence in the Niger Delta." Review of African Political Economy, Vol. 34, No 114: 637-660.

Wax, Emily, "French Peacekeepers Arrive in Congo: U.N.-Backed Mission Seeks to Quell Ethnic Fighting and Protect Civilians," The Washington Post Foreign Service, June 7, 2003.

_________, "Somalia Lawlessness Spills Into the Sea: Modern-Day Pirates Strike for Ransom and Cargo," The Washington Post Foreign Service, April 2, 2006.

Welsh, David, The Roots of Segregation, Cape Town: Oxford University Press, 1971.

Whitaker, Jennifer Seymour, How Can Africa Survive? New York: Council on Foreign Relations Press, 1988.

Williams, Chancellor, The Destruction of Black Civilization: Great Issues of A Race From 4500 B.C. To 2000 A.D. Chicago, IL: Third World Press, 1987.

Wiseman, John, "Leadership and Personal Danger in African Politics," Journal of Modern African Studies, 31, No. 4, December 1993.

Worger, H. William, et al, Africa and The West: A Documentary History from the Slave Trade to Independence, Phoenix, AZ: The Oryx Press, 2001.

Wright, Stephen (editor), African Foreign Policies, Boulder, CO: Westview Press, 1999.

Yergin, Daniel, THE PRIZE: The Epic for Oil, Money and Power, New York: Simon and Schuster, 1991.

Young, Crawford, Ideology and Development in Africa, New Haven, CT: Yale University Press, 1982

_____________, The Politics of Cultural Pluralism, Madison, WI: University of Wisconsin Press, 1979.

Zablotsky, Edgardo E. "Political Stability and Economic Growth."
http://www.cema.edu.ar/~eez/Publicaciones/DocumentosdeTrabajo/doc109.PDF accessed 11/25/2011.

SOME USEFUL WEBSITE ON AFRICA

1. Africa News on Line at http://www.africanews.org. This is one top source for up-to-date information on all of Africa, news from more than 60 different sources. New stories and news are added daily on this website. Pick any country in Africa or topical news section or visit a region within the continent of Africa. It covers all aspects of Africa.
2. Africa Policy Information Center (now Africa Action), at http://www.africapolicy.org. Analyzes and publishes policy relevant information related to the United States policy in Africa, bringing to light perspectives from grassroots organizations and government entities.
3. www.allafricannews.com. Source of news from Africa
4. www.africapolicy.org/docs98/reg9803.htm
5. www.agoa.gov/Resources/TRDPROFL.01.pdf
6. Report of the Commission for Africa. Available at www.commissionforafrica.org
7. www.galleries.media24.com/News24
8. Africa on Line at http://www.news.africaonline.nu
9. Trans Africa Forum www.transafricaforum.org
10. South Africa, Truth and Reconciliation Commission Websitehttp://www.truth.org.za
11. www.africanviews.org
12. www.africajournalismtheworld.com

BOOKS BY OLAYIWOLA ABEGUNRIN

1. Olayiwola Abegunrin, *Africa in Global Politics in the Twenty-First Century: A Pan-African Perspective*, New York: Palgrave Macmillan, 2009
2. Olayiwola Abegunrin, *Nigerian Foreign Policy under Military Rule*, 1966-1999, Westport, CT: Praeger Publishers, 2003.
3. Olayiwola Abegunrin, Nigeria and the Struggle for the Liberation of Zimbabwe: *A Study of Foreign Policy Decision Making of An Emerging Nation,* Stockholm, Sweden: Bethany Books, 1992.
4. Olayiwola Abegunrin, *Economic Dependence and Regional Cooperation in Southern Africa: SADCC and South Africa in Confrontation*, Lewiston, New York: Edwin Mellen Press, 1990.
5. Olayiwola Abegunrin and H.E. Newsum (Co-authored), *United States Foreign Policy Towards Southern Africa: Andrew Young and Beyond*, London & New York: Macmillan and St. Martin's, 1987.
6. Olayiwola Abegunrin and Olusoji Akomolafe (Editors), *Nigeria in Global Politics: Twentieth Century and Beyond; Essays in Honor of Professor Olajide Aluko*, Nova Publishers, 2006.
7. Olayiwola Abegunrin and Franklin Vivekananda (Editors), *The Political Ecconomy of South-South Cooperation: Towards A New International Economic Order*, Stockholm, Sweden: Bethany Books, 1998.
8. Olayiwola Abegunrin, Ralph Onwuka and Dhajoo Ghista (Editors), *African Development: OAU/ECA Lagos Plan of Action and Beyond*, Brunswick Publishing Company, 1985.

INDEX

B

C

E

F

G

H

I

J

N

O

P

Q

R

S

T

X

Y

Z